Timofey Agarin (ed.)

When Stereotype Meets Prejudice:
Antiziganism in European Societies

Timofey Agarin (ed.)

WHEN STEREOTYPE MEETS PREJUDICE:
ANTIZIGANISM IN EUROPEAN SOCIETIES

ibidem-Verlag
Stuttgart

Bibliographic information published by the Deutsche Nationalbibliothek
Die Deutsche Nationalbibliothek lists this publication in the Deutsche Nationalbibliografie;
detailed bibliographic data are available in the Internet at http://dnb.d-nb.de.

Bibliografische Information der Deutschen Nationalbibliothek
Die Deutsche Nationalbibliothek verzeichnet diese Publikation in der Deutschen
Nationalbibliografie; detaillierte bibliografische Daten sind im Internet über http://dnb.d-nb.de
abrufbar.

ISBN-13: 978-3-8382-0688-2

© *ibidem*-Verlag / *ibidem* Press
Stuttgart, Germany 2014

Printed in the United States of America

Contents

Note on contributors

Timofey Agarin is a lecturer in politics and ethnic conflict in Queen's University Belfast, where he is also the Director of the Centre for the Study of Ethnic Conflict. His research interest is in ethnic politics and their impact on transition from communism in Central Eastern European states. He is interested in the interplay of social and institutional change in postcommunism in issue areas of non-discrimination, minority protection, migration and civil society. Timofey has published in *Ethnopolitics, Perspectives on European Politics and Society, Ethnicities, Nationalities Papers* and *Journal of Baltic Studies.* He authored "A Cat's Lick? Democratisation and Minority Communities in the post-Soviet Baltic" (Rodopi 2010) and edited "Minority Integration in Central Eastern Europe: Between Ethnic Diversity and Equality" (Rodopi 2009, with Malte Brosig) and "Institutional Legacies of Communism: Change and Continuities in Minority Protection" (Routledge 2013, with Karl Cordell). Together with Matthew Kott, he is the founder of the collaborative research network "Romanis in Europe: Probing the Limits of Integration", sponsored by the University Association for Contemporary European Studies (UACES). Contact: t.agarin@qub.ac.uk

Huub van Baar is Assistant Professor of European Studies at the University of Amsterdam, and Research Fellow at the Amsterdam Center for Globalization Studies (ACGS), University of Amsterdam. He has published widely on the position, history, and political and cultural representation of Romani minorities, as well as on correlated issues of Europeanisation, citizenship, activism, securitisation, governmentality, and memory. He is the author of *The European Roma: Minority Representation, Memory, and the Limits of Transnational Governmentality* (Amsterdam: F&N, 2011) and the editor of *Museutopia: A Photographic Research Project by Ilya Rabinovich* (Amsterdam: Alauda Publications, 2012, with Ingrid Commandeur). He published on the Roma in the *Third Text, International Journal of Urban and Regional Research, City, International Journal of Cultural Policy, Citizenship Studies, Environment and Planning D: Society and Space* and *Journal of Ethnic and Migration Studies.*

Katharina Crepaz is a PhD candidate in political science at the University of Innsbruck, Austria. Her research interests include minority and human rights issues in the EU, the impact of European Integration and Europeanization on minority communities, as well as multi-level governance and regionalism as settings for minority empowerment.
Contact: katharina.crepaz@student.uibk.ac.at

Markus End is a PhD candidate at the Technical University Berlin. His project analyses the structure of meanings in modern antiziganism. He is the co-editor of *"Antizganistische Zustände"* series, published by Unrast. Markus regularly publishes reports and is an invited speaker at the *Documentation and Cultural Centre of German Sinti and Roma, Romnokher, AmaroDrom* and the *Phiren Amenca* network. His current project is analysing antiziganism in the German media, commissioned by the *Documentation and Cultural Centre of German Sinti and Roma*. More information is available at http://www.forschungsforum.net/user/98
Contact markus.end@gmail.com

Matthew Kott holds a DPhil in Modern History from the University of Oxford, and has previously worked at the Museum of the Occupation of Latvia in Riga, Latvia, and the Centre for Studies of the Holocaust and Religious Minorities in Oslo, Norway. From 2009 to 2011, he was coordinator for Romani studies at the Hugo Valentin Centre, Uppsala University. Since 2011 he is based at the Uppsala Centre for Russian and Eurasian Studies. His current research and teaching interests include the history of fascism and other forms of political extremism; the spread of racial biology; and antiziganism, with a particular focus on the Romani genocide—all with a comparative, regional focus on the countries of Baltic Sea region. His latest monograph (co-authored with Terje Emberland) is *Himmlers Norge: Nordmenn i det storgermanske prosjekt* (Aschehoug, 2012). Together with Timofey Agarin, he is the founder of the collaborative research network "Romanis in Europe: Probing the Limits of Integration".

Sara Memo is an independent consultant for the development and management of the EU co-funded projects in the area of socio-economic inclusion of vulnerable groups. Sara holds a doctorate in International Studies from the University of Trento, with the Doctor Europaeus Certificate received in April 2013. Her doctoral work undertook a comparative study of the legal status Romani groups hold across Europe and considered both the national and the transnational perspectives on Romani rights. She worked on her PhD project while at EURAC in Bolzano/Bozen, Corvinus University in Budapest and at the DG Employment, Social Affairs and Inclusion, European Commission in Brussels. Sara also holds an E.Ma Degree in Human Rights and Democratization from the European Inter-University Centre of Lido-Venice (2007) and an MA from the University of Padua in Political Science specializing in Institutions and Politics for Human Rights and Peace (2006). Her main research interests are in human and minority rights, children's rights, socio-economic rights and comparative legal methodology. Contact: sara.memo@gmail.com

Diana E. Popescu is a PhD candidate in Government at the London School of Economics and Political Science. She has an MA in Philosophy of the Social Sciences and an MSc in Political Science from Leiden University. Her doctoral work combines political theory with Romani studies, focusing on the tension between social inclusion strategies and the protection of Romani identity. Diana is particularly interested in challenges the Romani case poses to theoretical frameworks of social justice and multiple disadvantage, how these frameworks can be drawn together to offer lessons for social policy. Diana has also worked as a research assistant for an on-going project on welfare regimes and the social exclusion of Romanis in the Western Balkans at the LSE's European Institute. Outside academia, she works with children from disadvantaged backgrounds, collaborates with educational projects both in London and in a Romani ghetto in Bucharest, Romania. Contact: d.e.popescu@lse.ac.uk

Julija Sardelić is a CITSEE Research Fellow in the School of Law, University of Edinburgh. Julija has a standing working relationship with the research project 'The Europeanization of Citizenship in the Successor States of the Former Yugoslavia' (see http://www.citsee.ed.ac.uk). At CITSEE she has investigated the position of Romani minorities in the Yugoslav successor states and the effects of transforming citizenship regimes on Romani communities. Julija holds a PhD in Sociology, awarded for research on Romani minorities' social status before and after the disintegration of the Socialist Yugoslavia. Outside academia, she has been also working as a civil society activist in different Romani settlements in the post-Yugoslav region for more than a decade. She is also a member of the European Academic Network on Romani Studies. Contact: julija.sardelic@ed.ac.uk

Ioana Vrăbiescu is a PhD candidate in Romani Studies at the Department of International Relations in National School of Political Studies and Public Administration (NSPSPA), Bucharest. She holds an MA in International Relations (2011) and a BA in Philosophy from University of Bucharest (2002), she has also read Gender and Minority Politics at NSPSPA. Her research interests include ethics in international relations, feminist political theory, Roma identity politics, human rights and minority rights. As a feminist activist, Ioana is a founding member of the Front NGO; she is the editor of the online debate forum http://feminism-romania.ro and a regular contributor to http://www.criticatac.ro/ a critical platform.
Contact: ioana.vrabiescu@gmail.com

Introduction

Timofey Agarin

Queen's University Belfast

The exclusion of Romanis came to the wider European public's attention with the 2010 expulsion of European Union (EU) citizens, members of Romani communities from France. That event, however, has yet to change the ways in which we perceive and analyse issues of European integration, cross-border migration and protection of human rights. Romanis have no single voice in politics in any one EU member state, and no organization of states or international non-governmental coalition takes up their own interests seriously and lobbies for political change on Romanis' own terms. We are thus bound to see antiziganism as the predominant perspective on Romani communities' status across much of the continent. With no kin-state of their own and lacking opportunities to mobilise potent political or economic resources, Romanis remain poorly organised, disempowered, largely marginal communities who more often than not live in parallel to dominant societies. The traditional policies of group protection, cultural diversity and minority inclusion have failed to redress their social deprivation and exclusion, and have been largely unsuccessful in changing stereotypes shared across all European societies about Romani communities.

The view of Romanis as a "race of criminals" is widely shared across Europe. In the past, this stereotype was used to justify mass persecutions, violence against and discrimination of Romanis by individuals, officials of the state and political institutions alike. The discrimination which members of Romani groups face is a sensitive issue on the European agenda. Despite numerous attempts at finding a suitable solution, and despite great improvements in the fight against discrimination, little has yet been achieved. This is due in part to the fact that a widely-accepted definition of 'minority'—one that might also include the Romanis—is missing, and mostly because the importance of collective rights as a means to protect the cultural identity of minorities has often been underestimated. This collection of papers describes and assesses the attempted definitions of antiziganist prejudice, their applicability to individuals only loosely collected under 'Roma and Travellers', and the limits of recognition that accompany Romani interests in the public sphere.

1. The Scope of our Argument

Stereotypical representations of Romani communities abound in analyses of majority societies' relationships with Romanis today, just as they have been since Romani presence was first recorded in the annals of European history. Yet, much like members of dominant nations, Romanis too have sought international recognition of their plight by organising themselves into international non-governmental organisations of one sort or another, thereby lobbying for greater consideration of their interests, advancing claims for the recognition of their culture and advocating that interest representation should be done by people, not by the states of which they happen to be members. While international Romani organisations have sought to champion the idea of Romani individuals being united in a group with a strong common identity without creating either institutions of a state or promoting an inclusive way to establish a shared identity, individual Romanis have remained locked in the boundaries of territorial states. And because state institutions exercise considerable pressures on majority populations to identify in terms hardly comparable to those advocated by Romanis, they have effectively undermined Romanis' own perceptions about the individual equality of those in- and out-groups.

Diversity within groups has not helped either: customs, languages, religious affiliations, and citizenships vary across Romani communities, preventing them from forming a "united front" when facing similar sets of prejudice. This diversity requires activities to take place under the radar of broad political institutions, which in turn has led to a focus on local solutions to highly specific problems faced by small Romani groups. The limited participation of Romanis in these activities has only further supported the stereotype of the "Gypsy" challenging the principle of territorial politics, economic liberalism and the Westphalian state system. But, lacking many prerequisites for effective participation, Romani individuals and communities alike retract from engagement with the majority public, and thus enhance public perceptions of Romanis' self-exclusion, entrenching stereotypes about the "Gypsy" further and feeding the prejudice against the "Roma problem."

The distinction between Romani interests from those of non-Roma communities has been a part of European societies' strategy of dealing with Romani groups for centuries. The advance of democratic liberalism placed the onus on individuals to choose whether and how to participate in social, economic and political processes, diluting differences between various groups in societies that impact on the range of opportunities their individual members can choose from. And while intergroup differences are increasingly neglected in the light of presumably shared views about the benign role competition for economic resources played in satisfying individual needs, the more pressing is the need to think of opportunities individuals fail to enjoy because they are perceived as a member of a stereotyped group such as 'Roma'.

The distinction between Roma and non-Roma individuals, however, has made clear that only those interests and aspirations comparable to, or at least translatable into those of the majority could be achieved through interpersonal communication, social interaction and political participation. Both of these perceptions are said to have resulted from a covert agenda among neoliberal political economies, retrenching stereotypical representations of Romanis as "workshy", "deviant scroungers." Such stereotypes limit opportunities for non-Romanis to engage with Romanis and have forced a double lock of citizen disengagement: on an individual level, from discussing issues affecting all citizens alike, and at the level of communities, where Romanis ought to seek avenues to counteract the outsiders' views of the Romanis' radical difference from the majority.

And yet, from the inquiries which this volume makes into the origin of the prejudice about the "ways of a Gypsy", it is the stereotype about the irreconcilable otherness of the Romanis shared across majorities in European societies, which lies at the heart of Romani exclusion. Throughout this volume we point out that the institutions offering options for the accommodation of Romanis were framed on terms that serve dominant groups, and have been often identified as unlikely tools to reverse the effects of systemic discrimination and antiziganism which Romani individuals face in interactions with members of the majority. As contributions in this volume demonstrate repeatedly, Romanis do not participate in the societal processes which most of members of the majority take for granted, as a result of their concerns and interests not being reflected in and hard to translate into existing policies and institutional structures. If anything, political institutions supporting Romanis further undermine the options for Romani individuals' equal access and participation on their terms because they accommodate only those Romani interests that are easily translatable into or understandable for members of the dominant majority. And at a time when democratic decision-making has brought considerable advancement for interest representation of majority populations in European states, promoted limited state engagement with citizenries' and entrenched identity disputes, the stereotypical representation of Romani communities as unwanted "Others" has remained the same.

The interests and aspirations of Romanis often are believed to be at odds with the objectives of wider society, without much evidence about the veracity of these broad generalisations, either about Romanis or about the majority. This volume, therefore, puts the spotlight on antiziganism, uncapitalised throughout, but not as a narrow phenomenon that limits Romani inclusion. Since Berthold Bartel's publication of "Vom *Antitsiganismus* zum *antiziganism*" (2008), the term has become more established in the scholarly literature; furthermore, it distinguishes the work from those who insist, as is often common in some social and anthropological work, that Gypsy is a real, existing category of people. The "*zigan-*" root in English lays bare the ideational construct of the Gypsy "Other", as it is jarring one out of the linguistic comfort zone of semantic familiarity. We see the origin of Romani exclusion as being rooted in antiziganism as a form of group-based enmity that does not need "real" Romanis to reproduce stereotypes of and prejudice about individual representing the Romanis or the community as a whole.

The scholarship analysing issues faced by Romani communities has sought to insert the claim about collective identity into debates of individually experienced inequalities by members of these only tentatively established groups. Often, the importance of and respect for human rights are difficult to gauge in the discourse about collectivities. This is a complex process of pooling individual participation in shared political, social and economic processes and hence also generalising the scope of interests that are to be represented. As a result, authors discussing Romani exclusion often state explicitly that using collective group rights to participate can only be ensured on the basis of their recognised and protected cultural identity. Others, however, seek to establish the contradiction in terms between the group rights protection and the lack of uniformity within any cultural group that is to share an identity, such as Romanis. The last argument seems to be particularly potent as it can extend and defend the claim that the long-term recognition of Romanis' own perceptions of identity, needs and interests would be damaged despite the short-term improvement of their situation because of recognition. Interesting as these issues might be, our volume disregards these issues explicitly.

Why would anyone want to do that? We believe that in doing so we are not dodging our responsibility to engage with the problem itself. On the contrary, the papers collected here put the question squarely into the court of the advocates of collective and/or individual rights solutions: How legitimate can one speak of the interests of Romani individuals and communities if these are defined by non-Roma, and even then can be hand-picked by the representatives/elites of Romanis on the basis that some interests would feature higher in the list of their subjective priorities or appear to correspond to majority's expectations about what Romanis would need/want, etc. Often, such views are being projected upon Romanis in a negative or positive form so as to render legitimacy to the claim, identity and interests expressed. Rarely do such projections draw upon Romanis' own concept of community, group, and personhood. As the papers in this volume argue, general failure to engage with Romanis' own ideas, interests and identities on their own terms reproduces one of the basic mechanisms of exclusion, central to antiziganism: disengagement from social reality regardless of the factual inaccuracy of stereotypes underlying the imagined, outside community.

In leaving issues about rights and recognition outside of this volume relates to the difficulty in relaying the set of questions raised here to wider audiences. Given that Romani groups are highly diverse, a universal and univocal definition of "Who are the Romanis?" is difficult to establish. And any recourse to individual or group rights that can be projected upon the non-defined community of Romanis would be utterly flawed. Scholars of Romani studies, Romani advocates and Romanis themselves have found it difficult to create a unique, pan-European Romani voice in the present European context. Though no one expects a uniform appearance of Dutch, Germans or Swedes, there is an underlying expectation about a need for an immediate recognition of a person representing a group of Romanis. A great deal of inter-state as well as intra-state variance remains a challenge to talking about "the Romanis", though conventions are in place to favour "Roma" as the term used in European organisations to denote all members of Traveller, as well as Romani groups. With members of Romani communities residing across different nation-states and showcasing differences— at times, lineages that Romanis themselves refer to as those of a "tribe" or "clan"—it is impossible to claim any kind of group uniformity in order to ascertain wider political, social or rights for recognition.

2. The Objects of Stereotype and Prejudice

Attempts to pull Romani groups together in pursuit of recognition have been rather regular since the International Romani Union advocated the collective designation for all Romani-speaking groups as "Roma" in early 1970s. Of course, this denomination is not uncontested. There are groups with traditional and present-day endonyms such as Sinti, Manouches, Romanichal, Kale, etc., who disapprove of "Roma" as the proper term for all Romani groups. This reflects a close association between the term and a (more vocal) part of the community, most often associated with Eastern European, and particularly with Balkan Romani activists and their self-proclaimed leadership in the Romani nation-building project since the early 1990s. It is important to underline first and foremost the widespread presence of Roma and non-Roma Romani groups in all European countries, with the most significant concentration in Central and South Eastern European countries.

The presence of Romanis however, is not limited to Eastern Europe and struggles for an appropriate designation are not limited to the international forum, but can also be seen in individual countries. For example, the Romani Travellers of Norway (*Romanifolket*) have successfully lobbied to be recognised as a separate national minority from the Roma in Norway. In addition, the distinction between Travellers and Romanis is one that has often brought confusion to the discussion by emphasising the differentiated nomadic and non-nomadic groups. Indigenous Romani groups and communities can be found throughout all countries of the European Union. The demotion of borders within the EU, the current migration processes across Europe and a perceived increase in Roma mobility has made the groups' visibility part and parcel of the new European social integration agenda. Communities in the focus of this volume refer to themselves by many names: Gypsy, Gitano, Sinti, Romungro, and the like. And the states that are home to these respective groups, when drafting policies which target the latter, reproduce to some degree such self-designators or create new ones altogether.

Our collaboration on the pages of this volume sought to use the term that references the community without prescribing them any traits of identity, whilst acknowledging their distinctness and underlining that current policies targeting individuals, groups and entire societies are identity-based. While the emergent minority rights discourse established a generic term—the Roma—to describe all communities, stressing the similarity of their social status over the past decades, the object-like position of the Roma vis-à-vis the policies and practices of states, majority societies and the posited "irregularity" of their status have deserved a revision of this policy-inspired term for the purposes of academic research. We recognise that the preferred usage in scholarly contexts today is the noun "Roma" with related adjective "Romani" as is reflected in many online forums and discussions. Similarly, we acknowledge the noun "Romany/Romanies" as the historically accepted and socio-linguistically rooted most common point of reference for these groups. But in order to highlight our preference for an exogenous yet non-coercive, descriptive yet encompassing the wide variety of groups and individuals designated as the "Roma", the volume uses the term "Romani" as both a noun and an adjective of an individual.

Our preference for the term "Romanis" is therefore important for two reasons: First, "Romani" is both an adjective and a noun, comparable with other ethnic terms: Italian/Italians, German/Germans, Russian/Russians, etc., and is fully valid in English. This indicates the "substance" of being a Romani that is often denied in public references to an (allegedly) "artificial" denominator of "the Roma". We also think that whilst it is rarely questioned that the Finnish (as a collection of Finns) are distinct and do not overlap with the Finnish "nation" or "state", similar use of terms are seen as less than acceptable in the case of Romanis.

The second reason for which we prefer "Romani" as the reference point for academic research, rather than for advocacy, is precisely because it is an externally set referent, and as a concept does not really exist as set of tangible objects. Romanis are out there only by virtue of their existence in and as a part of the social world, and as such the Romani community is a discursively constructed rather than a materially constructed identity. Whether it is an interpersonal relation with other Romanis or non-Romanis, it is social interaction (or lack thereof) that creates and solidifies the projection of the (real or presumed) identity between individual group members who share practices, interests or are imagined as sharing these.

The "Roma"—the term commonly used today to designate all Romanis—is in our understanding a social and therefore purely rhetoric construct, which is a misnomer for something that purports to, but does not exist in reality. The word "Roma" is often deployed as a placeholder for a collection of details, not all of which will be found in that group or an individual "Roma." And, as we observe with words being used as both conceptual equivalents and *in lieu* of individual phenomena, the distinction between the two dwindles: We would often hear someone talk of "our community", "your nation" and "my country" as if these really existed outside highly personalised relationships with "Others". Similarly, many individuals who, in general terms "fit" the description of the "Roma" because they are marked by community boundaries, are actually defined to a much greater extent by shared identities and practices that distinguish them both individually and as a group from any member of society. Because the group—including its individual members—is marked by its exclusion from and lack of access to political, social, economic and cultural processes, we draw attention to practices and opportunities that the majority takes for granted when talking about the Romanis.

Thus, our concern is that it requires a lot of effort to talk of Romanis without falling into a rhetoric trap of antiziganism. For the purpose of this volume, the editor suggested the use of "Romani/Romanis" to reflect the diversity of groups that share some or all of the following attributes, often stated as characterising Romani population: the use of a common language (Romanes), the sharing of common origins, aspects of culture, and decisively the experience of marginalisation and discrimination resulting from their belonging to the group. For both these reasons, most contributions in the book refer to "Romani/Romanis" describing groups in general and collectively, whilst the term "Roma" is reserved specifically for those groups that have traditionally used this as a collective self-designation.

In employing the generic term "Romanis", we point to three interrelated and as such potent issues at the core of Romani exclusion: Namely, that antiziganist attitudes are commonplace in all European societies; that these are hard to reconcile with individual, face-to-face experiences which members of majorities have with Roma; and finally, that the community of those occupying an object-like position in societies represent an array of groups with few shared markers of identity, except for that of exclusion. However, it has been up to the authors to choose the term with which they are most comfortable.

3. Background of the Volume

This volume offers a building block to identify the limits of recognition that do not spring from cultural differences between majority and Romani groups, but reflect the sets of interests underlying the exclusionary practices that affect all members of society. As much as exclusion is a part of social interaction, all contributors to this volume argue that the most far-reaching repercussions for those who already have limited access to and resources for equal participation in social process tend to reproduce prejudices and coin further stereotypes when facing systematically marginalised communities such as Romanis. In fact, this volume brings to a head the summary of work from the Collaborative Research Network (CRN) "Probing the limits of integration: Romani and Traveller minorities in Europe." The CRN has been growing since early 2010 and has received recognition from the University Association for Contemporary European Studies in 2011 under the short title "Romanis in Europe". Following a number of European events bringing Romani migrants and the exclusion of individual Romanis from access to housing, education, labour market participation and healthcare, coordinators have pursued specific interests in evaluative research with the focus on policies of recognition, targeting Roma communities, allowing their geographic mobility and determining their relationship with national and European institutions.

Looking back at the three years of the CRN's activity, we have indeed promoted research collaborations and knowledge exchange through existing networks. We have also tapped into inter-disciplinary, comparative and cross-regional research on European institutions and societies. "Romanis in Europe" sees itself as an interdisciplinary network initiative that brings together scholars, researchers and practitioners sharing a specific interest in the limitations of existing European policies aimed at Roma integration. The key rationale of the "Romanis in Europe" network has been to deepen collaboration between disciplines in order to further our understanding of current Romani situations in Europe, the impact of Romani integration policies on communities and the potential which European institutions and policymakers have to enhance Romani participation in governance. This larger collaboration network brought together experts on European integration and social cohesion, cultural diversity and linguistic communities, non-discrimination and minority rights, improving the nature and value of the discussions we had within the network.

In more than one sense, participants of our network have actively broadened the scope of the debate we had originally envisaged: Our peer-support has united both the young and the established, social science and humanities scholars, resolute historians and political scientists, all of whom have so far missed a level, mutually-supportive and encouraging exchange concerning the limits of Romani integration in Romani studies. And our collaborations took us considerably further than we had expected, to studies of the origins of Romani exclusion and the reasons why it is omnipresent in EU member-states that praise themselves as being democratic and liberal.

Through CRN partnerships we sought a two-way knowledge transfer between our partners in Eastern, as well as in Western Europe. This included increasing dialogue among our members about research ideas, methods and skills within the broader agenda of European Studies in Western and Northern European academia. At the same time, we raised awareness of the importance the European integration project has for European citizens proper, how issue-specific networks can enrich the conceptual understanding of empirical findings delivered by research in and on Southern and Eastern European societies in local languages. Perhaps unsurprisingly, the "Romanis in Europe" saw growing interest in questions about the origin of exclusion being raised by scholars hailing from, even if not working in the recently acceded EU member-states.

And of course we are happy to see that there are further research outlets in development. We have seen the European Academic Network on Romani Studies (EANRS) emerging with a similar mandate and, crucially, with support from the European Commission, sponsoring greater engagement of academics representing different disciplines and methodologies in the study of Romanis. Importantly, the EANRS regularly brings its research outcomes to policymakers' attention and boasts an established relationship with the Council of Europe, the OSCE and a range of national policy-making bodies. The objectives of the "Romanis in Europe" network were much narrower: It sought to offer an inclusive platform for academic exchange, a forum that welcomes contributions that are difficult to translate into and are hardly picked up upon by policymakers and other "user communities".

Although it has at times been difficult to coordinate, the founding members of the network have pressed for setting an academic, rather than an advocacy agenda in its work. Our logo represents the scholarly search for the limits of Romani integration in Europe, whilst avoiding the usual sentimental coding. It is our belief that reasons for Romani exclusion lay deeper than policymakers—and potentially also publics—are willing to concede. Even more so, we were delighted to join forces with the Hugo-Valentin Centre of Uppsala University in October 2013 for the conference "Antiziganism: Discrimination, Marginalisation and Persecution of Roma." Four papers in this volume were presented at that event; two more originate from the joint conference "Roma Participation, Empowerment, and Emancipation" held at Corvinus University, Budapest, together with the Roma Education Fund, the EANRS and University of Bristol in May 2013.

All the papers in this volume address antiziganism as a practice ubiquitous for contemporary societies and crucial for the study of Romani exclusion. Yet, most contributors are less concerned with the impact antiziganism has on Romanis proper as they investigate the wider social and political repercussions of antiziganism for societies where Romanis live. In so doing, all collected papers straddle the issues raised in debates on diaspora and global civil society, theories of inclusion and exclusion, cultural distinction and policy analyses. All of them demonstrate that the trinity of minority group/national majority/political management of ethnic diversity is being challenged by an increasingly vocal transnational awareness of social problems on the ground. All the papers focus on interest, rather than identity- or territory-based forms of solidarity between citizens as those emergent ties between individuals, rather than ethnics that prompt political institutions to seek novel ways of accommodating those who are excluded.

4. Overview of Contributions

All the papers—although to varying degrees—challenge the state-centred, liberal multicultural idea of equality as the cornerstone of approaches to Romani integration which we have observed across the European continent over the past decade. Though the authors are resolute in their scrutiny of the reasons why practices aiming at Romani inclusion have (so far?) been unsuccessful, studying the differences of Romani situations across states and societies in Europe yields a unique perspective on three dimensions of exclusion as experienced by Romanis: first the denied right to practice citizenship; second, exclusion from the opportunity to participate in societal process on their own terms; and finally, exclusion marked by the stigma of ethnicity, barely different from the underlying racial stereotypes of poverty and marginality. This volume tackles these issues by drawing upon a range of case studies and theoretical approaches that cross-cut disciplines, countries and cultures, and adopts a multi-dimensional approach to studying issues that influence exclusion and integration of Romani communities in Europe.

Huub van Baar discusses the emergence of a specific form of antiziganism across contemporary Europe that seeks to legitimise the differential treatment of Roma and majority citizens on the grounds that differentiation is legitimate. This "reasonable anti-Gypsyism" is projected from political decision-making upon a wider society, not excluding social scientists' studies. Van Baar claims that ambiguity in presentation and articulation are indicative of the new type of antiziganism we observe across Europe of late. The following paper by Matthew Kott offers a detailed account of the recent registration of Romanis in Sweden and police reactions to media criticism. The paper argues that although policing has long considered the "Gypsy" as a criminal Other in the nation-state, even in a Nordic-type welfare state like Sweden, evidence—and not only traces—of institutional racism and structural antiziganism can be found in abundance once the focus of criminal investigation turns to Romanis. The third paper offering a meticulous investigation of a case study is that of Markus End, who analyses the structure of meanings in modern antiziganism. End's paper undertakes an in-depth analysis of one of the most radical manifestations of antiziganism in the National Socialist movement of the early twentieth century and argues that in order to gauge the reasons for pertinent antiziganism, research should instead turn to an analysis of the majority society, and even disregard "Roma" as they are nowhere to be found in antiziganist rhetoric.

Katharina Crepaz and Sara Memo focus on international instruments of Romani empowerment in their two papers. Crepaz points out that even though the European Commission has taken interest in issues related to Romani exclusion, Romanis are still largely viewed as passive recipients of policies and aid. Using a multi-level governance approach to resolving some of the coordination issues, she argues, could help to step away from the donor-recipient frame and facilitate our view of Romanis as actors in policy implementation. Thereafter, Memo discusses the impact of differences in the legal status of Roma across

the EU concerning opportunities available for Romani communities to participate in socio-economic processes. By taking a comparative constitutional perspective Memo suggests that the current move to recognise Roma as a "pan-
European minority" is unlikely to improve conditions on the ground for group
members, and hence the daily conditions of Roma in the lack of a complementary legal recognition. Ioana Vrăbiescu sets the tone for approximations to the
reality of Romani self-perception as well as misrepresentation of Romanis by
non-Romanis. Vrăbiescu asks about the underlying structures that tolerate
and, as such, leave antiziganism unchallenged in everyday practices that are
not that different between Romanis and non-Romanis. As Romani identity is
irrelevant for antiziganist rhetoric, so is the reality of practice and interest of
Romanis one might experience in the everyday. Thus, there is a moving target
of interest that seeks essentiality, yet in practice is elusive not because it is
bound to a group, but rather is a quality of an individual, Romani or otherwise.

Diana Popescu analyses the connections between antiziganism and exclusion,
focusing on the notion of moral exclusion. She shows that antiziganist stereotypes portray Romanis as undeserving others with the effect of rendering unequal treatment and exclusion acceptable to the majority. At the same time,
however, Popescu points out that the deprivation associated with social exclusion has the paradoxical effect of reinforcing negative stereotypes as regards
Romanis, making antiziganism and social exclusion deeply intertwined. The
paper by Julija Sardelić discerns different forms of antiziganism in the post-
Yugoslav space. It introduces the theoretical understanding of antiziganism as
a form of cultural racism and presses on with the argument that in different
post-Yugoslav states it is manifest in the ugliest of forms, such as hate speech,
violent attacks against Romani minorities, etc. At the same time, antiziganism
is latent and is an undercurrent in different discursive practices, directly or indirectly targeting Romani individuals. Finally, Timofey Agarin claims that European Union policies that address discrimination against Romanis and support
improvement in their everyday lives are in fact following the treaded path of
antiziganist reasoning. Not only has the focus on individual aspirations and the
withdrawal of state support from marginal communities left individuals from
marginal groups to their own devices. The focus on identities has disengaged

institutions of the state from addressing exclusion that is conditioned upon structurally salient issues.

Dear reader, I welcome you on this voyage across Europe: from Sweden, Romania, and the Netherlands, to the countries of the former Yugoslavia, and across time: from early twentieth century to policy blueprints that are likely to determine nascent European governance for Romani inclusion over the next few decades. The volume engages with theoretical issues—what is antiziganism and why we do not need a definition of it to know antiziganism when we see it—to point out the practical conundrum about the right not to be discriminated against. The expressions of antiziganism discussed in this volume are different, but they always describe Romanis and their interests, practices, identities as those incompatible with idealised images about a "good citizen", who is usually a non-Roma. This is where the stereotype that a Romani cannot be a member of society "like you and me" meets the prejudice that "s/he does not want to be like you and me". Whether or not the agents of antiziganism really understand the reasons for their sentiment is in a sense immaterial: What is important is the fact that policy decisions towards the Romanis have resulted from a mixture of long-established stereotypes and contemporary uncertainties about the ways of repackaging prejudice under conditions of an otherwise liberal society.

Acknowledgement

Papers collected in this volume have been presented at several conferences, partially sponsored by the CRN Romanis in Europe and I would like to acknowledge the University Association for Contemporary European Studies (UACES) for funding network's activities during the period of 2011-2014. Also, many thanks to Matthew Kott for support during the move of the network to its current host institution, the Centre for the Study of Ethnic Conflict, Queens University Belfast, and for the help in coordinating when my time was in short supply. My particular thanks for organizing the meeting of the network in March 2013 and moral support ahead of and after the Antiziganism conference in October 2013, both in Uppsala.

The Emergence of a Reasonable Anti-Gypsyism in Europe

Huub van Baar

University of Amsterdam

On 5 February 1995, four Romani men noticed a strange traffic sign, erected on the path to their segregated neighbourhood in the Austrian town of Ober-wart. On the sign was written 'Roma back to India'. When they tried to remove the sign, a powerful bomb exploded. The four Roma were killed on the spot.

Jörg Haider, the then leader of the far-right Austrian Freedom Party (FPÖ), was one of the first politicians who commented on the attack. In the second half of the 1990s, his political party and its anti-foreigner agenda were strongly on the rise in Austria. Haider speculated that the bombing was an internal Romani dispute and related to a circuit of Eastern European gangs and weapons trad-ers. The Austrian media appeared to be receptive with regard to such imputa-tions. Many daily newspapers speculated on the possibility that the Roma had unintentionally blown themselves up, apparently regarding the idea as plausi-ble. These imputations were not limited to the media. During the first 36 hours after the attack, the Austrian police were also basing their investigations on the scenario that the four Roma had fallen victim to a self-inflicted accident. Imme-diately after the attack, the police thoroughly searched all the houses of the Romani community; they found nothing suspicious. The media continued to praise these 'adequate efforts' for several weeks, even after the police had admitted that it was quite possible that the strategy of their criminal investiga-tion had been mistaken.[1]

In the autumn of 1997, Franz Fuchs, the perpetrator of the attack in Oberwart, was arrested by chance in the course of a routine traffic control. It turned out that between 1993 and 1996, he had committed more than twenty racially mo-tivated attacks in Austria, including one on the then mayor of Vienna.[2] Evi-dently, the Roma of Oberwart had been unjustly put in the dock.

1. The Europe That Has Come

Shortly after the Oberwart bombing, the British historian Tony Judt reflected on Haider's rapidly growing popularity and the political climate this represented. In an article in *The New York Review of Books* of February 1996, he refuted opinions that Haider's rise reflected the return of Austria's murky wartime past, as several commentators had suggested. According to Judt, Haider and his like did not stand for the ghost of Austria's past, but, rather, "for something far more serious: they are the ghost of Europe's yet to come".[3]

In this context, we should see the events involving the Roma in Austria in 1995 as characteristic of how this group are being treated in much of Europe today: they are instantaneously and habitually put in the dock. It is not only extremist groups and far right political parties that have voiced criminalizing allegations against the Roma. Moderate politicians, citizens, the police, policy-makers, and some sections of the media have also expressed such imputations. While this attitude could be seen throughout the 1990s, primarily in Central and Eastern Europe, it is a trend that is today omnipresent throughout Europe.

One astonishing example is the hysteria about the Roma as alleged kidnappers; a rumour that spread quickly all over the world in the autumn of 2013. On 16 October 2013, policemen 'discovered' a blonde girl in a Romani ghetto in the Greek town of Farsala. They were suspicious, and took the child pending further investigations. The girl's discovery generated sensationalist headlines in many parts of the world, the implication being from the outset that 'the blond angel' could not be a Romani child. Images and stories of this 'blonde angel Maria'—as she was dubbed by the media—were travelling the world as being about a child who had probably been stolen by the local Roma. The parents of children who had disappeared derived hope from her 'discovery' and some claimed to have recognised their missing daughter in Maria. Even some well-known cases of kidnapped girls widely covered in the media, such as that of the British child Madeleine McCann, who went missing in Portugal in 2007, were connected to the allegedly child-stealing Roma.[4]

In the same week that police discovered Maria, two similar cases made news elsewhere. In Dublin and Athlone in Ireland, the police took two 'blonde' children from Irish Romani families after neighbours expressed concerns about the familial links of these children with the elders of their households. In one of these cases, journalists were present when the police took the child into custody for further investigation.[5] In all three of these cases, the authorities drew upon DNA testing to ascertain genetic links between the children and elders in the households in which they lived. The children in Ireland turned out to be the natural offspring of the couples from whom they were taken. The Greek Maria had been born to Bulgarian Romani parents who had given her up in a case of informal adoption due to their poverty.

The myth that the Roma steal children has been widespread in European societies since the late Middle Ages, and re-emerges repeatedly, often in times of crisis. There are no known cases in which Roma have demonstrably been involved in kidnapping. In May 2008, a Romani woman living in Naples was accused of kidnapping children, though no evidence was presented to prove the allegation. Nevertheless, some politicians backed the accusation and just few days later, some 60 Italian citizens assaulted a Romani settlement housing around 400 Roma in Ponticelli near Naples in retaliation for the alleged kidnapping. Molotov-cocktails were thrown into the ghetto, resulting in its complete destruction.[6] Similarly, at the height of public concerns about Roma stealing children from the ethnic majority in October 2013, Serbian skinheads attempted the violent abduction of a 'blonde' Romani boy from his parents.[7] However, neither the 2013 Serbian case nor the 2008 arson in Italy, both cases of actual attacks on Romani communities, have been as widely reported as the alleged kidnappings in Greece and Ireland.

These Serbian and Italian cases, but also the less dramatic Greek and Irish ones, show what unsubstantiated allegations can do, particularly when media, politicians and police fail to condemn the abuse of stereotypical images, or even stimulate their further reproduction. Media coverage of the 'blonde angels' paid remarkably little if any attention to the question of the violation of the prohibition of ethnic profiling by the police and other authorities: if considering a child having a different appearance to its parents being seen to be a legitimate reason for the authorities to intervene in the private lives of a family and resort to DNA tests for 'answers' is not ethnic profiling,[8] what is? Where was the public uproar at police forces breaching the UN Convention on the Rights of the Child or the prohibition of children's separation from their parents without demonstrably good reason?[9] However, the Roma have appearances against them, and using unauthorised means to control or discriminate against them have been used or tolerated all too often.

2. Reasonable Anti-Gypsyism

Violent anti-Gypsyism has been a part of European social practice for a relatively long time now. In Bulgaria, the Czech Republic, Hungary, and Slovakia, for instance, extremist, neo-Nazi, and neo-fascist groups have repeatedly attacked members of Romani minorities and even murdered some of them. Since 2008, in these four countries alone, more than 120 attacks on Roma and their property have taken place.[10] Violent attacks have not, however, been limited to these countries; we have also seen assaults on Roma in, for instance, France, Greece, Italy, Lithuania, Romania, and Serbia.

The majority of Europe's politicians and citizens, including those in the countries mentioned, reject these violent manifestations of anti-Gypsyism. But another trend as alarming as this violence is manifesting itself in Europe, as the recent cases of alleged kidnapping clearly illustrate. Across the continent, we are currently witnessing the troublesome emergence of what I call a 'reasonable anti-Gypsyism'.[11] A widely supported movement among non-Roma seeks retaliation under the pretext that the Roma frequently exhibit undesirable behaviour. The argument goes that you are rightfully entitled to act against the Roma and treat them differently, because they cause inconvenience, indulge in criminal activity and can generally be expected to cause trouble. It is not 'we', but 'they' who violate rights and fail in their duties. This 'reasonable anti-Gypsyism' manifests itself throughout politics and wider society.

For quite some time, phrases like 'the inadaptable', 'the indecent' or even 'the criminal' have been used or promoted to refer to the Roma in several Central and Eastern European countries.[12] Moderate politicians rarely oppose the use of these labels, and sometimes even incorporate them in policy proposals and measures. Recently, this troublesome approach has also made inroads into Western European practices. More often, and almost self-evidently, politicians, the police, and citizens consider the Roma to be a 'security problem'—a menace to public order requiring unorthodox and in part drastic measures.

A clear example of such measures is the expulsion of EU citizens of Romani background from France. The media across Europe paid extensive attention to these expulsions during the 'hot summer' of 2010, when President Sarkozy clashed furiously with the European Commission over this issue.[13] Despite their controversial character and despite protests from the European Commission and human rights organisations, these expulsions continued unabated and recur until this day. Since Romania and Bulgaria's EU accession in 2007, about 50,000 Romanian and Bulgarian Roma have been expelled from France.[14] Until the presidential elections of 2012, it was Sarkozy's right-wing government that was responsible for carrying out the expulsions; since then, Hollande's socialist government has continued the policy. If anything, this makes it clear that the political conviction of those in power does not do much to change the way the Roma are treated in France. In September 2013, Manual Valls, Minister of the Interior in the Hollande government, claimed that Roma "do not want to integrate" and that their lifestyles are "clearly in confrontation" with the French way of life. He added: "the majority [of Roma] should be delivered back to the borders. We are not here to welcome these people".[15] Valls' stance echoes the statement of Sarkozy's party colleague Jacques Myard, who said in 2010 that the key issue of the "European Roma problem" (sic) was the Roma's "excessive mobility" and "medieval lifestyle". Myard suggested that the EU should seriously reconsider its free movement directive in response to this alleged 'Roma problem'.[16]

Many have begun to consider these expulsions and other rigid measures against the Roma as normal in Europe. During the first fifteen years after 1989, the official approach to the Roma concentrated primarily on social inclusion and human and minority rights. At the moment, however, the approach is increasingly focused on enforcing public and social order and on the fight against crime. Opinion polls in France and elsewhere in Europe show that the majority of the population supports the controversial Roma policies of their political leaders and,[17] thus, that many in Europe tend to sustain or tolerate the 'reasonable anti-Gypsyism' that has emerged. The maintenance of the French policies demonstrates that the collective, ethnicity-based expulsion of Romani migrants from an EU member state—a practice which violates European law on free movement and erodes the EU's principle of equality—has been tolerated in principle so as to continue despite widespread criticism. France partially legitimises the expulsions with references to alleged disturbance of public order by the Roma.

As I have argued elsewhere, the framing of the Roma as a security issue is part of a political problem and of the legitimisation of anti-Gypsyism.[18] We need to consider, at least partially, the on-going securitisation of the Roma against the background of changing police practices. Extensive research of police practices in France, conducted by Didier Fassin over the course of 15 months, shows that Romani migrants had particularly often been faced with stop-and-search procedures as part of both established and newly introduced proactive policing measures. Despite this, offenses committed by Roma had rarely been identified.[19] Moreover, policy measures such as the French expulsions, as well as related policy measures observed throughout Europe, are unsuccessful, as they target symptoms. Policies commonly fail to challenge the key reasons why Roma migrate to Western Europe: poverty, unemployment, discrimination and hopelessness.

The one-sided focus on enforcing order, and the fight against crime, sustain and even reinforce anti-Gypsyism. Part of the widespread stereotyping is made up of the ingrained view that the Roma are a nomadic, roaming pack of thieves who maintain their own secret codes, refuse to integrate, and escape the sanctions of the authorities by constantly roving Europe.[20] Several of these stereotypes have recently appeared in media throughout Europe. The Roma are stereotypically represented as criminals, as disturbers of public order, or as well-organised clans or gangs who operate clandestinely and transnationally across Europe. For example, in 2012 the Swiss weekly magazine *Die Weltwoche* published on its cover a photograph of a Romani boy pointing a gun at the specta-

tor under the headline "The Roma are coming—Raids in Switzerland". The related article was called "They come, they steal and they go".[21] Absurd and disturbing as this Swiss case might appear, we can readily find an even more
serious one in a more recent case from the Netherlands.

3. 'Transgressing Roma': The Return of the *Zigeuner*

Two studies produced at the University of Utrecht in the autumn of 2013 went
viral in headlines across the Dutch and Belgian media with headlines on 'Romani criminality'. Two studies by Dutch academics are at the eye of the storm.
Annemiek Dul wrote a thesis on the relationship between human trafficking and
what she calls the 'internal dynamics of the Romani culture'.[22] Dina Siegel,
Professor of Criminology, produced another study, entitled *Mobiel banditisme*
(*Mobile Banditry*).[23] Between March 2012 and April 2013, Siegel conducted
research on so-called 'itinerant criminal groups' from Central and Eastern Europe operating in the Netherlands. The department 'Police and Science' of the
Dutch Policy Academy supported both studies; it co-supervised Dul's thesis
and commissioned the report written by Siegel's research team at the University of Utrecht.

In her thesis, and in what resembled a press release in the Dutch daily newspaper *Trouw*, the young scholar Dul suggests that some elements in "the Romani culture" stimulate crimes such as human trafficking.[24] She claims that the
Romani culture "creates a normative framework in which many women consider it as normal to work as prostitutes".[25] What Dul calls the "moral codes of
the Romani community" would radically undermine perspectives on Romani
integration and opportunities for their participation. These moral codes, she
states, would justify abuse within the Romani community, such as child prostitution and human trafficking.[26]

However, the attention paid to Dul pales into insignificance compared to the
impact of Dina Siegel in the news. In the second half of September 2013, Siegel
repeatedly appeared in newspapers, on primetime newscasts, and in several
talk shows in the Netherlands and Belgium. Everything started with a long news
report in the Dutch weekly newspaper *Vrij Nederland* in which Siegel claimed

that the Roma are overrepresented among Central and Eastern European 'itinerant criminal groups' operating in the Netherlands.[27] According to Siegel, one needs to break down the so-called "*zigeuner* taboo" and clearly state the ethnic background of those "itinerant criminal groups".[28] Only then, she stated, "we will not stigmatize the entire group of Eastern Europeans or even all the Romanians in the Netherlands".[29]

However, Siegel failed to take into account the stigmatising effects of her own analysis on the 'entire group' of Roma. Her statement that "the *zigeuner* has returned" ('*de zigeuner is terug*') and, thus, that the stereotypes are correct, turned out to be grist to the mill of those who spread hate speech via the internet and far-right groups. On the website of the far-right Belgian political party Vlaams Belang, for instance, Siegel's research report was immediately presented as a study that "smashes the *zigeuner* taboo (*zigeunertaboe*) to smithereens".[30]

Zigeuner, the often-used Dutch and German term for 'Gypsy', etymologically refers to an untouchable, unclean being; a pariah. Not surprisingly, many Roma consider it to be a term of abuse. Despite Romani and pro-Roma attempts to ban the use of this label in German and Dutch-speaking societies, these endeavours have never been fully successful. Indeed, we are now faced with the opposite trend, in which scholars such as Siegel present *zigeuner,* usually written with a lower-case letter 'z', as a legitimate alternative marker for 'Roma'.[31]

This tendency is not limited to the Low Countries. For several years, significant numbers of Romanians, including policymakers and politicians, have called for the reintroduction of *Ţigan*, the Romanian equivalent of *Zigeuner*, in official government documents and narratives.[32] The term 'Roma' is confusing, they argue, because it resembles the word 'Romanian' too much. Most importantly, they say, the Roma's 'bad behaviour' abroad being responsible for even a tenuous connection between the Roma and Romanians in general is bound to bring Romania's image into disrepute, or worse, damage it considerably. This suggestion 'to call a spade a spade' is evident in both the Romanian and Dutch cases. In short, we can reintroduce or maintain this use of derogatory labels for Roma without any problem, because many of them behave 'indecently' anyway. Consequently, analyses based on this argument which explain complex socioeconomic, historical and political problems concerning the Roma in behaviouristic terms, are articulations of anti-Gypsyism. They are presented, however, as a 'reasonable anti-Gypsyism' to which 'decent' citizens cannot have any serious objections.

4. Criminology at a Time of Reasonable Anti-Gypsyism

One salient detail related to Siegel's research is that it had not been published at the time of her public statements and the resulting attention in the media. Remarkably, the newspapers and news bulletins reproduced her claims without having consulting her research report in the first place.

What was the basis for Siegel's claims? Her report relies on small-scale qualitative, rather than quantitative, analyses that her research team conducted, mainly with police officers, in and outside the Netherlands. Several masters' students on her team visited Romania and Bulgaria for about a week, but made only a few short visits to a Romani ghetto during that time.[33] This type of research in no way justifies the landslide claims made by Siegel to the Dutch and Belgian media. When she stated, in the Belgian late-night talk show *Reyers Laat,* that 80 per cent of the Central and Eastern European criminal gangs operating in the Netherlands are Romani, she added that she dealt with "estimates" in her research.[34] But when scholars present estimates without adequate quantitative investigations as percentages, science turns into a kind of crystal ball gazing. Moreover, Siegel reportedly links the wealth of some Romani families, as evidenced by the exorbitant tombstones of some Roma in one Bulgarian cemetery, to their criminality.[35]

The improper handling of most of Siegel's research sources—whether they are ethnographic, juridical, historical, or theoretical—is the most remarkable aspect of the report. In general, her research does not corroborate the most remarkable claims she made about the Roma in the media. Statements that Romanian and Bulgarian police officers made about the Roma are simply taken as true, while the report also includes sources that remark that the police themselves are "the biggest mafia in Bulgaria" and "the most corrupt body in Romania".[36] What these claims imply for the quality and reliability of the police sources used remains entirely unclear. Moreover, an analysis of the threefold relationship between the statements made by police officers, proactive and other police practices, and the ways in which police officers perceive the Roma is lacking in the report. Consequently, the report does not provide adequate insight into the institutional and societal climate in which police officers make statements about the Roma.

As for the juridical sources, the report is based on an analysis of 907 Dutch criminal files.[37] Nowhere, however, do the authors of the report explain exactly how these files have been analysed, what kind of selection criteria were used to identify them or whether there were any difficulties pertaining to their examination. For instance, have police and officers of the judiciary registered nationality and ethnicity in these criminal files, and if so, how exactly? How exactly have the researchers combined the information about the nationality and ethnicity of offenders with the report's central concern with regard to mobile banditry? The report offers no answers to these crucial questions, neither does it exhibit any transparency.

What is clear, however, is that both Siegel and Dul have made wide-ranging claims about 'the Roma', 'the Romani culture' and 'Romani families' on the basis of a small number of cases that were poorly analysed. Though both studies warn against generalisations, both authors indirectly suggest that the Roma are both perpetrators and victims. Without a properly nuanced presentation of results, they claim that Roma exploit other Roma, in particular through the trafficking of women, forced marriage and forcing children to beg and steal. In short, some Roma enrich themselves at the expense of many of their fellow Roma. Moreover, 'criminal Romani families' hand down these patterns of behaviour from one generation to the next.[38]

In South Africa and the United States, blacks are overrepresented in crime statistics, yet only racists would claim that their involvement in crime is their own fault or the result of inherited criminality, and that these trends have nothing to do with the complex histories of segregation, apartheid and inequality. Although the overrepresentation of the Roma in criminal activities has not been proven at all, scholars such as Siegel are nevertheless holding them responsible for this alleged phenomenon. References to a still on-going history of exclusion, marginalisation and extremely negative and stereotypical representations of Roma are lacking, or are only mentioned incidentally.

The claim that "criminal Romani families" are a separate category of "mobile bandits" is one of Siegel's most disputable hypotheses.[39] Uncritically following the classification of some Flemish criminologists, who distinguish a "gypsy type" among "itinerant criminal groups",[40] Siegel categorises some criminal families on the basis of their ethnic background. Though one can speak of criminality in the context of extended families, nothing justifies labelling a specific category of criminal families as Romani, as Siegel does. When one adds the label 'Romani' and thereby designates a specific type of criminal as "criminal Romani families", one suggests that the ethnic Romani background is responsible for the criminality of those families. By so doing, the phenomenon of 'itinerant criminal groups' is seen only through the glass of Romani culture, and consequently, criminality among the Roma is explained racially.

The fact that criminal behaviour occurs among the Roma is not under discussion here. Neither do I question that some problems are handed down from one generation to the next, even though, in analysing this, we also need to take into account the role of complex historical, political and socioeconomic backgrounds. However, what should be under discussion is the way in which the accumulation of deep-seated and repeatedly reproduced stereotyping of the Roma has led to abuses in the way they are treated, in the media and in policy building and implementation regarding them.

5. Governing Europe, Enforcing Social Order

The contentious idea that we might have generations of "criminal Romani families" has led to criminal investigation practices in which police officers have traced the family trees of Romani families, as has recently been uncovered in Sweden.[41] Such highly problematic and illegal governmental practices have not, however, been limited to Sweden. In 2010, journalists and scholars revealed that both the French Gendarmerie and a Dutch municipality had extensively, and for a long time, created ethnic profiles of Roma and compiled databases illegally.[42] Moreover, in an interview circulating on the web, a Dutch police inspector states that he is combatting 'Roma-criminality' ('*Roma-criminaliteit*') as if to do so is an uncontroversial and accepted concept or phenomenon.[43] Elsewhere, the same inspector, who is responsible for the dissemination of knowledge about the Roma among the Dutch police and municipalities, presents family trees of 'Romani clans' to clarify the 'problem' of 'Roma without borders'.[44]

Seeing the Roma only through the lens of security and criminality, the police have been led astray by highly problematic genealogical methods of criminal investigation. Do we dare to question such practices? We seem to turn a blind eye to them under the pretext that when it comes to the treatment of some groups, complex social problems could better be solved in an "unorthodox way". Without a doubt, research into criminality should be possible, and one should be able to identify the proportion of minorities among criminals. Similarly, within the limits of the law, the police should be able to map criminal offences committed by the members of minorities. However, proactively compiling databases and using investigative methods that equate group membership with a tendency to crime is both unhelpful and illegal.

In the context of contemporary police practices, Fassin has argued that we are confronted with an ambiguous shift from law enforcement to what he calls "enforcing order":

> Instead of enforcing the law, as they would describe their activity, the officers patrolling in the disadvantaged neighbourhoods are actually enforcing a social order characterized by swelling economic inequality and expanding racial discrimination.[45]

The enforcement of social order requires adequate management and deployment of measures such as the proactive screening of *potential* offenders.

These measures have become part of a more general governmentality targeting ethnic and religious minorities in Europe.[46] In the context of policing, Fassin puts forward:

> Over recent decades, the general evolution of policing worldwide has been toward the harsh version of law enforcement. Or more precisely, this harsh version has been almost systematically imposed as a form of government of the most precarious and marginalized groups, notably working-class communities and ethnic minorities. A key element in this process has been the spread of a securitarian ideology, backed by discourses that fan public fears to justify more repressive policies, a rise in police numbers, and the escalating severity of penalties, regardless of whether there is an objective increase in crime and criminality, and often even when they are falling. The geographical segregation of the poorest groups [...] has considerably aided this shift, both by allowing police action to be focused on specific neighbourhoods, and by rendering this reality invisible to the majority.[47]

Fassin's observation of the shift from law enforcement to enforcing social order fits with the more general trend I have noticed when it comes to the treatment of Roma in Europe, particularly with regard to the shift toward enforcing public and social order and the fight against crime. The troublesome emergence of a reasonable anti-Gypsyism in Europe gives succour to this trend (and vice versa).

Science, police officers and the media should be responsible for combatting anti-Gypsyism, rather than fostering it, either directly or indirectly. The continuous reproduction of negative images of Roma, uncritical analyses and the incorporation of stereotypes in reporting and even policies, are encouraging the reasonable anti-Gypsyism that currently dominates throughout European society. However, 'reasonable' and 'unreasonable' anti-Gypsyism are not disconnected phenomena; they are merging seamlessly on a scale, and represent gradations of violence. The seemingly more humane reasonable anti-Gypsyism ambiguously stimulates a negative approach to the Roma and renders both dubious policy and police practices legitimate, allowing the transgression of legal boundaries at no peril. Moreover, the case of the continuing French expulsions and the ethnic profiling in Sweden, France and the Netherlands might lead to violent anti-Gypsyism being seen as legitimate by the more extremist elements in society.

The Roma are the last minority in Europe that can be discriminated against without limit—shamelessly, and often without punishment. Only time will tell how long we can continue to permit this troublesome situation in Europe. Contrary to the current trend, it would be wiser to vigorously distance ourselves from this situation if we wish to avoid more escalation than we are already facing in contemporary Europe.

References

1   For the wider context of the attack, see, for instance, ERRC, *Divide and Deport: Roma and Sinti in Austria*, Budapest, European Roma Rights Center, 1996. See also Susan Tebbutt, "Germany and Austria: The 'Mauer im Kopf' or virtual wall," in Will Guy, ed., *Between Past and Future: The Roma of Central and Eastern Europe* (Hatfield: University of Hertfordshire Press, 2001), 268-84.

2   Martin Schwarz, "Lebenslange Haft für österreichischen Bombenbauer," *Berliner Zeitung*, 11 March 1999.

3   Tony Judt, "Austria and the Ghost of the New Europe," *New York Review of Books*, 43:3, 15 February 1996, 26.

4   Helena Smith, "Two face charges over blond-haired girl found in Gypsy camp," *The Observer*, 20 October 2013. See also "Maria: Greek Roma couple charged with abduction," *BBC News*, 21 October 2013.

5   Henry McDonald, "Blonde girl, 7, removed from Roma family in Ireland," *The Guardian*, 22 October 2013. See also Cormac McQuinn, "Gardia took Roma child (2) without telling the HSE," *Irish Independent*, 11 November 2013.

6   See OSCE, *Assessment of the Human Rights Situation of Roma and Sinti in Italy: Report of a fact-finding mission to Milan, Naples and Rome on 20-26 July 2008* (Warsaw: Organization for Security and Cooperation in Europe, 2009), 4, 6, 23, 28.

7   Sladana Aničić, trans. Selma Muhić, "Serbia: Skinheads try to abduct fair-skinned child from Romani family," *Romea*, 23 October 2013.

8   See also ERRC, *Legal Factsheet: Child Protection—What Should States Do?* (Budapest: European Roma Rights Center, 2013).

9   United Nations Convention on the Rights of the Child, articles 2 and 9.

10   See, e.g., Amnesty International, "Wake-up call for a giant: The EU must end discrimination against the Roma," 4 April 2013. See also the website of the European Roma Rights Center, at which the attacks against Roma are well documented.

11   Compare Huub van Baar, "Europe's Romaphobia: Problematization, Securitization, Nomadization," *Environment and Planning D: Society and Space* 29:2 (2011), 203-12. See also Huub van Baar, "Roma worden weer zigeunerboeven," *Trouw*, 26 October 2013.

12   Huub van Baar, *The European Roma: Minority Representation, Memory and the Limits of Transnational Governmentality* (Amsterdam: F&N, 2011), 191-231, 317-21. See also Georgia Efremova, "Integralist narratives and redemptive anti-Gypsy politics in Bulgaria," in Michael Stewart, ed., *The Gypsy 'Menace': Populism and the New Anti-Gypsy Politics* (London: Hurst and Company, 2012), 55-63; Gwendolyn Albert, "Anti-Gypsyism and the extreme-right in the Czech Republic 2008-2011," in Stewart, *The Gypsy 'Menace'*, 137-65; Lidia Balogh, "Possible responses to the sweep of right-wing forces and anti-Gypsyism in Hungary," in Stewart, *The Gypsy 'Menace'*, 242-44.

13   See, for instance, Ian Traynor, "Roma deportations by France a disgrace, says EU," *The Guardian*, 14 September 2010. See also Lizzy Davies, "France defends Roma expulsion policy," *The Guardian*, 15 September 2010.

14   For the context of the expulsions, see, for instance, Van Baar, "Europe's Romaphobia"; Helen O'Nions, "Roma Expulsions and Discrimination: The Elephant in Brussels," *Eu-*

ropean Journal of Migration and Law 13 (2011), 361-88; Horia Barbulescu, "Constructing the Roma People as a Societal Threat: The Expulsions of Roma from France," *European Journal of Science and Technology* 8 (June 2012), 279-89; Owen Parker, "Roma and the Politics of EU Citizenship in France: Everyday Security and Resistance," *Journal of Common Market Studies* 50:3 (2012), 475-91; Andrew Korando, "Roma Go Home: The Plight of the European Roma," *Law and Inequality* 30:1 (2012), 125-47.

15   "French minister Valls defends call for Roma expulsions," *BBC News*, 25 September 2013. See also "Majority of French believe Roma should leave France," *France24*, 28 September 2013.

16   Myard interviewed by Riz Kahn, "Expelling the Roma", *Al Jazeera*, 3 August 2010. See also Van Baar, "Europe's Romaphobia".

17   See, e.g., FRA, *Data in Focus Report: The Roma* (Vienna: European Union Agency for Fundamental Rights, 2009).

18   Van Baar, "Europe's Romaphobia".

19   Didier Fassin, *Enforcing Order: An Ethnography of Urban Policing* (Cambridge, Polity, 2013). Fassin carried out his research between 2005 and 2007 and, thus, before Romania and Bulgaria entered the EU. Fassin had repeatedly tried to continue his research into police work. However, his requests (of 2007-08 and of 2009-10) had been rejected by the French Ministry of the Interior, which has almost complete control over research into police practices and into those of other state-funded security professionals. He concludes: "The procedure for approving a simple study that involved observing police work therefore becomes a matter for the central administration and the minister's office—ultimately where such requests are actually blocked" (*Enforcing Order*, 17). This trend implies that research into police practices has become close to impossible in France. We have seen similar developments to hinder and strictly control research into police work in other European countries.

20   Elsewhere, I have explained how the intersecting processes of stigmatization, securitisation, and 'nomadisation'—the latter being the problematisation of the Roma in terms of nomadism—have led to new forms and practices of anti-Gypsyism throughout Europe. See Van Baar, "Europe's Romaphobia" and Huub van Baar, "Homecoming at Witching Hour: The Securitization of the European Roma and the Reclaiming of their Citizenship," in Daniel Baker and Maria Hlavajova, eds., *We Roma: A Critical Reader in Contemporary Art* (Utrecht: Valiz/BAK, 2013), 50-73.

21   "Die Roma kommen: Raubzüge in der Schweiz," *Die Weltwoche*, 12 April 2012. Phillip Gut and Kari Kälin, "Sie kommen, klauen und gehen," *Die Weltwoche*, 12 April 2012.

22   Annemiek Dul, *Broederschap of pooierschap? Een onderzoek naar de invloed van de interne dynamiek van de Roma gemeenschap op de aanwezigheid van mensenhandel*, MA Thesis (Utrecht: Universiteit Utrecht and Korps Landelijke Politiediensten, 2013).

23   Dina Siegel, *Mobiel Banditisme: Oost- en Centraal Europese rondtrekkende criminele groepen in Nederland*, Reeks Politiewetenschap no. 72 (Apeldoorn/Utrecht: Politie & Wetenschap/Universiteit Utrecht, 2013). The English translation of this report appeared in February 2014 under the title *Mobile Banditry: East and Central European Itinerant Criminal Groups in the Netherlands* (The Hague: Eleven International Publishing). I refer to and quote from the English translation.

24 Perdiep Ramesar and Martijn Roessingh, "Romacultuur maakt slachtoffers," *Trouw*, 18 October 2013.
25 Dul, *Broederschap of pooierschap?*, 47, my translation.
26 Ibid., 43, 47, my translation.
27 Harry Lansink, "Het zigeuner-taboe," *Vrij Nederland*, 21 September 2013.
28 Siegel interviewed by Harry Lansink, "Het zigeuner-taboe," 30.
29 Ibid., 31, my translation.
30 Website Vlaams Belang, "'Het zigeunertaboe'", http://www.vlaamsbelang.org/nieuws/10302 (as of 5 October 2013).
31 For the expression of a similar idea, see Stefan Popa, "De zigeunercode moet gekraakt worden," *de Volkskrant*, 28 September 2013. The Romanian-Dutch novelist Popa suggests that Central and Eastern European Roma, now they are migrating to Western Europe, are becoming 'zigeuners' again.
32 See, for instance, István Horváth and Lucian Nastasă, eds., *Rom sau Țigan: Dilemele uniu etnonim în spațiul românesc* (Cluj-Napoca: Institute for Research on National Minorities and Soros Foundation Romania, 2012). See also Irina Diana Mădroane, "Roma, Romanian, European: A Media Framed Battle over Identity," *Critical Approaches to Discourse Analysis across Disciplines* 5:2 (2012), 102-19.
33 Siegel, *Mobile Banditry*, 16, 145-51.
34 *Reyers Laat*, 24 September 2013.
35 Siegel, *Mobile Banditry*, 94-96.
36 Siegel, ibid., 126.
37 Siegel, ibid., 18.
38 Siegel, ibid., 27.
39 Siegel, ibid., 131.
40 Stijn van Daele and Tom vander Beken, "Exploring Itinerant Crime Groups," *European Journal of Criminal Policy Research*, 16 (2010), 9-10.
41 Niklas Orrenius, "Över tusen barn med i olaglig kartläggning: Registreringen av Romer," *Dagens Nyheter*, 23 September 2013. See also, "Police report themselves for illegal Roma registry," *The Local*, 23 September 2013.
42 For the French case, see "MENS, le fichier ethnique illégal sur les Roms," *Le Monde*, 7 October 2010. See also "Unlawful gendarmerie database on Roma people," *Statewatch*, October 2010. For the Dutch case, see Veerle Vroon, "93 Roma-jongeren, waarvan 62 leerplichtig: Roma etnische registratie in Nederland," *De Groene Amsterdammer*, 21 September 2010.
43 Wander Rooijackers, "De bestrijding van Roma-criminaliteit vergt een lange adem," *de Website voor de Nederlandse Politie*, 3 August 2009, http://www.websitevoordepolitie.nl/passie-voor-het-vak/de-bestrijding-van-roma-criminaliteit-vergt-een-lange-adem-440.html (as of 10 September 2009).
44 Walter Hilhorst, "Roma zonder grenzen", http://www.ciroc.nl/presentaties/presentatie_hilhorst.pdf (as of 4 March 2012).
45 Fassin, *Enforcing Order*, xv, see also 92-93, 215-18.
46 For these changes and its specific impact on the Roma, see Van Baar, *The European Roma* and Huub van Baar, "Socio-economic Mobility and Neo-liberal Governmentality in Post-socialist Europe: Activation and the Dehumanization of the Roma," *Journal of Ethnic and Migration Studies*, 38:8 (2012), 1289-1304.
47 Fassin, *Enforcing Order*, 216.

It is in their DNA: Swedish Police, Structural Antiziganism and the Registration of Romanis

Matthew Kott
Uppsala University

Throughout 2013, there have been numerous stories in the domestic and international media about the strained relationship between the authorities in many European countries and Romani minority communities—the former of which are often under pressure from the prolonged economic and political crisis in the EU, and the latter of which may be in a state of flux due to a prolonged trend of Romani migration on a scale last seen following the emancipation of Roma slaves in the Romanian principalities in the mid-nineteenth century. In the public debate, Romanis are often presented in terms of being a socially disruptive "Other" that threatens to undermine law, order, and general morality, potentially causing societal breakdown. As former Labour Home Secretary David Blunkett recently stated in an interview with BBC Radio, "We have got to change the behaviour and the culture of the incoming community, the Roma community, because there's going to be an explosion otherwise. We all know that."[1]

Such attitudes have a long history and say a great deal about structural racism and perceptions of the Romani "Other" in modern nation states. What follows here will be an examination of a particularly illustrative case from Sweden, where a police register of some four thousand Romanis recently came to light. In my analysis, there will be a discussion of the persistence of institutionally racist cultural practices within the Swedish police force, and how this relates to the broader phenomenon of what can be termed "structural antiziganism" in an otherwise successful and liberal national welfare state like Sweden.

1. The News Story and Prevarications of the Police

On the morning of Monday, 23 September 2013, one of the leading Swedish daily newspapers, *Dagens Nyheter*, presented its main front-page story with

45

the following headline: "The police register thousands of Romanis. *Dagens Ny-heter* exposes: This is how the police conduct the illegal mass surveillance of Swedish families".[2] The story revealed the existence of a computerised database stored on a server belonging to the police authorities in Skåne (Scania), the southernmost region of Sweden. The database file, "Total", was saved in a folder evocatively named *"Kringresande"* (Itinerants). This database comprised a register of 4,029 persons from all over Sweden, organised in such a way as to show family relations; in effect it was a massive genealogical tree. Many of those included in the database were deceased. The oldest persons registered were born in the 1890s. Furthermore, details of over a thousand children made up a quarter of the database entries. Some were registered by the police when they were only a few months old. The sole feature shared by the persons included in the database was that they were all either themselves Romanis, or had been in a relationship with a Romani partner.[3]

According to the Swedish Data Privacy Act (*Personuppgiftslagen*), it is expressly forbidden to collect data about ethnicity, except in a few prescribed circumstances.[4] The Police Data Act (*Polisdatalag*) clarifies that gathering data about a person solely because of "race or ethnicity" is illegal.[5] It was also asserted that such a register also constituted a breach of the individual's right to privacy under Article 8 of the European Convention on Human Rights.[6] Since a significant proportion of those in the "Total" database could not realistically be under suspicion of any crime (being either deceased or small children), *Dagens Nyheter* presented this as a clear-cut case of illegal data gathering on ethnic grounds by the Skåne Police.

Even though Sweden had had no direct experience of Nazi rule during World War II, the country's significant history of racial biology and eugenics makes news of police mapping the family trees of a particular ethnic group a highly sensitive issue. All media outlets picked up the story, as Swedish Romani citizens throughout the country were interviewed about their fears of being included in the register, which conjured up disturbing family memories of the 1940s.[7]

Academics and other experts were also asked to comment on the widening scandal.[8] National Police Commissioner Bengt Svensson called the register "unacceptable", declared that there was no support in the legislation for such a register, and said the Skåne Police would request an internal investigation under the leadership of a public prosecutor.[9] Later that same day, the governmental Commission on Security and Integrity Protection said it would launch its own investigation into the database and possible violations of privacy.[10]

The next day, *Dagens Nyheter* continued to develop its scoop by revealing that there existed a second register of 997 names in the same folder, "*Kringresande*". Unlike "Total", which was an advanced database produced using IBM's i2 Analyst's Notebook advanced investigative intelligence analysis software, this second list was a simpler Excel file. Like "Total", however, this register also focussed on persons connected to the Romani community in Sweden. Often these individuals had no direct connection to criminality, such as the widely respected human rights activist from Gothenburg, Soraya Post.[11] As an internal police investigation was being initiated by the department of the Prosecutor-General's Office for police cases (*Riksenheten för polismål*), a range of other state bodies—the Equality Ombudsman (*Diskrimineringsombudsman*), the Office of the Chancellor of Justice (*Justitiekansler*), and the Swedish Data Inspection Board (*Datainspektionen*)—were discussing the ways in which they would coordinate their own activities with this, and the aforementioned inquiry of the Commission on Security and Integrity Protection.[12]

The initial reaction to *Dagens Nyheter's* revelations by the Skåne Police was complete denial. On the morning of 23 September, police press spokesman Lars Förstell told the media in no uncertain terms, "No such register exists". Later that same day, when it became apparent that this was not the case, the new explanation was that the database existed, but it was not a "register". Instead it was said to be an "analytical file" (*analysfil*), whereafter the Skåne Police went into crisis management mode.[13] In the late afternoon, a press conference about the "alleged register" (*påstått register*) was called in Malmö. Representatives for the leadership of Skåne Police expressed their regrets that some persons may have been caused distress by the news of a police database that included information on young children. Nevertheless, the police line was that this was an "analytical file" that was created as part of the normal intelligence gathering during a criminal investigation, and by no means was to be viewed as an ethnically-based register. Children and others not suspected of any crime were included in order to map the social networks of those under investigation. If any breaches of the Police Data Law had been committed, these concerned incomplete entries (e.g. not making explicitly clear who was suspected of criminal activity, and who was merely part of their social context) or failure to properly weed data that was deemed irrelevant for the investigation.[14] Thus, the police leadership in Skåne admitted that technical mistakes had been made, but not that anything fundamentally illegal had been done. Nevertheless, the aforementioned statements by National Police Commissioner Svensson forced the Skåne Police into a position where they had no option but to request an internal inquiry to test the database's legality.

On 25 September, it was further revealed that the Skåne Police had previously denied, when directly queried by the responsible oversight authorities, that they were systematically collecting any sensitive data at all. *Dagens Nyheter* published a facsimile of the written reply to the Commission on Security and Integrity Protection dated 23 April 2012, i.e. during the period when the database of Romani individuals was actively being built up by members of the Skåne Police.[15]

Justice Minister Beatrice Ask apologised personally (albeit not officially in the name of the state) for the registration of Romanis by the police, and admitted that it could indeed be an expression of racism.[16] National Police Commissioner Svenson, following a meeting with politicians in Stockholm, ordered all police districts in the country to report back on whether there were any other similar databases to be found.[17] Svenson also thought it strange that, although such sensitive personal information is only to be kept on file by police for a limited period of time, permission to extend the period of use for the database was granted twice by local superiors within the Skåne Police without any concerns being raised.[18] When asked later about why he approved the extension for the registration of Romanis, the head of the criminal police in Skåne, Stefan Sintéus, denied having had any detailed insight as to what the database that he had approved contained.[19]

Some members of the police force outside of Skåne, however, began to come to their colleagues' defence. Among the most vocal was Peter Springare, head of the serious crimes unit for the Örebro Police. Springare defended the use of tracing family trees—including children—in investigative work, and said it was a commonly used method in the Swedish police. This made him highly critical of Svenson's statements condemning the register when the story first broke.[20]

At the same time, the Skåne Police presented a more detailed explanation for the gathering of this information: namely that this mapping of social networks was part of the criminal investigation into a conflict between two Romani families in the satellite town of Staffanstorp, part of the Malmö–Lund metropolitan area in Skåne.[21]

When Sigurd Heuman, chairman of the Commission on Security and Integrity Protection appointed to undertake the inquiry into the legality of the database, offered his first impressions to *Dagens Nyheter* on 1 October, he said that this explanation was not complete. Even though the initial impetus may have been a "clan feud" (*släktfejd*) in Staffanstorp, the police in Skåne soon began registering many other individuals as well, including persons from Stockholm, Gothenburg, and all over Sweden. "In principle, the register concerns only Romanis, or persons married to Romanis," Heuman explained. Furthermore, it was revealed that not only a limited number of investigators within the Skåne Police had access to this database, but also third parties were allowed to query the database, including the state Migration Board (*Migrationsverket*) that deals with immigration and asylum matters. According to Heuman, the database of Romanis looked very much like a "handy thing to have" (*bra-att-ha-register*) for the police.[22]

Later in October, the rationale behind the registration presented by the police became more complex. The initial mapping of the 2009 conflict was extended in early 2011 to take in details of members of four Romani extended families—this time originating from Italy, Poland, former Yugoslavia, and Romania—also resident in Staffanstorp. This expansion occurred in conjunction with a spate of burglaries, confidence tricks, and other crimes in Skåne. Some sources suggested the presence of automatic weapons and a potential escalation of the intergroup conflicts. Later in 2011, the police dragnet expanded to include suspects of an invoicing fraud scheme, which eventually led to a trial in Malmö in October 2013.[23]

Throughout the weeks of media coverage, the Skåne Police consistently denied any serious wrongdoing. The police district's Chief Legal Counsel, Monica Nebelius, repeatedly appeared in the media to dismiss the accusations made by *Dagens Nyheter*. In a televised debate on the public service television broadcaster SVT's prime-time public affairs programme *Agenda* she stated in a debate with the editor-in-chief of *Dagens Nyheter*, Peter Wolodarski:

> We have no register of Romanis. This is a construct [*tankekonstruktion*] created by *Dagens Nyheter*. We have no register based on ethnicity. What we do have, however, is a collection of information [*uppgiftssamling*] and that is based on criminality.[24]

By and large, the initial reactions of the general public in Sweden to the revelations by *Dagens Nyheter* were ones of shock and outrage that such a thing more reminiscent of 1943 could happen in 2013. In a show of solidarity with their Romani compatriots a demonstration protesting the activities of the Skåne Police took place in central Stockholm already on the evening of 23 September. Not only activists from both left-wing and liberal political organisations, but also representatives from a range of Romani and non-Romani NGOs came out to publicly condemn "racial profiling" by the police.[25] Aside from persons working within police structures, such as the aforementioned Nebelius or Springare, few voices in the public debate questioned the fundamental assertions that the register was essentially "racist", and therefore also "illegal".[26]

National Police Commissioner Svenson, Justice Minister Ask, and Integration Minister Erik Ullenhag (whose portfolio includes liaising with national minorities like Sweden's Romanis) all concurred in quickly and decisively condemning the existence of such an ethnically-based register.[27] Indeed, as one commentator has put it, "The police and their critics seem to live in different worlds, with completely different perceptions of reality."[28] How then is it possible that significant sections of police are of completely divergent opinions? When trying to explain this strong denial in the face of both damning facts and a largely unanimous public discourse, a good place to start can be that it represents a self-reinforcing interaction between institutional and structural racism.

2. Institutional and Structural Racism

Policing is one of the areas of state and society where institutional racism has been identified as a problem.[29] In the Swedish case of the registration of Romanis by the Skåne Police under examination herein, I would argue that this is also an example of a particular form of structural racism, namely, structural antiziganism. Although "structural" and "institutional" racism are at times used as synonyms,[30] they are really separate, albeit related phenomena. Both these types of racism have in common that they—in contrast to individual prejudice—are "embedded in the institutions and structures of social life",[31] and thus are perpetuated without conscious actions by individuals. Put another way, these are forms of racism that are neither intentional, nor individualist.[32] *Institutional racism* as the older, more established term, refers to policies and practices, particularly within public institutions, that differentiate on the basis of essentialised ethnic or physical characteristics (i.e., "race"). Robin Oakley defines it as follows:

> The term "institutional racism" should be understood to refer to the way institutions or organizations may systematically treat, or tend to treat, people differently in respect of "race". The addition of the word "institutional" therefore identifies the source of the differential treatment: this lies in some sense within the organization rather than simply with the individuals who represent it. The production of differential treatment is "institutionalized" in the way the organization operates.[33]

Thus, institutional racism is the product of the internal institutional culture of an organisation like the police. As Niklas Luhmann and his followers have described, this "culture" exists alongside the formal organisational structures and provide a way of justifying the existence of the organisation, while also providing a framework in which the organisation understands and engages with broader society and specific societal issues.[34] This internal culture is built upon a variety of intangible elements, such as symbolic traditions, language (e.g.

professional jargon), and *esprit de corps*, which impart and perpetuate a common internal identity that transcend the individuals that make up organisation at any given time.

Institutional racism is thus not just a question of discriminatory official policies (an example of "direct" institutional racism[35]), but also concerns routine practices and informal aspects of institutional culture.[36] Even if the former are formally abandoned, institutional racism can persist due to the continued reproduction of the latter.

Structural racism occurs when discrimination is so ingrained in many aspects of daily life that it is nearly "invisible" to those not targeted by it. Individuals who are otherwise not overtly racist in their worldview can thus uphold structural racism without being aware of it, simply by following the hegemonic norms prevalent in the society in which they live. In all societies, however, institutions rarely operate autonomously as if in a vacuum. Hence the need to consider the concept of *structural racism*, current definitions of which arise in part from systems theory. As John A. Powell explains:

> It is a product of reciprocal and mutual interactions within and between institutions. Institutional racism shifts our focus from the motives of individual people to practices and procedures within an institution. Structural racism shifts our attention from the single, intra-institutional setting to inter-institutional arrangements and interactions. Efforts to identify causation at a particular moment of decision within a specific domain understate the cumulative impact of discrimination.[37]

In this way, the institutional racism that can be found in one organisation can be seen in relation to the policies, perceptions and practices that inform the culture of other actors in a given society—and indeed, the society as a whole. Thus, for example, institutional racism in police, cannot be treated as if it arose on its own; instead it must be understood as an outcome of a series of interactions with many other societal institutions, e.g. the justice system, social services, the education system, healthcare, religion, employers, etc.

In the age of nation states that arose in nineteenth-century Europe, in society after society this has entailed the project to construct a unified national "we" that transcended former local, class, and estate boundaries. Inevitably, the nation-building process of this new in-group has required the formulation of an out-group, the "Other", to whom the members of the national "we" can compare their relative similarity. Amongst the various social, cultural, and ethnic groups that almost all European nation states were Orientalised and racialised into the archetypal "Others" were the Jews and the "Gypsies".

The "Gypsy" is a notional construct of European majority societies arising from centuries-long interactions—including cultural clashes and mutual misunderstandings—with various Romani minorities and other groups that have at times occupied a similar social niche, often accompanied by an itinerant way of life. This construct of the "Gypsy" is of a dual nature. On the one hand, it represents the strange and exotic ethnic "Other", at once both fascinating and potentially threatening. In the modern, scientific era such attributes as darker skin colour, language, and cultural practices were liable to become racialised.

On the other hand, the "Gypsy" is also the social outsider, identified with behaviour considered disruptive to societal law and order. Violence, crime, deceit, immorality, lack of hygiene, and impiety are some of the negative attributes ascribed to "Gypsies". A romanticised view of the "Gypsy" as child-like "noble savage"—singing and dancing by the campfire, unspoilt by the drudgery and cares experienced by the hard-working, orderly majority—inspired both imitation (in the form of "Bohemianism"), but also contempt (by branding them as workshy parasites and mentally deficient). The associations with criminality, disease, and nomadism also became essentialised, making "Gypsies" into, at best, undesirables, and, at worst—as a security threat (e.g. as potential spies for foreign powers). These rootless Outsiders could thus be driven away with impunity, since they supposedly felt no loyalty for settled society anyhow and *Wanderlust* allegedly being "in their blood".

Whilst the perception of the "Gypsies"—as with the anti-Semites' construct of the "Jews"—can have very little to do with how Romanis actually are, the fact that Romani minorities have consistently been the object for projections of "Gypsiness" across time and space has means that Romani identity formation has nonetheless taken place in a kind of dialectic with the majorities' idea of the "Gypsy". Antiziganism can be defined as the fear, mistrust, prejudice, or hatred directed against individuals or groups identified as belonging to the category "Gypsy" (Ger. *Zigeuner*, Swed. *zigenare*, etc.) and has almost always accompanied expressions of nationalism across Europe albeit to varying degrees.

In the construction of the nation state, one of the key elements is the harnessing of the state's monopoly on violence for the purpose of legitimating and upholding the hegemonic order against the really or potentially threatening "Other". As such, modern policing has had a central role in the internal consolidation of the nation and nationalizing state against internal "Others", in much the same way as modern, citizen-based standing armies have guaranteed the national state's integrity from external dangers. In this way, the "Gypsy" became one of the foci for police in nation states almost from the very beginning.

The growth of modern nation-states led to changes in policing, as the state was eager to not only define, but also increasingly to control its citizens. The Romanis and other itinerant traders that had had an important niche in pre-industrial, corporatist societies were increasingly seen as undesirable vagrants that disrupted the work of state bureaucracies and the growth of capitalism. "Gypsy" behaviour was increasingly criminalised on social and economic grounds, and local police officials were often invested with significant powers to determine who was a "Gypsy" and how to protect the local community from this menace. As recent research on Wilhelmine Germany has shown, this soon led to police forces compiling registers of persons considered "Gypsies" as a prophylactic measure for preventing crime. It also encouraged collaboration amongst police across jurisdictional boundaries, as well as promoting a standardisation of procedures at a national level.[38]

In the late nineteenth century, new fields of knowledge, such as psychology and racial biology were making their influence felt within policing. Inspired by Cesare Lambroso's criminal biology, several practitioners in Germany and elsewhere felt they had found a genetic explanation for the phenomenon of "Gypsy criminality". Antisocial behaviour such as crime, vagrancy, and prostitution was determined by heredity. Thus the offspring of the essentially antiso-cial "Gypsies" were biologically predetermined to be criminals, or at the very least a burden to society.[39] As Wolfgang Wippermann observed, in late nine-teen-century Germany, the presumption of innocence did not apply to anyone considered a "Gypsy".[40] The same was largely true elsewhere as well.

In the interwar period in Europe, the "Gypsy plague" was a concern of so many of the national police forces that roving bands of "Gypsies" became an idea-tional archetype for transnational organised crime networks. As such, the "Gypsy plague" was repeatedly the subject of discussions amongst the Inter-national Criminal Police Commission, i.e. Interpol. At the ICPC's Copenhagen conference in 1935, a member states backed the initiative proposed by repre-sentatives of the SS-ified police force from Nazi Germany regarding the crea-tion of an international registry of "Gypsies" in Vienna. This database would contain genealogical details and help map the relational networks of "Gypsies" across Europe, based on a pooling of information from the various existing registries created at the local and national levels.[41]

All this coordinated surveillance of "Gypsies" as natural born criminals by police was a contributing factor to the continent-wide genocide of Romani and Trav-eller groups across Axis-dominated Europe in World War II. In this genocide, local police authorities often had great leeway for decision-making, and thus were highly complicit in the outcome of life or death for local Romani popula-tions.[42] Furthermore, this antiziganist prejudice amongst the police and judici-ary did not disappear along with the defeat of Nazism. In post-war, democratic West Germany, police officials accused of participating in Nazi crimes against Romanis were initially able to successfully argue in their defence that their "Gypsy" victims were persecuted not on racial grounds, but as criminal and asocial elements according to the laws of the time. As a result these policemen were acquitted of wrongdoing by the courts.[43]

For the police in many countries of Europe, "Gypsies" constituted a threat to law, morality, and order. The association of "Gypsy bands" with criminality and the déclassé, marginalised elements of society dates back at least to the sev-enteenth century.[44] This was also an era of brutal anti-Gypsy laws in many parts of Europe, with punishments including forced deportation and extrajudicial execution. The need to solve the "Gypsy plague" gained genocidal proportions during the World War II. Even after the war, the perceptions of the "Gypsies" as a problem group continued to predominate in many societies, perpetuating structural antiziganism generally, and institutional racism within the police in particular.

3. Swedish Public Authorities and the Criminalisation of Romanis

As elsewhere, the state in Sweden has a long and ignominious history of laws and regulations that persecute "Gypsies"—using various terms such as *zigenare*, *tattare* (from misidentification with "barbarian" Tatars),[45] etc. Throughout the 1600s in Sweden a body of legislation directed against "Gypsy" criminality culminated with the so-called "Tattarplacat" of 1637, which accused Romanis of all manner of crimes harmful to peace and order (including theft, black magic, fraud, prostitution, and blasphemy). In the first instance all "Gypsies" were order to leave the country by a certain date, after which any "Gypsy" man found would be summarily executed without trial, while woman and children would be forcibly deported. Without mincing his words, Allan Etzler—writing during World War II—called this law an immediate "plan for extermination" (*utrotningsplan*).[46]

These pre-modern policies, however, ebbed out over time. As the modern nation-state developed, new measures and rationale produced new forms of repression. In Norway, which was in a union with Sweden throughout much of the nineteenth century, the work of Eilert Sundt was pioneering. In 1848, this founder of Norwegian social anthropology was tasked by the Ministry of Justice and Police to present a report on the "so-called *Fantefolk*" (one of the exonyms for Romani Travellers in Norway). The result was published in 1850 with the telling title: *Description of the Fant or Vagabond People in Norway: A Contribution to the Knowledge of the Lowest Ranks of Society*.[47] Sundt later followed this treatise up with several annual reports. To this day, the sociological and linguistic data collected by Sundt are still useful as a source for how the Romani minority lived in Norway at the time; however, his reports also dealt with various ways of "solving" the Romani "problem". In later years Sundt advocated radical measures such as forced labour camps to turn Romanis into "proper citizens", and openly criticised the police's laxity with regards to how they dealt with *fanter* and vagabonds.[48] All of this can be seen as setting a precedent in Scandinavia, since Sundt collaborated widely with experts from Sweden and Denmark as well.

Sweden passed a new vagrancy law in 1885. As on the Continent, now local police could arrest persons with no fixed address or with irregular sources of income. This legislation in essence criminalised the semi-nomadic way of living that the Romani population had developed, forcing them out of such economic niches as travelling pedlars and tradesmen. At the same time, non-Romani persons who became socio-economically marginalised through lack of employment opportunities were increasingly branded as *tattare* after being arrested for vagrancy. Suggested solutions for this problem included labour colonies and the institutionalisation of children. The equation *tattare/zigenare* with the "socially excluded" underclass continued in the Swedish legal discourse into the 1920s, when the first country-wide registration of "Gypsies" by the police was undertaken as part of a parliamentary inquiry on vagrancy.[49]

In 1914 a new, temporary aliens law was enacted in Sweden, delineating who was considered undesirable and to be denied entry. Developing further the discourse of the aforementioned vagrancy legislation, the first article of the new law expressly forbade entry to foreign "Gypsies" (*zigenare*) and other foreigners who intended to make their living by begging or as itinerant performers of music or with trained animals. Furthermore, foreign travelling tradesman or pedlars were also banned, as were gamblers, former convicts, and anyone else unable to make a respectable, honest living (*"saknar möjlighet att här ärligen vinna sin försörjning"*). It was the responsibility of all such persons upon their arrival to report to the local police for immediate deportation.[50] The purpose of this law is clearly to prevent any new Romanis from entering the country, since both the ethnic category "Gypsies", and all manner of traditional occupations of Romanis are mentioned.[51] These "temporary" measures from the 1914 legislation to restrict Romani immigration were repeated largely verbatim in subsequent aliens laws from 1927, 1937, and 1945. From the outbreak of World War I until the immigration ban on "Gypsies" was lifted in 1954, only an estimated three foreign Romanis were able to enter the country.[52]

The growing influence of racialist thinking in the Swedish public discourse—the State Institute for Racial Biology was founded by act of parliament in Sweden in 1921—strengthened the perception that not only foreign "Gypsies" constituted a threat to society, but also the Romanis already resident in Sweden as well. According to historian Gunnar Broberg, the term *tattare* became a sort of catch-all term for the "dark and evil" elements that explained why such a "great and strong" nation like Sweden was being held back in its development. Professor Herman Lundborg, the first head of the Institute for Racial Biology, was apparently obsessed with trying to map out the influence of inferior groups using data collected from parish registries, anthropomorphic measurements, and photographs.[53]

The combination of racial and social stigmatisation led to a first countrywide "inventory of *tattare*" (*tattarinventering*). This was organised by the parliamentary standing committee on poor relief (*Fattigvårdslagstiftnings-kommitté*) in 1922 in conjunction with the preparation of their recommendations for revising the vagrancy legislation. Since the parish registry books were deemed to underrepresent of the true number of *tattare*, the police districts around Sweden were provided with a special form—"formulär Ta"—to fill out regarding those identified as *tattare* in their respective jurisdictions. The standing committee was pleased by the result of the police registration, which in its opinion presented a good picture of the social conditions under which the *tattare* then lived.[54] The total number of *tattare* and *zigenare* identified but the police in 1922 was 1,833, whereas the parish registries reported 2,575 *tattare*, *zigenare*, and "equivalent" ("med dem jämställda").[55]

Throughout the 1920's and '30s the so-called *tattarplågan* (the Swedish variation on the theme of the "Gypsy plague"), was to reappear in various public and media discussions about crime, poverty, and eugenics. For example, *tattare* were discussed as undesirable social and racial elements in the parliamentary debates surrounding the Swedish sterilisation laws of 1934 and 1941.[56] A full page article in *Dagens Nyheter* from 1935 entitled "The *Tattare* Plague Costs 10 Million per Year" is rife with antiziganist stereotypes about the burden to society posed by "Gypsy" criminality and parasitism. The caricature illustrating the article also reproduces the imagery of antiziganism.[57] Later, in 1942, the prominent ethnographer Carl-Martin Bergstrand even published a book with the title *Tattarplågan*.[58]

Even though Sweden remained formally neutral in World War II, the country was thus not immune to the generally heightened atmosphere of antiziganism that accompanied and facilitated the unfolding genocide against Romanis throughout Axis-dominated Europe. Based on its own domestic structural antiziganism—that is, without the direct stimulus of occupation or alliance with Nazi Germany, as elsewhere—it was decided that the "Gypsy plague" and its associated social problems were to be solved in Sweden.[59] The main state institution entrusted this task was the National Board of Health and Welfare (*Socialstyrelsen*), a state agency that during the interwar period was largely responsible for building up the Swedish welfare state. Its remit at the time included aspects of medical policy, social welfare, and labour deployment. As such, it helped formulate and implement the sterilisation laws;[60] ran a forced labour colony for prostitutes (usually charged under the vagrancy laws)[61] and during the war built up a network of internment camps for suspect aliens (both foreign communists and alleged collaborators with the Nazis).[62] In almost all its areas of responsibility—even the internment camps for politically unreliable foreigners[63]—the Board came to see Romanis as problematic.

The Board initiated a second "inventory" of *tattare* and *zigenare* that would provide the basis for a permanent registry of those considered "Gypsies" in Sweden.[64] This registration was divided up into two separate actions: one for *tattare*, and one for *zigenare*. The latter was conducted on 31 May 1943 by the local police authorities.[65] This resulted in the registration of 453 "Gypsies", and a summary of the results were published by the Board in 1944.[66]

The registration of *tattare*, however did not proceed as smoothly, due to the fact that there was a dispute as to how this category should be defined: based on anthropological (i.e. racial) criteria, or social ones. Gunnar Dahlberg, then head of the Institute of Racial Biology, was ordered to carry out an anthropological survey of inmates of prisons, workhouses, and asylums for chronic alcoholics in order to determine whether *tattare* differed from other Swedes. His result was negative, which complicated the task of registering *tattare*.[67] Allan

Etzler, an historian who had previously worked within the prison system, criticized Dahlberg's findings as flawed, as they did not take into account ancestry and culture;[68] indeed, Dahlberg's conclusions could easily be predicted, since his sample was selected based on who the staff of these various penitentiaries identified as a *tattare*,[69] i.e. regardless of the individual's self-identification. Despite these difficulties in definition, a preliminary "inventory of *tattare*" yielded a total of 7,668—albeit many of these were also persons identified by the authorities as being of *tattare* background, but who did not necessarily consider themselves as belonging to families with Romani heritage.[70]

The authorities in other Nordic countries at the time tended to share the views of Etzler, rather than Dahlberg. In 1942, two Danish doctors made a "social-biological study" of the "Gypsies" in Denmark, in order to determine how best to deal with the social marginalization associated with this group. The resulting monograph, *Gipsies in Denmark*, published in during the German occupation is remarkable for two reasons: firstly, it is published in English; and secondly, the authors at times take issues with the conclusions of the leading Nazi German authority on the "Gypsy problem", police "criminal biologist" Robert Ritter. On the other hand, the book follows much of Ritter's methodology, and includes extensive genealogical tables discussing the hereditary nature of social problems like criminality and mental infirmity amongst the Danish "Gypsies".[71]

The authorities in Nazi-occupied Norway, particularly the police, were keenly interested in Sweden's practical experience in coming to grips with the "Gypsy plague". Already in mid-June 1943, the head of the Norwegian Criminal Police sought contact via diplomatic channels with the Swedish Board regarding the registration of *tattare* and *zigenare*. The officials of the Board obliged, sending to the Norwegian Police explanatory information, and even a copy of the form used by Swedish policemen in the registration of *zigenare*. This was then used as a model for the questionnaire to be used in the Norwegian Police's own planned registration of Romanis.[72] Seeing as Police Minister Jonas Lie—a trusted colleague of Heinrich Himmler—was from 1943 discussing various increasingly genocidal ways of "solving" his country's Romani "problem",[73] the fact that Swedish government officials promptly provided helpful information to the SS-controlled police in occupied Norway is possibly indicative of the extent of institutional and structural antiziganism in the Swedish civil service at the time.

The collection of detailed data about Romani individuals continued in the post-World War II period. For example, several volumes of personal information were assembled as part of the state's "Gypsy inquiry" (*Zigenarutredning*) of 1954,[74] and later regarding the question of allowing Romani refugees from eastern Europe in the late 1960s. Some local police forces, such as in Malmö, still kept separate records of Romani suspects in the 1990s.[75] In various municipalities, the social services also kept files on Romani families; in Stockholm, the registration of "full" and "half-Gypsies" was carried out by the social services as late as 1996.[76]

As a result, various public authorities in Sweden—particularly the police and social services—had long institutional traditions of ethnic registration of Romanis as a "problem group", as well as existing datasets of sensitive private data that revealed social and family relations. The long-term effect of this was to build up an environment where both institutional and a more general, structural antiziganism were normalized and internalized within the Swedish state sector and amongst its employees.

One branch of the state sector which repeatedly came to exploit these data collected by the authorities was academia. Over the decades, researchers, particularly social anthropologists and ethnologists, have dipped into the records assembled and archived by the state to produce monographs whose findings have been detrimental to the public attitude towards Romanis. In some cases, such as Adam Heymowski's influential dissertation from 1969, wherein he concluded that *tattare* were a social isolate of déclassé Swedes, and not a Romani cultural group, were probably well-meaning in their positivism.[77] Others, such as the work of Birgitta Svensson and Karl-Olov Arnstberg in the 1990s, appear to intentionally give a "scientific" justification to negative antiziganist stereotypes.[78] Both of these authors used the concept of *samspel* ("interplay") to reflect Romanis'—supposedly intentional and mocking—manipulation of majority society's laws, structures, and mores to their own ends. Arnstberg's book is also based on extensive access to the personal information in the aforementioned files of the social services in Stockholm. Although he has anonymised the individuals involved as required by good scholarly practice, his publication nonetheless is a textbook example of how such a collection of sensitive data can be exploited in ways that are detrimental to Romanis, both as a community, and as individuals.

Even after Romanis (romer) were officially recognised in law as one of Sweden's five national minorities from 2000, aspects of institutional racism and structural antiziganism have been slow to change within parts of the Swedish state. For example, following the accession to the EU of Romania and Bulgaria in 2007, Romani beggars from these countries began to appear in cities across southern and western Europe, particularly in Italy and France. The arrival of new Romani migrants prompted outbursts of antiziganism from private citizens, and later, also the authorities and could also be evidenced when migrant beggars begun to arrive in Scandinavia in 2009.

In July 2010, the public service broadcaster Sveriges Radio revealed that the police in Stockholm had been routinely rounding up for deportation citizens of new EU member states on the grounds that they had been begging. This was despite the fact that they had the right to reside in Sweden for up to three months in the first instance, and that begging is not illegal in Sweden. In the ensuing public debate, Minister for Migration Issues, Tobias Billström, defended the actions of the police, arguing that it was right to expel from Sweden foreigners who arrived with no intention of earing an "honest" (ärlig) living. According to Billström, begging was neither an honest, nor reasonable way of supporting oneself, and that those that came to Sweden to beg were abusing the spirit of the EU's right to freedom of movement.

Billström also introduced arguments about "organised" begging and human trafficking. Nevertheless, the discussion revolved mainly around 26 Romanian Romani street musicians, deported in 2010 by the police for "begging" and lacking "honest means of supporting themselves" (ärlig försörjning). Whilst the current Aliens Law does allow for the expulsion of foreigners for begging, busking is not usually equated with begging by the police when the musicians are not Romani. Furthermore, the criterion of an "honest living" had no legal status since the provisions of the nineteenth century vagrancy laws were abolished in 1965. Thus, it was clear that even in 2010 that the Stockholm Police was working within an antiziganist discourse that had its roots in laws from 1885 and 1914. Furthermore, this institutional antiziganism was given strong, albeit not uncontested support from the government minister in charge of immigration, for whom resignation after this scandal was never even seriously considered. This provides an inkling of the extent of structural antiziganism in the Swedish state sector.[79]

4. Analysis of the Registration Scandal: The Usual Suspects

In this historical context, the fact that police in Sweden had been keeping a database of Romanis as a reference aid in their investigative work should come as little surprise. Indeed, Romanis in Sweden had long suspected that this was the case.[80] It has already been posited that the interconnected concepts of institutional and structural antiziganism can offer a good starting point for explaining the Romani registration scandal of 2013. The following analysis will seek to test the two parts of the premise.

With regards to institutional antiziganism, one needs to look at the internal culture within the police force: Do Swedish police routinely employ practices that expect outcomes on the basis of race or ethnicity? And, in the specific case of Romanis, is there any evidence of internalisation of the antiziganist trope of "Gypsy criminality"? Not long before the Romani registry came to light, there was a major public debate about how prevalent and systematic the use of sorting persons by ethnic criteria was within the Swedish police as a whole.

Previously, the Skåne Police had earned opprobrium when it was revealed as having an internal idiom that deemed racialist labelling of suspects as acceptable practice. During disturbances in the Malmö neighbourhood of Rosengård in 2008, riot police were recorded as having called stone-throwing youths of immigrant background "fucking monkeys" (apejävlar). In 2009, it came to light that racist formulations ("Neger Niggersson") were used in made-up names of example suspects for internal police training courses. Later, it was also exposed that investigators could look up suspects in the police database using search terms like "*neger*".

Whilst revelations such as these could force an apology from the police leadership, the offending actions were blamed on a few bad apples. At first these bad apples were hard to identify, and therefore internal investigations led nowhere; later, however, reprimands and sanctions became more commonplace. So common, in fact, that one representative for the police officers' union in Skåne, Stefan Olsson, claimed that this sharpened policy on racist language was negatively affecting the workplace environment.[81] It has also since been revealed that the Skåne Police criticised the introduction of the new Police Data Law, as investigators had wanted to be able to search for matches based on ethnicity, which would be banned.[82]

In late 2012 and early 2013, a major joint operation was undertaken by the Migration Board, the Police, and the Prison and Probation Service (*Kriminalvården*). The goal was to reduce the number of illegal immigrants in the country without residency permits. Known by the acronym REVA, the operation embedded Border Police with regular police doing routine checks for minor crimes and infractions. This allowed persons caught in the dragnet to be quickly handed over for deportation if a background check revealed a lack of proper residency status. One such place where REVA was deployed was in checking for persons travelling without valid tickets in the Stockholm subway system. Apart from the metropolitan Stockholm area, REVA was also rolled out in Skåne.

Complaints from the public, experts, and politicians accused the police working for REVA of mainly stopping and checking persons of "foreign appearance" (*utländskt utseende*)—i.e. that the police were engaged in illegal racial profiling.[83] Even though the police leadership steadfastly denied any racial profiling was being applied, amongst the police there were also voices that raised concerns over REVA and its psychological toll on the officers involved.[84] After the aforementioned Billström debate, the Romani community also from an early date viewed the REVA operation with concern.[85]

After the Romani registration story reached the headlines in 2013, there was a discussion of the use of databases that map networks of ethnic communities in the media. As mentioned above, the gathering of certain types of sensitive personal data is strictly controlled in Swedish law. Yet a senior police investigator like the aforementioned Peter Springare could defend the use of registering members of an ethnic community in a criminal investigation. Indeed, if it was a case of organised crime—he mentioned the example of an Albanian gang in Gothenburg—it was necessary information gathering to understand social relationships within the criminal organisation. Furthermore, he said that National Police Commissioner Svenson had encouraged the creation of regionally-based police analytical teams like the one accused of building up an illegal ethnic registry in Skåne. Springare sought to portray such databases as part of normal investigative practice, even if he formally condemned the registration of persons on a purely ethnic basis. [86]

Thus, a decade into the twenty-first century, practices of categorisation based on racial or ethnic criteria were still widely present in the institutional culture of the Swedish police. Even if the values system was slowly changing in the ranks of police,[87] how far does this change among police officers reflect on wider antiziganist attitudes in society? In a debate broadcast live on the main daily news analysis programme of the national public service broadcaster *Sveriges Radio*, Springare made the claim that, based on his long professional experience, "Romani criminality" differed from how crimes were perpetrated by other groups, since Romanis tended to involve their entire family in illegal activities—for example using children as a covering distraction. Thus, the registration of children, even toddlers, by the Skåne Police in its investigative research was understandable, even though he admitted technical mistakes may have been made in how the database was formulated and updated.[88]

Such statements, coupled with the aforementioned sorting of suspects by Romani ethnicity,[89] demonstrate that antiziganism is also still entrenched in the police officers' mentality.[90] Nevertheless, there were also voices from the police community that sharply criticised the registration of Romanis. Gunno Gunnmo, a former policeman that has in recent years been one of the key personnel in government inquiries on Romani issues, expressed his disappointment with his former colleagues.[91] Some serving police officers also spoke out about racism and antiziganism within the police.[92]

The extent to which the Skåne Police saw what had been done as fundamentally wrong is, however, unclear. In December 2013, it was revealed that an unknown amount of data from "*Kringresande*" was moved to a new, unidentified database.[93] How this material will be used in the future is not known. What can be said is that the tradition of "inventarising" Romanis as potential "Gypsy criminals" has not ended yet within Swedish policing.

The reasons for the Skåne Police being able to act with such apparent impunity lies with the way the much of the rest of the state apparatus reacted to the question of the Romani register. When the Commission on Security and Integrity Protection presented its final report on 15 November, Sigurd Heuman reiterated that the register looked very much like a "good to have" tool, and that it broke the law in several aspects. Yet, he said it was not, according to the letter of the law, an ethnically-based register, since the information was gathered with the suspicion of criminal activity as its point of departure. This point was seized upon by Monica Nebelius, who saw this as clearing the Skåne Police of accusations of a compiling a racist database.[94] Soon afterwards, the investigation of the two police officers suspected of being primarily responsible for the database was closed without indictment, since the public prosecutor felt there was not a strong enough case to bring any criminal charges to court.[95]

Finally, despite Sweden's constitutional protection for public sector whistle-blowers (*meddelarfrihet*), there was also an investigation into the legality of the leak to Dagens Nyheter that exposed the entire scandal. The chief prosecutor investigating the case was Mats Åhnlund—the same prosecutor who investigated the legality of the actions of the policemen who allegedly created the database. In mid-January 2014, it was announced that the investigation of the leak would also be closed without pressing any charges, even though aspects of the leak clearly broke the law.[96] Åhnlund's line of argument in not pressing charges against any individuals within the police for creating the database was that it was not possible to locate individual criminal responsibility, since the registration of Romanis was obviously the result of a "higher order failure of the system" (*överordnade systemfel*). Chancellor of Justice Anna Skarhed explained the decision to not seek charges relating to the leaking of information to *Dagens Nyheter* by referring to the greater public interest and the need to safeguard democratic principles in society.[97]

Taken together, the overall picture this presents is one where significant parts of the state sector in Sweden are still infused with structural antiziganism. As such, it is little wonder that Nebelius and the Skåne Police leadership would feel vindicated in thinking that nothing fundamentally wrong had been done in registering over 4,000 Romanis over a period of several years.

Conclusion

As the paper demonstrated, the revelation of the Romani register in Sweden can, but should not be seen as an isolated event. It can be easily situated within a policing tradition in Sweden that includes viewing "Gypsies" as potential criminals *per se*, and where the racist modes of categorisation are accepted as legitimate tools in upholding law and order. This internal police culture is mutually reinforced by the persistent structural antiziganism permeating other significant parts of the Swedish state apparatus.

It is worth reminding the reader that Sweden is not alone in this problem of institutional and structural antiziganism. As the scandal in Sweden unfolded in the autumn of 2013 other examples of police antiziganism appeared, first in Greece, then Ireland. The story of police raiding a predominantly Romani neighbourhood in Larissa led to the discovery of a blonde girl living with a Romani family spread quickly in the international media.[98] This created a spate of reports of alleged "kidnappings" of non-Romani children by "Gypsies"—another classic antiziganist trope.[99] Days after the Greek police announced the discovery of "Maria", the Irish police removed a blonde child from a Romani family in the Dublin neighbourhood of Tallaght.[100] A second child was also briefly taken into care by the Irish police in Althlone, also on suspicion of having been kidnapped.[101] In none of these instances did it turn out that the children had actually been kidnapped; in the Irish cases, the biological ties to the families were clearly established despite the children's differing appearance. Yet the Greek and Irish police were clearly unwilling to take the Romani parents' claims as believable in the first instance, and chose to instead fall back on centuries-old myths of "Gypsy child stealing".[102]

The problem in Sweden and elsewhere in Europe in 2013 is not that Romanis have any genetic predisposition towards criminality, as antiziganist constructs would have us believe. On the contrary, given prominent role of the idea of "Gypsy criminality" in the development of modern policing, one could say that antiziganism is programmed into the very DNA of police forces of nation states.[103] Indeed, the problem is that the persistence of institutional and structural antiziganism means that law enforcement agencies continue to project upon Romanis the image of ideal-type criminal outsider, as they have for over a century. Due to this strong "hereditary predisposition", regrettably, it is unlikely that antiziganism will disappear from policing in Europe any time soon.

References

1   Quoted in: "David Blunkett in riot warning over Roma migrants", BBC News website, 12 November 2013, http://www.bbc.co.uk/news/uk-politics-24909979 (as of 13 November 2013).

2   "Polisen registrerar tusentals romer. DN avslöjar: Så bedrivs den olagliga massövervakningen av svenska familjer", *Dagens Nyheter*, 23 September 2013.

3   Niklas Orrenius, "Över tusen barn med i olaglig kartläggning", *Dagens Nyheter*, 23 September 2013.

4   Personuppgiftlagen (SFS 1998:204), §13 and §16. Available online at: http://www.riksdagen.se/sv/Dokument-Lagar/Lagar/Svenskforfattningssamling/Personuppgiftslag-1998204_sfs-1998-204/ (as of 14 November 2013).

5   Polisdatalagen (SFS 2010:361), ch. 2 §10. Available online at: http://www.riksdagen.se/sv/Dokument-Lagar/Lagar/Svenskforfattningssamling/Polisdatalag-2010-361_sfs-2010-361/ (as of 14 November 2013). Cf. Orrenius, "Över tusen"; Niklas Orrenius, "Förbjudet att registrera på etniska grunder", *Dagens Nyheter*, 23 September 2013.

6   Orrenius, "Över tusen"; Mikael Delin and Staffan Kihlström, "Polisen anmäler sig själv", *Dagens Nyheter,* 24 September 2013. Cf. the text of the Convention, which can be found at: http://conventions.coe.int/treaty/en/Treaties/Html/005.htm (as of 25 November 2013).

7   Cf. Niklas Orrenius, "Sara, 2, hamnande i registret som spädbarn", *Dagens Nyheter*, 23 September 2013. In this article one interviewee also compares with the registration of ethnic groups in former Communist states.

8   The author himself was also interviewed for *Aktuellt*, the main television news programme of the public service broadcaster SVT, on 23 September 2013.

9   "Bengt Svenson: 'Det är helt oacceptabelt'", press release, 23 September 2013, http://polisen.se/Aktuellt/Nyheter/Gemensam/juli-sept/Bengt-Svenson-Det-ar-helt-oacceptabelt/ (as of 25 November 2013).

10   "Granskning inledd med anledning av tidningsartiklar om ett register över romer", press release, 23 September 2013, http://www.sakint.se/Pressmeddelande-23-september-2013.pdf (as of 25 November 2013).

11   Niklas Orrenius, "Hundratals romer i nytt register", *Dagens Nyheter*, 24 September 2013.

12   Delin and Kihlström, "Polisen anmäler". For example, the Data Inspection Board decided not to initiate its own investigation until that of the Commission on Security and Integrity Protection was completed: "Säkerhets- och integritetsskyddsnämnden utreder polisens registrering", press release, 24 September 2013, http://www.datainspektionen.se/press/nyheter/2013/sakerhets-och-integritetsskyddsnamnden-utreder-polisens-registrering/ (as of 28 November 2013).

13   Orrenius, "Hundratals romer"; Lisa Röstlund and Kenan Habul, "Polisen: 'Är inget register utan en fil'", *Aftonbladet*, 23 September 2013, http://www.aftonbladet.se/nyheter/article17523725.ab (as of 25 November 2013). The reporters from *Aftonbladet* say that Förstell had first admitted to the register's existence when questioned on 22 September, i.e. before the story broke in *Dagens Nyheter*, only to deny it on the 23rd.

70   Matthew Kott

14   Video footage from the beginning of the press conference can be found of the website of the Swedish Police at: "Film från presskonferens om påstått register hos polisen", 23 September 2013, http://polisen.se/Skane/Aktuellt/Nyheter/Skane/juli-sept/Film-fran-presskonferens-om-pastatt-register-hos-polisen/ (as of 25 November 2013).
15   Niklas Orrenius, "Skånepolisen teg om sina register", *Dagens Nyheter*, 25 September 2013.
16   Mats J. Larsson, "Ministern: Det kan handla om rasism", *Dagens Nyheter*, 26 September 2013. By contrast, *Svenska Dagbladet* reported that Ask apologised "å Sveriges vägnar" (in Sweden's name) for the registration: Hannes Delling and Mikaela Åkerman, "'Märkligt att ingen slagit larm'", *Svenska Dagbladet*, 26 September 2013.
17   Jens Kärrman, "Polischefen: Alla län ska göra en extra kontroll", *Dagens Nyheter*, 26 September 2013.
18   Delling and Åkerman, "Märkligt".
19   Niklas Orrenius, "'Registrets användning utvidgades'", *Dagens Nyheter*, 1 October 2013.
20   Delling and Åkerman, "Märkligt".
21   Larsson, "Ministern".
22   Orrenius, "Registrets användning".
23   "Bakgrund: Därför skapades registret", newswire item, *Tidningarnas Telegrambyrå*, 23 October 2013. Cf.: "Polisen försvarar omstritt register", *Svenska Dagbladet* website, 23 October 2013, http://www.svd.se/nyheter/inrikes/polisen-forsvarar-omstritt-regis-ter_8649266.svd (as of 16 December 2013).
24   Karl-Johan Karlsson, "Polisen: 'Har inget romskt register'", *Expressen,* 28 October 2013.
25   Bengt O. Björklund, "Många protesterade på Mynttorget", *É Romani Glinda* no. 5 (2013), 7.
26   One exception that proves this rule is, for example, the opinion piece by philosophy professor Per Bauhn: Per Bauhn, "Okritisk hållning till rasism", *Svenska Dagbladet*, 27 October 2013. Bauhn gives the Skåne Police the benefit of the doubt, and cautions against mechanistically labelling various phenomena as racist, as this can actually make it difficult to combat "the real racism" (*den verkliga rasismen*) that exists in society.
27   Cf. Bauhn, "Okritisk".
28   Stefan Lisinski, "Kritiken verkar inte gå hem", *Dagens Nyheter*, 19 Decmeber 2013.
29   For an evaluation of the situation in the UK in the wake of the Stephen Lawrence case, see: Oakley, "Institutional Racism". Generally, cf.: Tracy Roberts, "Race and the Criminal Justice System", in George Ritzer and J. Michael Ryan (eds), *Blackwell Encyclopaedia of Sociology* (Chichester: Wiley-Blackwell, 2011), 489–90.
30   Cf. Mikaila Mariel Lemonik Arthur, "Racism, Structural and Institutional" in George Ritzer and J. Michael Ryan (eds), *Blackwell Encyclopaedia of Sociology* (Chichester: Wiley-Blackwell, 2011), 491.
31   Arthur, "Racism", 491.
32   John A. Powell, "Structural Racism: Building upon the Insights of John Calmore", *North Carolina Law Review* 86:3 (2008), 795. Cf. Robin Oakley, "Institutional Racism and the Police Service", *The Police Journal* 72:4 (1999), 289.
33   Oakley, "Institutional Racism", 290.

34   Wil Martens, "The Distinctions within Organizations: Luhmann from a Cultural Perspective", *Organization* 13:1 (2006), 89.

35   Arthur, "Racism", 491.

36   Oakley, "Institutional Racism", 290–1.

37   Powell, "Structural Racism", 796.

38   Simon Constantine, "Particularities of Persecution: The Policing of Gypsies in Saxony 1871–1914", *Immigrants & Minorities*, individual article published online (2013), http://dx.doi.org/10.1080/02619288.2013.820578 (as of 19 December 2013), 1–24.

39   Peter Widmann, "The Campaign against The Restless: Criminal Biology and the Stigmatization of the Gypsies, 1890–1960" in Roni Stauber and Raphael Vago (eds), *The Roma: A Minority in Europe. Historical, Political and Social Perspectives* (New York and Budapest: CEU Press, 2007), 19–29. Wolfgang Wippermann, *"Wie die Ziguener": Antisemitismus und Antiziganismus im Vergleich* (Berlin: Elefanten, 1997), 113–15. Bogdal, 337ff.

40   Wippermann, 113.

41   Regula Ludi, "Swiss Policy towards Roma and Sinti Refugees from National Socialism: Defensive Walls Instead of Asylum" in Donald Kenrick (ed.), *The Gypsies during the Second World War*, vol. 3: *The Final Chapter* (Hatfield: University of Hertfordshire Press, 2006), 124–5.

42   For a discussion of this in the case of the Baltic states, see: Matthew Kott, "The Fate of the Romani Minorities in Estonia, Latvia, and Lithuania during World War II: Problems and Perspectives for Romani Studies and Comparative Genocide Research" (forthcoming).

43   Bogdal, 409–10.

44   Bogdal, 116ff.

45   Allan Etzler, *Zigenarna och deras avkomlingar i Sverige: Historia och språk* (Stockholm: Geber, 1944), 44. Cf. Bogdal, 40.

46   Etzler, 69, 71.

47   Eilert Sundt, *Beretning om fante- eller landstrygerfolket i Norge: Bidrag til kundskab om de laveste samfundsforholde* (Chrisitiania [Oslo]: Brøgger, 1850).

48   On Sundt and the Romani minority, see: Øyvind Midbøe, *Eilert Sundt og fantesaken* (Oslo: Universitetsforlaget, 1968).

49   Selling, 45–8.

50   Norma Montesino, *Romer i svensk myndighetspolitik—ett historiskt perspektiv* (Lund: Lunds Universitet, Socialhögskolan, 2010), 17–18.

51   Cf. Selling, 58.

52   Ingvar Svanberg and Mattias Tydén, "Zigenare, tattare och svensk rashygien" in Jahn Otto Johansen, *Zigenarnas Holocaust* (Stockholm; Stehag: Symposion, 1990), 162.

53   Eva F. Dahlgren, *Fallna kvinnor: När samhällets bottensats skulle lära sig veta hut* (Stockholm: Forum, 2013), 46. For a discussion of the complex relationship between the use of photography in Gypsylorism, racial biology, and policing practices (including the eventual Nazi genocide) in the case of interwar Germany, see: Eva Rosenhaft, "Exchanging Glances: Ambivalence in Twentieth-Century Photographs of German Sinti", *Third Text* 22:3 (2008), 311–24.

54   Birgitta Svensson, *Bortom all ära och redlighet: Tattarnas spel med rättvisan* ([Stockholm]: Nordiska museet, 1993), 157–8.

55 Gunnar Broberg and Mattias Tydén, *Oönskade i folkhemmet: Rashygien och sterilisering i Sverige* (Stockholm: Dialogos, 2005), 147.

56 Broberg and Tydén, *Oönskade*, 147–52.

57 A partial facsimile of this article is reproduced in: Svensson, 175.

58 Carl-Martin Bergstrand, *Tattarplågan: Tattarna i svenskt folkliv* (Gothenburg: Gumperts, 1942).

59 Broberg and Tydén, *Oönskade*, 153; Thom Axelsson, "Tattarna och deras begåvning: Tekniker för styrning under det tidiga 1940-talet", in Johannes Fredriksson and Esbjörn Larsson (eds.), *Att rätt förfoga över tingen: Historiska studier av styrning och maktutövning* (Uppsala: Historiska institutionen, Uppsala universitet, 2007), 178.

60 Regarding its role in "biologising" (i.e. racialising) the *tattare* as a problem group, see: Broberg and Tydén, *Oönskade*, 150–2.

61 Dahlgren.

62 Tobias Berglund and Niclas Sennerteg, *Svenska koncentrationsläger i Tredje rikets skugga* (Stockholm: Natur och kultur, 2008). Berglund and Sennerteg make the comparison to concentration camps—an interpretation that is contested.

63 See, for example the case of two young Norwegian Romani sisters passed to the Board for internment by the Norwegian exile authorities for as belonging to a typical vagabond family, and for having allegedly been seen in public in the company of German soldiers: Riksarkivet (Stockholm), Statens Utlänningskommission (SUK), Lägerarkiv Kjesäter, BII:1 (Avvisningar osv. 1942–43), 14676 and 14677.

64 Broberg and Tydén, *Oönskade*, 153.

65 Note of Anders Twengström, National Board of Health and Welfare, 7 July 1943, photocopy in the collections of Center for Study of the Holocaust and Religious Minorities (HL-senteret), Oslo. This is a copy of a document held in the Riksarkivet (Oslo), files of the Norwegian Criminal Police (Kripo). Cf. Etzler, 126–7.

66 Etzler, 127.

67 Broberg and Tydén, *Oönskade*, 153–4; cf. Note of Twengström.

68 Broberg and Tydén, *Oönskade*, 155–6.

69 Svensson, 35.

70 Broberg and Tydén, "Zigenare", 172. The summary of this registration were published by the Board in 1945.

71 Erik D. Bartels and Gudrun Brun, *Gipsies in Denmark: A Social-Biological Study* (Copenhagen: Munksgaard, 1943).

72 Photocopies in the collections of the Center for Study of the Holocaust and Religious Minorities (HL-senteret), Oslo. These is are copies of documents held in the Riksarkivet (Oslo), files of the Norwegian Criminal Police (Kripo).

73 Bernt Rougthvedt, *Med penn og pistol: Om politiminister Jonas Lie* (Oslo: Cappelen Damm, 2010), 314–19; Terje Emberland and Matthew Kott, *Himmlers Norge: Nordmenn i det storgermanske prosjekt* (Oslo: Aschehoug, 2012), 483–4.

74 On this see: Selling, ch. 4.

75 Niklas Orrenius, "Polis: 'Foton på romer lades i särskilda lådor'", *Dagens Nyheter*, 24 September 2013.

76 Niklas Orrenius, "Romer kontrollerades i sina egna hem", *Dagens Nyheter*, 27 September 2013.

77   Adam Heymowski, *Swedish "Travellers" and Their Ancestry: A Social Isolate or and Ethnic Minority?* (Uppsala: Uppsala University, 1969). Heymowski later revised his views somewhat: Adam Heymowski, "Resande eller 'tattare': En gammal minoritet på väg att försvinna", in Ingvar Svanberg (ed.), *I samhällets utkanter: Om "tattare" i Sverige* (Uppsala: Centre for Multiethnic Research, 1987), 13–21.

78   Svensson, *op cit.*; Karl-Olov Arnstberg, *Svenskar och zigenare: En etnologisk studie av samspelet över en kulturell gräns* (Stockholm: Carlssons, 1997). Arnstberg has in the 2000s increasingly become associated with xenophobic and anti-immigrant discourses favoured by the political far right in Sweden.

79   Selling, 176–80. Billström remains migration minster at the time of writing in 2014.

80   Mikael Dellin, "Skandalen har raserat många romers förtroende för staten", *Dagens Nyheter*, 25 Sept. 2013. A prominent Romani activist had expressed to the author suspicions about police registration in private conversation already several years before this story broke.

81   "Inget åtal för 'Niggersson'", *Svenska Dagbladet* website, 2 July 2009, http://www.svd.se/nyheter/inrikes/inget-atal-for-niggersson_3152311.svd (as of 16 January 2014); "Skånepolisen hämmas av språkkrav", *Svenska Dagbladet* website, 8 April 2010, http://www.svd.se/nyheter/inrikes/skanepolisen-hammas-av-sprakkrav _4539445.svd (as of 16 January 2014).

82   Roger Haddad, "Skånepolisen ville söka på etnicitet", *Svenska Dabladet* website, 29 October 2013, http://www.svd.se/opinion/brannpunkt/skanepolisen-ville-soka-pa-etnicitet_8666166.svd (as of 16 January 2014).

83   Maltide Niang, "Politiker rasar mot kontroller av papperslösa", SVT website, 22 February 2013, http://www.svt.se/nyheter/sverige/politikerna-rasar-mot-kontroller-av-papperslosa (as of 15 January 2014); Henrik Bergquist, "Kontroller i t-banan bryter mot folkrätten", *Svenska Dagbladet* website, 1 March 2013, http://www.svd.se/opinion/brannpunkt/kontroller-i-t-banan-brott-mot-folkratten_7945848.svd (as of 15 January 2014); Jonas Bergström and Anders Österberg, "Hudfärg ska inte vara polisens riktmärke", *Svenska Dagbaldet* website, 20 March 2013, http://www.svd.se/opinion/brannpunkt/hudfarg-ska-inte-vara-polisens-riktmarke_7963246.svd (as of 15 January 2014).

84   Lisa Röstlund, "Poliser: 'Rasprofilering skadar poliskåren'", *Aftonbladet* website, 27 February 2013, http://www.aftonbladet.se/nyheter/article16324378.ab (as of 15 January 2014).

85   "Redaktören har ordet", *É Romani Glinda* no. 6 (2012), 2.

86   Jens Kärman, "'Vi har uppmuntrats att arbeta på det här sättet'", *Dagens Nyheter*, 25 September 2013.

87   Orrenius, "Polis: 'Foton på romer'".

88   "Registrering av romer—bara vanligt polisiärt underrättelsearbete?", *Studio Ett*, 25 September 2013, Sveriges Radio website, http://t.sr.se/1al3hFV (as of 16 January 2014). Springare talks of how "Romani criminality" differs from around 13:00 in this recording.

89   Orrenius, "Polis: 'Foton på romer'".

90   Former policeman Mikael Lundh admitted in a public discussion that, while serving in the Stockholm police, "I myself was one of those who discriminated against Romanis": "ÉRG:s Romska kulturdagar på Sensus", *É Romani Glinda*, no. 6 (2013), 6.

91   Gunno Gunnmo, "Besviken på sina egna", *É Romani Glinda*, no. 5 (2013), 4.

92   Orrenius, "Polis: 'Foton på romer'"; Martin Marmgren, "Nu behöver polisen en egen Lex Maria", SVT Debatt website, 25 September 2013, http://debatt.svt.s e/2013/09/25/nu-behover-polisen-en-egen-lex-maria/ (as of 16 January 2014);

93   Mikael Delin, "Uppgifter om romer flyttas till nytt register", *Dagens Nyheter*, 14 December 2013.

94   Niklas Orrienius and Mikael Delin, "Beslut: Polisens register över romer olagligt", *Dagens Nyheter*, 16 November 2013.

95   "Utredning om polisregister nedlagd", *Svenska Dagbladet* website, 20 December 20+13, http://www.svd.se/nyheter/inrikes/utredning-om-polisregister-nedlagd_88414 92.svd (as of 16 January 2014).

96   Mikael Delin, "JK lägger ned sin utredning", *Dagens Nyheter*, 17 January 2014.

97   Peter Wolodarski, "Fortsätt att vissla, säger justitiekanslern", *Dagens Nyheter*, 19 January 2014.

98   E.g. "Maria: Greek Roma couple charged with abduction", *BBC News* website, 21 October 2013, http://www.bbc.co.uk/news/world-europe-24605954 (as of 20 January 2014).

99   For a blatant example of the antiziganist media discourse, see: William Turvill, "Three Roma arrested after ANOTHER unidentified child is found 'kidnapped' in Greece", *Daily Mail* website, 23 October 2013, http://www.dailymail.co.uk/news/article-2473971/3-Roma-Gypsies-arrested-ANOTHER-child-kidnapped-Greece.html (as of 20 January 2014).

100   "Blonde girl, 7, removed from Dublin Roma family", *BBC News* website, 23 October 2013, http://www.bbc.co.uk/news/world-europe-24626422 (as of 20 January 2014).

101   "Child removed, then returned to Roma family in Athlone", *TheJournal.ie* website, 23 October 2013, http://www.thejournal.ie/athlone-roma-child-1143089-Oct2013/ (as of 20 January 2014).

102   This phenomenon has also been widely criticised, e.g.: Louise Doughty, "An angel kidnapped by Gypsies? In the absence of all the facts, age-old libels are being replayed", *The Guardian* website, 22 October 2013, http://www.theguardian.com/commentisfree/2013/oct/22/angel-kidnapped-by-gypsies-libel-replayed (as of 20 January 2014); Oksana Marafioti, "Roma Writer: Actually, Stealing Children Isn't Our Favorite Pastime", *TIME* website, 23 October 2013, http://ideas.time.com/2013/10/23/roma-writer-actually-stealing-children-isnt-our-favorite-pastime/ (as of 20 January 2014); Tom Sykes and Barbie Latza Nadeau, "Roma Face Persecution Across Europe In New Baby Stealing Panic", *The Daily Beast* website, 24 October 2013, http://www.thedailybeast.com/articles/2013/10/24/roma-face-persecution-across-europe-in-new-baby-stealing-panic.html (as of 20 January 2014); Peter McGuire, "Do Roma 'Gypsies' Really Abduct Children?", *The Huffington Post UK* website, 24 October 2013, http://www.huffingtonpost.co.uk/peter-mcguire/roma-gypsies-children_b_4152869.html (as of 20 January 2014); Jesse Walker, "The Legend of the Child-Snatching Gypsies: An old fear rears its head again", *Reason.com* website, 30 October 2013, http://reason.com/archives/2013/10/30/the-legend-of-the-child-snatching (as of 20 Jaunary 2014)

103   At the height of the registration scandal, a satirical comedy group even suggested that in the interests of public safety there should be a register created of all the family members of the Skåne Police, even newborn children, since obviously have "the baton in

their blood": Per Svensson, "De har batongen i blodet", *Sydsvenska Dagbladet* website, 24 September 2013, http://www.sydsvenskan.se/kultur--nojen/de-har-batongen-i-blodet/ (as of 20 January 2014).

Antiziganism as a Structure of Meanings:
The Racial Antiziganism of an Austrian Nazi

Markus End

Technische Universität Berlin

The phenomenon of hatred against so-called "Gypsies"[1] has existed in different forms for more than half a millennium. Throughout this time, the lives and the health of those stigmatised as Gypsies have been threatened by violence of the majority. Antiziganism showed its true potential for destruction in the Holocaust committed against half a million Roma, Sinti and other people that were collected under the despicable common Gypsy name. Antiziganism remains the cause for stigmatisation of people referred to as Gypsies, for their segregation and discrimination, as well as for physical attacks on Roma, Sinti, Pavee and other people.

This paper seeks to forego mistakes that have been made in the past scholarship in identifying core matters within antiziganism. It aims at a multilevel analysis and offers an explanation of antiziganism separate from approaches focussing on the perceived cultural differences between Roma and members of the majority society. To achieve this, we must change the optic and shift our perspective on antiziganism away from the object of discrimination, i.e. the Roma, to that of the majority society. Especially at the level of European advocacy for Romani rights, one witnesses the fight against antiziganism focussed on Roma entirely to the detriment of the awareness about antiziganism's origin in the majority society. This paper offers a definition of antiziganism that keeps check on the source of antiziganism and sees it as

> a historically developed and self-stabilising social phenomenon, consisting of three interrelated social processes. First, a homogenising and essentialising perception of specific social groups under the stigma of "Gypsies" or other related terms; second, the assignment of characteristics to those stigmatised in the manner underlining their deviance from the majority society; third, structural discrimination and subjection to violence resulting from general ascendancy to the attributes discerned above. [2]

The first two aspects describe the ideological level that—theoretically—can take place without actually targeting people. The social structures and actions that aim to discriminate, exclude, threaten, hurt and kill Roma, Sinti, Kalé, Pavee or others, make up the bulk of the third aspect, marking these as an essential part of antiziganist attitudes and clearly illustrating why it is such a problem for any society. It is important to keep in mind that although individuals are performing those negative actions, they are not the result of responses to behaviours and/or characteristics of actual people. Rather, the practices of those motivated to follow an antiziganist action pattern result from the ways in which the majority society is shaped and structured to allow, if not to endorse such behaviour.

It is also important to differentiate the image of the Gypsy, from that of individual Roma, Pavee and others that exist in society. The origin of this image refers us back to the first two aspects of the definition offered. The first significant factor allowing for antiziganism reflects on the background processes of homogeni- sation and essentialisation. By homogenising a group, racists declare that "if you know one, you know them all" and as a result, all Gypsies become (more or less) the same. The process involves not only the construction of the out- group, such as the "other" or Gypsies, but purports an equally homogenised picture of the in-group and, in the case presented here, Germans. In accord with this worldview, being a Gypsy or a German is something that determines and shapes one's whole life, devouring individuals of their individuality and cat- egorising them in dichotomous typologies. Individuals thus categorised have little chance of un-becoming Gypsies or Germans, but bear those labels as their heritage and from one generation to the next.

Historically, imperatives of homogenisation and essentialisation have been communicated through the discourse of racial belonging and the resultant cat- egorisation. However, in the contemporary world, concepts such as "culture", "mentality", "ethnicity", "origin" and so on are deployed for exactly the same reason, and perpetuate the logic of alterity.[3] In the context of anti-Roma racism, the "Gypsy" is most commonly used to draw the line between "races" and "cul- tures". Some languages use terms that derive from the Greek *athinganoi*, for example *Zigeuner, gitano, cigány* and so on.[4] As awareness for the stigmatis-ing content of those terms grows, antiziganists prefer the use of more covert terms such as "mobile groups", "vagabonds" (*Landfahrer* in German, *gens du voyage* in French), or "inadaptables" (*nepřizpusobivý* in Czech).[5] Even terms that are commonly used for self-identification by members of some groups, such as "Roma", are regularly misused in antiziganist rhetoric.

The second aspect of the definition comprises the ascription of specific char-acteristics of social deviance to the constructed group. It allows not only for the out-group to be seen as an inverse projection of the in-group; the members of an in-group are posited as a standard of positive normativity. What one thinks of Gypsies, therefore, is not distilled from experiences with, or in reflection upon the behaviour of (any one) existing group of Roma, but is the projection of the norm-setting majority about the existing social norms and values that are in danger of being breached by the out-group. The Gypsy, therefore, serves as a projective counter-image of the "good citizen" to enforce values and norms in the majority society, to ensure majority members behave, are emphatic and follow the common norm. Since forms of behaviour and feelings that violate the "norm" exist in society, members of the majority must project those violations upon the figurative Gypsy. The authorities follow suit and help establish the figure of the Gypsy as the model of non-conformist, deviant behaviour.[6]

The fact that people's actual behaviour is not the origin of the stereotypes as-cribed to and the prejudices associated with the Gypsy-figure does not mean that they are accidental. In reality, they bear the weight of the majority society's basic norms and values derived not out of experience but from negating the normative ideal. Clichés, stereotypes and "knowledge" about Gypsies is pro-duced and re-produced in the minds of European majority societies' individuals as inverted images of their own cultural industries. Even though the longstand-ing norms and values in question in Western societies have been changing gradually over recent decades, the image of the Gypsy has stayed largely the same. According to their respective contexts, some stereotypes may vary; yet literary studies in particular offer a picture of a very stable Gypsy stereotype over past centuries.[7] These Gypsy images change depending on the context in which they are communicated, messages implied therein and aspired outcomes of co-optation, yet the intent of these images remains intact. The description of a Gypsy in antiziganist texts maintains and develops the stable structure of meanings that can be analytically reconstructed.[8] This paper unveils the combination of abstract meanings that underlie antiziganist stereotypes and images and thus draws reader's attention to the abstract structure of antiziganism.

I discuss the tropes of antiziganism by reflecting on the structure of meanings found in the work of Tobias Portschy, the highly recognisable leader of the then-illegal *Nationalsozialistische Deutsche Arbeiterpartei* (NSDAP, National Socialist German Workers' Party, or Nazi Party), in Austrian Burgenland.[9] The resolution of the "Zigeunerfrage" (The "Gypsy Question" akin to the "Jewish Question"), an issue hotly debated in the Burgenland region during the early 1930s was one of the party's priorities. This section of the NSDAP differed from others located in other German-speaking territories, first and foremost because it constructed a concise and appealing reasoning for upholding antiziganist sentiments in public. Thus, though Portschy was not a famous figure of the Nazi party, the pamphlet he published in 1938 as the Governor of the Burgenland is among the most radical manifestations of National Socialist antiziganism.[10] This paper discusses his approach to, understanding of and the impact on tenets of antiziganism; it concludes with several observations on the parallels evident in majority relations with Roma today.

1. Homogenising and Essentialising

The paper focuses entirely on just one piece of literary work. There are several good reasons for such an in-depth analysis. First, Portschy's pamphlet points out the specific antiziganist structure of meanings that can be found in nearly all expressions of antiziganism, even today. Second, whilst the text was created during the National Socialist era, a time particularly renowned for its group-based enmity, many of these discourses, including those on race have been discussed in the past but only spurious attention was granted to aspects of antiziganism. Finally, the situation of the Burgenland was highly unique to the German Reich. Society in this borderland region was defensive of its claim to truly belong to Germany and hence went to greater lengths to establish its belonging to the German nation at the cost of excluding the rest, such as the Roma.

To set the stage, we should note how Portschy conveys the image of a homogeneous and essentialised other. Portschy's text employs an interesting tool to maintain the importance of racial purity, i.e. the concept he uses to explain homogeneity and essentiality. In arguing against the inclusion of the Gypsies into society, he states

> As we know today, different types of blood do not mix, but rather only aggregate with one another in groups. Therefore the Gypsies would live on as half-, quarter- and one-eighth-Gypsies, and would endanger the level of our culture in the frontier land to the extreme. *The unity of the soul of the German people would be lost. We would become an ambivalent people.*[11]

Up to this point, these descriptions are merely the usual racist images about sanguine purity. Including Gypsies into the body of the German people is akin to contamination, though interestingly Portschy also reflects on Gypsies' own purity when they incorporate Germans:

> Still today very often criminal and deviant persons are cast out of the German village community. [...] If as a result of this enduring rejection by farmers, these people until now have sought and found connection with Gypsies, then criminal and criminal unite and racial degradation triumphs. This, and only this is the reason why so many blond heads are to be found in colonies of Gypsies.[12]

Portschy considers blond heads to be Gypsies, because they live in a Gypsy colony, and they are criminals like the Gypsies. So the interesting point is that in Portschy's view, "Gypsy blood" does not suffer from, i.e. does not change as a result of "contamination". Group characteristics stay the same, as does their own identity. So in Portschy's notion of the Gypsy, we find a reflection of the "dialectic of racially-based discrimination"[13]. Following Wulf D. Hund, we see here one of several examples of antiziganist process of out-group crystallisation: First, through the creation of a homogenous group that is defined by essentialist markers such as "race", "ethnicity" or "culture" and, second, through the ascription of deviant characteristics onto those stigmatised, creating a double-bound definition of mutually reinforcing in- and out-groups. One definition works through the essentialist marker (which reflects the social construction process), the other via the characteristic ascribed without individual experience. Similar processes are at play in all socially relevant prejudices, yet the double-bound definition has been particularly powerful in the history of antiziganism.[14]

Throughout the centuries, the term "Gypsy" has been used to either describe a group perceived of as a people, a tribe or something similar, or for a group defined by a supposedly deviant social behaviour. Obviously, this double definition indicates the main function of antiziganism which is the fortification of the normative codes intended for the in-group.

The two steps necessary to establish a racist stereotype, as set out in the beginning of the paper, often fail to proceed smoothly in the real world. An antiziganist worldview is oftentimes obstructed if antiziganists believe in the ideological backbone of their views, yet the world around them does not correspond to these viewpoints. However, like other bigotry-infested groups, antiziganists establish that their own perceptions of the world are correct within the limited realm they are able to experience. As a result, people speaking Romanes while working as farmers, or blond heads living like Gypsies pose a threat to an antiziganist worldview. The first case is relatively easy to deal with and Portschy gives the best example here:

> There are some rare cases where a Gypsy dissociates himself from his community and pursues honest work. But if one believes that this person will persistently live up to the way of life of our people, he would be very wrong. Sooner or later [...] the longing for his people takes over, he lets work be work, the *nomadism* and the *parasitic* behaviour win out and suddenly he is an old Gypsy again. Based on this fact, it is obvious that the *mode of life* of the Gypsies is *racially* conditioned and they cannot change the way they are.[15]

So in this case, as is clearly stated, the essentialising and the homogenising take of racism is the strongest. Interestingly, the inverted relationship is not given here: as we have seen in the citation above, the author claims that persons who should have belonged to the German race can still be reduced to Gypsies, just because they are believed to behave like a Gypsy and thus betray their people's code of conduct. We can therefore safely conclude that Portschy chooses the definition of his target group with the maximal extension: Gypsies are all those who can be reduced to the essence of and thought of as a part of a homogeneous group of Gypsies, as well as all those who behave in what he deems to be a Gypsy way.[16]

But Gypsies are not only separated from the Germans; they are set up as an ultimate juxtaposition to being German. As Portschy puts it: "Good and Evil [...], Germanness and Gypsyness cannot be reconciled but exist in a continual antagonism."[17] This opposition seems to be a fundamental one. Though "*Deutschtum*" and "*Zigeunertum*" are not readily translatable into English, the use of these abstract terms makes clear that we are dealing with an anti-group prejudice as a *Weltanschauung* and the notion of opposing ways of existence are inherently defining the two groups. In Portschy's view, every German represents Germanness and every Gypsy the Gypsyness, both imagined as homogenous groups, delimited from one another by essentialising markers.

In the following I distinguish three of the basic tropes of modern antiziganism: the tropes of non-identity, archaic parasitism, and the lack of discipline all attributed to the imagined Gypsy.[18] These three tropes define the principles of essentialisation and homogenisation that grant antiziganism its structure and its meanings. The following section of the paper does not engage in the analysis of Romani cultures in general, or any individual group in particular, but follows up on patterns of antiziganism that we find in antiziganist texts in many contemporary European societies.

2. The Ascription of "Non-Identity"

The central element of the antiziganist structure of meanings is typically expressed in a banal way: "Gypsies do not have a stable identity. On the contrary, they are characterised by ambivalence." To put it into a slightly more abstract way, "Gypsyness is the identity of non-identity." As we have seen above, the antiziganist structure of meanings is always marked by duality and it reflects on the majority society as well as on the projected Gypsy. The National Socialist antiziganism has always imagined the group in racial terms, so Portschy employs his racial image of the Germans, and even of Germanness to distinguish Gypsies as different from the rest. This expression is the key part of the core ideology of antiziganism, expressed as "Germans have a stable, rooted, fixed and undivided identity."

The first and primary mode of conveying identity upon modern European subjects was through affiliation in religious communities. In the early modern period, people were required to have the same religious denomination as their landlords and nobility. At the time there existed no place for ambiguity with regard to religion, nor was there any possibility for an individual to challenge her religious identity or contemplate being areligious. Yet, effectively, such transgressions have been attested to imagined Gypsies in contemporary writings of the day: Gypsies are either without religion, or have swapped religious identity as they pleased and thus followed more than one canon at the same time. The role of the Gypsy in this antiziganist view was not only just about having (an)other denomination than oneself: The idea of the Gypsy occupied a position outside the complex system of identities held together by reference to one religious community.

We find this pattern in Portschy's text in various iterations. Interestingly, the old religion-based stereotype of non-identity still makes its way into his pamphlet. He states that "there is no trace of true religiousness among them,"[19] though his identity as a Nazi should be in conflict with that of a religious person. Another notion of this trope is: "Gypsies belong exclusively to the *Roman Catholic Church*. But only because of their material advantage [...]. They let their children be baptised three or four times, if there is the possibility of receiving more christening presents."[20]

By denying religiousness, therefore, the Gypsy figure is denied identity. In the first example it is done directly, in the second, via the opposition of a true (for the Germans, Protestant) belief versus a purely superficial alignment with the Church, expressed as "belonging" out of material interests. In this example,

Portschy's antiziganist ideology combines the anti-Catholic rhetoric of National Socialism.

The same position outside the system of identities was assigned to Gypsies in the realm of ethnic groups and national identities. In the antiziganist mode of thinking, Gypsies do not have a nationality, being neither German, nor any other nationality like French or Polish. Rather, it is established that they have no nationality—they do not belong anywhere and are not rooted at all. The place assigned to the Gypsy-figure in the identity-system based on categories of nationality is that of non-identity.[21] Further, as the most important identity marker for Portschy is obviously the German "race", the trope of "race" plays a similarly important role for the image of Gypsies: "Gypsies know that they form a foreign body within the space of the German people [...]"[22] Gypsies are not seen as another people living "here", they are perceived as a foreign body within the space designated for the "German people". The contradiction is therefore clear: "Whoever knows Gypsies, knows that they are a people of no-mads, not of farmers."[23] For Portschy, the link to the soil has a metaphysical connection to past generations of one's own people and forms a recourse to their identity, making "farming" not only a way to grow grain, but a backbone for community identity. Hence, he must oppose offering the people perceived as Gypsies land to plough and live off:

> To give them ground and soil would be such a crime as to incorporate them into the body of our people, because German blood and German soil shall remain free and pure [...].[24]

So, as long as the Gypsy lacks that connection to the soil, Portschy is convinced that he has no identity at all. The opposition of Gypsies and farmers that Portschy uses makes sure that the stigma of the Gypsy is defined by his, i.e. Gypsy's non-identity. This also points to another element of contemporary antiziganism, the ascription of parasitism.

3. The Logic of the "Archaic Parasitism"

The second central element of antiziganism is the trope I refer to here as "archaic parasitism". Its expression takes the following form: "Gypsies do not produce their food themselves. They get it from their hosts by ignoring the basic rules of economy." Of course, there is a counter-narrative for the majority society: "Germans earn their bread by working hard". Portschy once again:

> The Gypsy is a pure *parasite*: he does not long for the possession of ground and soil to permanently cultivate it with his own hand's work, just as he does not long to earn his bread by his own hand's work [...]. He roams from village to village, *begging* and *playing*, and *stealing* what is necessary from the fields.[25]

This is the archetypical antiziganist logic of material reproduction. The image of the German self is not that of a modern industrial society, but that of landed labourers moulded into a *Volksgemeinschaft*, working without any mediation of money, leadership, or machines. The opposite of this image is that of a Gypsy who avails of the products created by others without having done anything himself, ignoring common social norms of property, work and mutual obligation.

This opposition also helps in explaining the analytical difference between the structure of meanings on the one hand, and the stereotypical images on the other. The stereotypical images of black people, Jews and Gypsies regarding the subject of work appear rather similar here: they are lazy and avoid real work. However, once the meaning is revealed, we can better understand what antiziganists mean when they say "Gypsies are unwilling to work". Portschy calls Gypsies "parasites" (*Schmarotzer*) repeatedly, implying that while the majority produces food, the Gypsy consumes it. This comparison is at the core of many Gypsy-related stereotypes, such as begging, petty thievery, living from their music, social fraud or fortune-telling. The German produces the food; the Gypsy eats it—a perfect illustration of a parasitic relationship.

The function of these narratives in this case is different from that of the workshy Jewish or black person. The meaning of Jewish laziness in modern antisemitism is also that the Jew consumes the food that the majority society produces. But the imagined form of procurement is different from that of the Gypsies: The construction of Jews is defined by means of stretching, perverting, or overdraw-ing achievements and rules of civilisation, disproportionality empowering Jews. Accordingly, they are associated with powerful modern institutions, the stock exchange, bank, interests or the media, which makes Jews too civilised and thus hideous.

The construction of laziness with the imagined black person is different again. In Eurocentric racism, black people live directly off nature without any need for labour.[26] They are imagined as part of a rich environment and so are seen as somewhat animalistic, proximate to nature and thus in no way parasitic. In con-trast, the idea of material reproduction in Gypsies is built around their ignorance about and will to undermine civilization: they do not own property and thus need not understand what is dear to society; they fail to grasp societal norms and are alien to the rule that one needs to work for living. Gypsies are therefore imagined as pre-modern humans. The import of economic considerations for the mechanics of antiziganism employs the metaphor of an archaic parasite, which lives off the products of others' hard labour without due gratitude and care.

4. The Supposed "Lack of Discipline"

This trope typically expresses itself as follows: "Gypsies tend to directly satisfy their desires. They are not able to discipline themselves." In comparison, "Ger-mans discipline themselves, and plan for the future." In many ways, Gypsies are the symbol of a lack of discipline, organisation, or planning, in contrast to the Germans' industrious nature. This trope is connected to the disciplinary actions undertaken by institutions of the state in early modern Europe, even more obviously than the previous two tropes. It finds its expression in Portschy's words where he references: "*They are without measure in the con-sumption of alcohol and drugs* [...]."[27] He describes Gypsy sex life in terms of "*concubinage*", "*incest*" and "*premature marriage*" ("*Wilde Ehen*", "*Inzucht*", "*Frühehe*", p. 18, original emphasis); and he is worried about Gypsies' fertility because of their "lust" ("*Sinneslust*", p. 24). Excessive use of drugs and unre-stricted sexuality are symbols for undisciplined desires, reflecting upon the Gypsy style of consumption—direct, voracious, contemporary and not driven

by any rationality. In the antiziganist worldview, Gypsies play music without no-
tation, have sex without restriction, spend all their money on festivities and do
not think about tomorrow, much less the distant future. The Germans, on the
contrary, live to work, save their money and love discipline:

> Today, there is an effort to keep the workplaces of German workers clean,
> tidy and nice. How much more must we be attentive to these issues, by
> keeping the school tidy and teaching the kids neatness and order.[28]

But that effort is endangered by the Gypsy-image: "We German children had
to sit on the same bench with the filthy and lice-ridden Gypsy kids in school."[29]
Alas, even in this area of life, Gypsies pose a threat to the German, his health
and his cleanliness, because of the imagined lack of discipline among Gypsies.

Conclusion

Antiziganism is a powerful and deeply-rooted ideology that gained a foothold
in the public psyche during the establishment of Western European societies
and has changed little since. It should be understood as a specific form of racism that led to discrimination and violence against Roma and other people stigmatised as Gypsies throughout the centuries. In its most extreme form, antiziganism took the form of genocide during the Second World War. At its core,
there is the image of the Gypsy that represents a figure non-existent in reality,
but made up from the inverted norms and values underpinning Western European societies. The idea behind this norm of a Gypsy necessary for antiziganism is structured around the set of meanings I have discussed above—non-
identity, archaic parasitism and lack of discipline—all of which dis-identify
Roma and others stigmatised as Gypsies from the rest of society.

Although my paper used the example of writings by a Nazi political leader ex-
tolling his views around 80 years ago, the meanings found in his work map
precisely onto contemporary antiziganist sentiments. All the issues discussed
are shockingly similar to contemporary antiziganist propaganda where the images projected onto Roma and other people stigmatised as Gypsies build upon
negative perceptions of the in-group, rather than on real experiences with Romani people. It is crucial then to understand those patterns in their diachronic

perspective in order to identify why they manifest themselves to this day. Most importantly, it is necessary to stress that those characteristics ascribed to Roma originate from and are reproduced by majority societies, not as a reaction to the behaviour or characteristics of real groups. That is why the shift of perspective from the Romani group to that of the majority society is the precondition for our understanding of antiziganism.

References

1   I use the term "Roma" for people, who self-identify as such, while "Gypsy" is used in citations and projections of an image shared across the European societies for this group and for others.

2   For discussion of the German term "Antiziganismus" see Markus End, "Antiziganismus. Zur Verteidigung eines wissenschaftlichen Begriffs in kritischer Absicht," in Alexandra Bartels et al., eds., *Antiziganistische Zustände 2. Kritische Positionen gegen gewaltvolle Verhältnisse* (Münster: Unrast, 2013), 39-72.

3   See Pierre-André Taguieff, "Die Metamorphosen des Rassismus und die Krise des Antirassismus," in Ulrich Bielefeld, ed., *Das Eigene und das Fremde. Neuer Rassismus in der Alten Welt?* (Hamburg: Hamburger Edition, 1998), 221-268.

4   This does not mean that those terms are not used by individuals to self-identify in some contexts; needless to say, the meaning implied in most such cases is radically different.

5   See František Kostlán, "Czech Republic: Romani personalities condemn the term 'inadaptables'," trans. Gwendolyn Albert, http://www.romea.cz/en/news/czech/czech-republic-romani-personalities-condemn-the-term-inadaptables (accessed on February 11th 2014).

6   See Leo Lucassen, *Zigeuner. Die Geschichte eines polizeilichen Ordnungsbegriffes in Deutschland 1700-1945* (Köln: Böhlau, 1996).

7   For some interesting works in the field of literary studies see Claudia Breger, *Die Ortlosigkeit des Fremden: "Zigeunerinnen" und "Zigeuner" in der deutschsprachigen Literatur um 1800.* (Köln: Böhlau, 1998); Nicholas Saul, *Gypsies and Orientalism in German Literature and Anthropology of the Long Nineteenth Century.* (Oxford: Legenda, 2007); Wilhelm Solms, *Zigeunerbilder: Ein dunkles Kapitel der deutschen Literaturgeschichte. Von der frühen Neuzeit bis zur Romantik.* (Würzburg: Königshausen & Neumann, 2008); Herbert Uerlings and Iulia-Karin Patrut, eds., *"Zigeuner" und Nation: Repräsentation—Inklusion—Exklusion* (Frankfurt/M. et al.: Peter Lang, 2008).

8   Klaus Holz, *Nationaler Antisemitismus. Wissenssoziologie einer Weltanschauung* (Hamburg: Hamburger Edition, 2001), 133-140.

9   For more information on Portschy's biography see Ursula Mindler, *Tobias Portschy. Biographie eines Nationalsozialisten. Die Jahre bis 1945* (Eisenstadt: Amt der Burgenländischen Landesregierung, Hauptreferat Landesarchiv und Landesbibliothek, 2006); Ursula Mindler, "Die Kriminalisierung und Verfolgung von Randgruppen in der ersten Hälfte des 20. Jahrhunderts am Beispiel der österreichischen 'Zigeuner'," in Christian Bachhiesl and Sonja Maria Bachhiesl, ed., *Kriminologische Theorie und Praxis. Geistes- und naturwissenschaftliche Annäherungen an die Kriminalwissenschaft* (Wien et al.: LIT, 2011), 59-79.

10 Tobias Portschy, Die Zigeunerfrage (Eisenstadt, 1938). All page numbers throughout the paper refer to this text.

11   *"Wie wir heute wissen, gibt es keine Vermischung verschiedenen Blutes, sondern nur eine Gruppierung. Die Zigeuner würden daher in Halb-, Viertel- und Achtelzigeunern fortleben und das Niveau unserer Kultur im Grenzland ungemein gefährden. Die Einheit der deutschen Volksseele ginge verloren. Ein zwiespältiges Volk würde entstehen [...]"* (30) (Emphasis in the original delivered in expanded letter-spacing).

12   *"Oft werden verbrecherische und verkommene Personen aus der deutschen Dorfgemeinschaft noch heute geradezu ausgestoßen. [...] Wenn diese infolge der hartnäckigsten Ablehnung durch das Bauerntum Anschluss bei den Zigeunern heute noch sucht [sic!] und bisher auch fand [sic!], dann vereinen sich eben Verbrecher mit Verbrecher [sic!] und die Rassenschande feiert Triumphe [sic!]. So und nur so sind die vielen Blondköpfe in der Zigeunerkolonie zu erklären."* (31) (Emphasis in the original delivered in expanded letter-spacing).

13   Wulf D. Hund, "Das Zigeuner-Gen. Rassistische Ethik und der Geist des Kapitalismus," in Wulf D. Hund, ed., *Zigeuner: Geschichte und Struktur einer rassistischen Konstruktion* (Duisburg: DISS, 1996), 11-35, here 32.

14   Michael Zimmermann, "Zigeunerpolitik und Zigeunerdiskurse im Europa des 20. Jahrhunderts," in: Michael Zimmermann, ed., *Zwischen Erziehung und Vernichtung. Zigeunerpolitik und Zigeunerforschung im Europa des 20. Jahrhunderts* (Stuttgart: Steiner, 2007) 13-70, here 24-27.

15   *"In ganz seltenen Fällen kommt es vor, daß ein Zigeuner sich von seinen Artgenossen lossagt und einen [sic!] redlichen Erwerb nachgeht. Wenn man aber glaubt, daß dieser Mensch sich nun dauernd in die Lebensweise unseres Volkes einlebte, ginge man weit fehl. Über kurz oder lang ergreift ihn [...] die Sehnsucht nach den Seinen, er läßt die Arbeit Arbeit sein, das Nomadenhafte und das Schmarotzertum siegt in ihm und er ist plötzlich wieder der alte Zigeuner. Aus dieser Tatsache ist aber ganz klar zu ersehen, daß die Lebensweise der Zigeuner rassisch bedingt ist und daß sie eben nicht aus ihrer Haut herauskönnen."* (12) (Emphasis in the original delivered in expanded letter-spacing).

16   At least one further explanation was in currency during the Third Reich period that would have resolved the contradiction at hand. Expectedly, it involved a stronger emphasis on racial theory. Robert Ritter's theory saw the pure Gypsy as less dangerous than the 'half-breed'. The 'half-breed', he thought, were the off-springs of Gypsies and a special group within the German people, who were deviant because of their genetic defects due to the mixture of races tracing back up to ten generations. Since their intermixing, the vagrants reproduced themselves and mixed with the pure Gypsies, thus creating the most dangerous people. So Ritter tries to rescue the racial thinking by concluding that every deviant behaviour is a result of blood contamination.

17   *"Gutes und Böses [...], Deutschtum und Zigeunertum sind einmal miteinander nicht zu versöhnen, sondern dauernd in Widerstreit."* (37)

18   Markus End, "Die Wirkungsweise der antiziganistischen Vorurteilsstruktur," in Alte Feuerwache e.V. Jugendbildungsstätte Kaubstraße, ed., *Methodenhandbuch zum Thema Antiziganismus für die schulische und außerschulische Bildungsarbeit* (Münster: Unrast, 2012), 28-34.

19   *"Von einer echten Religiosität findet sich bei ihnen keine Spur."* (13)

20   *"Die Zigeuner gehören ausschließlich der römisch-katholischen Kirche an. Dies allerdings nur am materiellen Vorteile wegen. [...] Auch lassen sie ruhig ihre Kinder drei-*

und viermal taufen, wenn Aussicht auf mehrere Patengeschenke besteht." (13) (Emphasis in the original delivered in letter-spacing)

21   For discussion of non-identity as attributed to the antisemitic idea of the Jew, see Klaus Holz, "Die antisemitische Konstruktion des Dritten und die nationale Ordnung der Welt," in Christina von Braun and Eva-Maria Ziege, ed., *Das bewegliche Vorurteil. Aspekte des internationalen Antisemitismus.* (Würzburg: Königshausen & Neumann, 2004), 43-61.

22   *"Die Zigeuner wissen, dass sie einen Fremdkörper im deutschen Volksraum bilden [...]"* (14)

23   *"Wer die Zigeuner kennt, weiß, daß sie ein Nomaden- und kein Bauernvolk sind."* (31)

24   *"Ihnen daher deutschen Grund und Boden zu überlassen, wäre nicht minder ein Verbrechen, als sie unserem Volkskörper einzuverleiben, denn das deutsche Blut und der deutsche Boden sollen rein und frei erhalten bleiben [...]"* (32) (Emphasis in the original delivered in expanded letter-spacing).

25   *"Der Zigeuner ist ein reiner Schmarotzer; er sehnt sich nicht nach dem Besitz von Grund und Boden, um ihn dauernd durch seine Arbeit zu kultivieren, wie überhaupt sich durch seiner Hände Arbeit sein Brot zu verdienen [...]. Er wandert bettelnd und spielend von Dorf zu Dorf, stiehlt dabei für das [sic!] ihn Nötige auf den Feldern."* (14) (Emphasis in the original delivered in expanded letter-spacing).

26   Hitler's proposition about the so-called "Südrassen" in his speech on anti-Semitism that shows similar logic in the argument: Reginald H. Phelps, "Hitlers 'grundlegende' Rede über den Antisemitismus," *Vierteljahreshefte für Zeitgeschichte* 16:4 (1968): 390-420, here 400-402.

27   *"Maßlosigkeit beim Genusse von Alkoholien und narkotische(n) Verkommenheit [...]."* (23) (Emphasis in the original delivered in expanded letter-spacing).

28   *"Heute strengt man sich an, die Arbeitsstätten unserer deutschen Arbeiter sauber, rein und schön einzurichten; wieviel eher muß man darau [sic] bedacht sein, die Schule sauber zu halten und den Kindern die Reinlichkeit und Ordnung beizubringen."* (20)

29   *"Mußten wir deutschen Kinder doch auf einer Bank mit den verdreckten und verlausten Zigeunerkindern in der Schule sitzen."* (4)

The Road to Empowerment:
A Multi-Level Governance Approach

Katharina Crepaz
University of Innsbruck

The Romani issue is relevant for the European Union from a number of per-spectives[1]. As was the case with the EU's interest for minority protection in general, the issue of Romani protection first arose in a security policy context[2]. Heterogeneous populations and ongoing tensions between societal groups could lead to outbreaks of ethnic violence, which may have destabilizing effects not only for the affected region, but for the Union as a whole.

Finding a balance in endangered societies is therefore a vital means of conflict prevention. In the early 1990s, the Balkan Wars saw ethnic conflict resulting in genocide—the eastward enlargement thus had to encompass strategies for dealing with possible future sources of conflict. In a related manner, minority protection is also connected to the free movement of EU citizens and migration from outside the Union. Outbreaks of ethnic violence may lead to migratory movements; however, other push-factors need to be taken into account, e.g. economic migration and migration in response to perceived discrimination. In the run up to EU-enlargement, Romanis were increasingly in the focus of at-tention due to the EU's interest in promoting respect for minorities and anti-discrimination regulations in the candidate states.[3] Since the Eastern Enlarge-ment, Romanis as asylum seekers from outside the EU are also matter of con-cern, but many Romanis are now EU citizens, constituting the EU's largest transnational minority, whose social and economic exclusion is viewed as a key issue to be addressed.[4]

The Romanis constitute a special case, as they are a transnational minority, and may be an autochthonous minority, an immigrant minority or even both categories in the same country. There is also a considerable gap between Romani and non-Romani populations in a number of areas; one of the major concerns are health and housing issues, as well as high levels of unemploy-ment and high school drop-out rates. As the Romanis lack a kin-state to lobby for them in a more traditional way, the European institutions, and in particular the European Parliament and the Commission, have taken up the role of Romani advocates. In its documents on the matter, the Commission stresses the need to involve subnational authorities, as well as civil society actors and Romani activists. However, this involvement still has significant shortcomings in practice, as the evaluation of the member states' implementation of the EU *Framework* shows.

Since the admission of Romania and Bulgaria in 2007, free movement of citizens and migration policy have become a growingly important frame used for assessing Romani issues in a wider Europe: In order to prevent—mainly but not only—Romani migration, member-states such as Germany have demanded restrictions on visa-free travel for citizens of Western Balkans countries. Bulgarian and Romanian Romanis leave their countries to escape poverty and discrimination, and as a result, the EU should address the situation in the new member states in order to address what is often perceived as a "problem of free movement of European citizens". Creating better living standards in the countries of origin is a first step to consolidation of the migration policy dimension now that the remaining legal barriers have been abolished as of January 1, 2014. Migration has transferred the Romani issue from being a mere Eastern European problem to representing an important matter for the whole Union, and the EU was required to take action[5].

Due to their relevance in a number of issue areas, the Romanis are the first minority in whose promotion and protection the Commission actively takes a stand, and demands action. While in the new member states some claims regarding minority protection have been made during the period of accession, no monitoring has taken place for the old member-states. This is different in the case of the Romanis, and therefore represents the first instance of a real EU-wide interest in minority protection. The Romanis are thus a "European" minority not only due to their presence in many EU countries, but also due to the Commission and the European Parliament as EU institutions acting as their main advocates. In representing both an immigrant and an autochthonous minority (sometimes even both in the same country), the Romanis also defy the often made distinctions to justify different protection standards.

Romani issues and the implementation of protection standards therefore do not only provide an interesting field of research on an important minority, they also have implications for the development and future paths of minority protection as a whole. Finally, they provide an insight as to what extent the EU can really influence policies in the member states, and how the desired outcomes might be achieved. Obviously, top-down norm implementation is not enough, there is also a need for a closer cooperation of civil society groups and local authorities to put drafted standards into practice. This is the reason why this paper adopts a Multi-Level Governance approach: As is the case with a range of European policies, Romani protection is not happening at only one level through only one institution. Group protection is a multi-level, multi-actor process of action. These multi-level and multi-actor characteristics can be identified throughout the policy-making process, from the first drafts to best practices to their implementation and evaluation. A multi-level view is therefore necessary to trace policy outcomes back to their origins, identify possible catalysts for change and options available to veto-players to sabotage compliance.

I will first give an overview of measures taken by the EU level on the sector of Romani protection and the improvement of living conditions, arguing that while improvements have certainly been made, the Commission is not fulfilling its goal of strong member-state involvement, especially in regards to regional and local authorities as well as civil society. By adopting a multi-level view, I will then try to show how these important actors could be involved more strongly, and that norm diffusion can be a "bottom-up" as well as a "top-down" process. In a multi-level system, actors may collaborate freely without permission from nation states; this could facilitate progress, especially on issues like minority protection where member states are often reluctant to comply. If Romani NGOs as well as civil society activists are involved in a dialogue from the beginning, and so make their contribution to all stages of the policy-making process, they could shift positions from mere recipients of protection to "makers", which in turn could lead to empowerment. Finally, a short example of an existing collaboration between supranational and subnational level will be reviewed.

1. Europeanization of the Roma issue—Measures taken at EU Level

The Romanis nowadays constitute the largest minority in Europe. The Union commits to the principle of "unity in diversity", and outlaws discrimination on the grounds of ethnic or social origin or membership of a national minority in the article 21 of the EU *Charter of Fundamental Rights*. Article 22 further states that "the Union shall respect cultural, religious and linguistic diversity"[6]. Especially since the Eastern Enlargement of 2004, minority issues have gained in relevance and made their way to the EU's agenda, in particular in making protection of minorities a prerequisite for EU accession. The case of Romanis constitutes a special case, not only due to their nature as a transnational minority, but also due to the Union's specific advocacy of measures going beyond the principle of non-discrimination, and its demand for old as well as new memberstates to draw up protective measures. Different policy areas are affected by the lack of a uniform approach to Romani issues across the EU in issues of migration policy, free movement of citizens, security policy, minority protection and anti-discrimination policy.

Gradually, the Romanis have come into the focus of attention more and more. In the progress reports on the CEECs states, the Commission specifically addressed Romani protection issues and criticized shortcomings. In a first collaboration, the Decade of Roma Inclusion 2005—2015 brought European countries (new EU member-states, as well as candidates and countries who did not possess candidate status) together with the relevant bodies in the UN, the Council of Europe, the OSCE and NGOs or civil society platforms. Originating from a joined Open Society Institute and EU conference in Budapest, held in 2003, the Decade of Roma Inclusion includes Bulgaria, Croatia, the Czech Republic, Hungary, Macedonia, Romania, Serbia, Montenegro, and Slovakia.

In its 2010 document *The social and economic integration of Roma*[7] the Commission commented on the 2009 launch of the *European Platform for Roma Inclusion*, composed of member states, civil society organizations, EU and international organization officials to provide a forum for the exchange of good practice and experience and to stimulate cooperation. The Platform drew up the 10 *Common Basic Principles for Roma Inclusion*: constructive and non-discriminatory policies, explicit but not exclusive targeting, an intercultural approach, aiming for the mainstream, awareness of the gender dimension, transfer of evidence-based policies, use of Community instruments (legal, financial and coordination instruments), involvement of regional and local authorities, involvement of civil society, active participation of the Romanis[8]. The Commission as well as the Council have therefore stressed the need to include regional and local authorities, and for the members to share best practices. While making use of Community instruments, active participation of both civil society organizations and the Romanis themselves are introduced as basic principles; transforming the role of the Romani community from mere recipients of outside help to actual shapers of their own policies.

The European level can set a common aim that has to be reached by all member states, yet it is up to the local and regional levels to find measures to reach the goals set by the commission, and to supervise their implementation. Involvement of Romani organizations and civil society is necessary to ensure sustainable developments and changes that are supported by the local populations.

The Commission concludes that "In line with these Principles, Roma issues should be systematically mainstreamed into all relevant European and national policies"[9]. This means that protection policies should be integrated and considered during the policy-making process at different levels; even policies that do not have a specific Romani focus need to be checked regarding their compatibility. Besides underlining the responsibility of the national level, the Commission also tries to involve other important stakeholders, such as civil society groups and local and regional authorities. In accordance with a multi-level governance approach, international relations no longer only occur between the state and the supranational level, but they may also happen between supranational and non-state actors. By connecting directly with different levels, the Commission can enter policy-making processes in a more direct way, especially in the context of local authorities, where important decisions regarding Roma are often made. The mainstreaming approach is an interesting development, as it does not entail specific Romani policies, but an outlook on Romani issues in all policy-making processes; Romanis are therefore not singled out, but included in measures benefitting all members of the community. By using such an inclusive mainstreaming strategy, the implementation of measures and the fight against prejudice could be facilitated.

In 2011, the Commission issued the *EU Framework for National Roma Integration Strategies up to 2020*, noting that "determined action, in active dialogue with the Roma, is needed at both national and EU level"[10]. The *Framework* endorsed is seen as "a means to complement and reinforce the EU's equality legislation and policies by addressing, at national, regional and local level, but also through dialogue with and participation of the Roma, the specific needs of Roma regarding equal access to employment, education, housing and healthcare"[11]. The *Framework* therefore also stresses the need for involvement of local and regional authorities and the benefits of a strong and participatory civil society.

The mainstreaming approach is also present, as the specific needs of Romanis should be considered in the policy-making processes for the four different fields. The areas of employment, education, housing and healthcare have been identified as four target areas in which significant differences between Romani and non-Romani populations can be observed, and where the EU aims to further the closing of these gaps. While the Commission stresses that the *Framework* is "the EU's response to the current situation", it also highlights that it "does not replace Member States' primary responsibility in this regard"[12]. The European level can therefore try to draw up strategies for addressing the situation; but even though the Romanis are a "European" minority, they still remain citizens of the respective member states as well, an important aspect that should not be forgotten in the discussion about the EU and its policies regarding Romanis.

The supranational area can provide a forum for collaboration, exchange of best practices and civil society involvement; however, on the ground implementation is in the hands of the member states and in those of their respective regional or local representatives. Member states are expected to close employment, housing and health gaps, and ensure that all Romani children at least complete primary education. Social housing and healthcare as well as primary education are often in the hands of local or regional authorities (e.g. in Germany, where education policy is a competence of the *Länder*). Collaboration between the EU and subnational levels is therefore vital to ensure progress. The Framework is also interesting from a minority protection policy point of view; while the *Decade of Roma Inclusion* included only member-states from the CEECs and countries in the Western Balkans, the *Framework for National Roma Integration Strategies* demands that *all* EU member states with Romani population develop such strategies, funding and monitoring mechanisms. Besides Malta, all members have Romani populations on their territory—the *Framework* is therefore the first instance for an EU-wide demand for minority protection measures. Old and new member states are expected to adhere to the same principles and norms of protection, which constitutes a new setting in minority protection policies.

The inclusive policy-making process could therefore also provide us with new insights on possible policy learning, as no external incentives for compliance are given. According to the principle of subsidiarity, common goals and aims are set by the Commission, but the concrete measures needed and their implementation lie in the hands of the member states or their respective regional and local representatives. As mentioned above, the identified target areas fall into subnational competence in various member states, and collaboration between EU and regional or local levels might prove to be more effective in contexts where it faces not only discussion, but active practical implementation.

In addition to calling on the member states' responsibility, the *Framework* also specifically addresses the issue of "empowering civil society", which refers to "strengthening the involvement of civil society by encouraging institutionalized dialogues with Romani representatives to become involved and take responsibility for policy formulation, implementation and monitoring on regional, national and local level"[13]. The *European Platform for Roma Inclusion* is expected to play an important role through the exchange of good practices, the provision of analytical support and the stimulation of cooperation. The strong desire for civil society involvement, as well as split responsibilities for implementation and monitoring, point at a multi-level governance framework as an appropriate frame for analysis. Different levels as well as different actors are included in the policy-making process, and remain present also in the implementation phase. This is an important development in regards to stakeholder participation: Minorities are often marginalized at the national level, and therefore often excluded from influencing political decisions, even those that directly concern them. Stronger collaboration between the supranational and the subnational levels could help to strengthen representation, and to design better fitted policy solutions.

In 2012, the Commission evaluated the progress made on national integration strategies in its communication *National Roma Integration Strategies: a First Step in the Implementation of the EU Framework*. The Commission again denotes the "primary responsibility" of the member- states: "[...] action to support Roma lies first and foremost in their hands"[14]. Discrimination is outlawed by EU law, but these measures alone are not enough, and need to be strengthened through member-state participation.

The communication also evaluates which member-states have already become involved in which fields. The situation of Romani children is particularly alarming: in Greece, France, Italy, Romania and Bulgaria, at least 10% of Romani youngsters aged 7 to 15 are not attending school, according to data collected by the Fundamental Rights Agency. Regarding involvement of regional and local authorities, the Commission criticizes that local authorities and other stakeholders were not engaged enough in the drafting of the strategies. Since "concrete programs are implemented at regional at local level"; this means that civil society and subnational entities are not involved enough in drawing up measures, but they are expected to carry them out. From a multi-level governance perspective, civil society and relevant stakeholders should be involved both in the input as well as in the output stages of policy development. Member-states show lacking commitment also when looking at funding, as they usually do not allocate specific budgets for measures relating to the *Framework*. Most countries rely almost exclusively on EU funding, which indicates that Romanis are still not being looked at as an issue of national salience.

In its concluding remarks, the Commission notes that "regional and local authorities are indispensable for delivering change and need to be fully on board when the strategies are reviewed and implemented"[15]. It also demands a more active role for Romani civil society: "Civil society, and in particular Roma organizations, should not be considered as passive recipients of change, but should be called upon to play an active role in generating it". This is a very important point, as it suggests a shift in the Commission's approach: Romanis are no longer just a marginalized minority, who is in need of protection, they are also called upon to be shapers of their own destinies. Of course, there are many structural constraints that limit this point of view; political involvement is certainly difficult when someone is in a daily struggle of poverty and discrimination. However, it is a highly important difference regarding framing, and regarding stakeholder involvement: the multi-level nature of the European polity allows the Commission to enter into a direct dialogue with civil society and Romani organizations, excluding levels which might counter European involvement. In actively participating during the policy-making process, minorities can make their voices heard, and influence possible future measures.

All the measures described above call for member state involvement, and even for important input from subnational authorities or regions, as well as civil society actors or NGOs. As Peter Vermeersch[16] argues, the EU is likely to be successful on its quest to improve the Romani situation: it has access to funding with which it can influence domestic policies, it considers the management of ethnic relations an important security concern, and it collaborates closely with civil society organizations who are able to add pressure "from below". However, there are not only positive sides to EU involvement: the more the EU gets involved, the more nationalist actors in member states might try to frame the Romanis as a "European" problem, which does not need to be worked on nationally. Vermeersch finds that

> while other citizens belong to the nation states, the Roma belong to Europe, thus latching onto the alleged 'Europeanness' of the Roma (and their alleged lack of national belonging) in order to exclude them symbolically from their own national space and frame them not only as 'Europeans' without any attachment to any particular nation state, but also as ethnic outsiders and cultural deviants.[17]

By using this kind of framing, Romanis are viewed as a special case, which could legitimize the use of special measures, as becomes apparent in the explanations given by the French government for expulsions of Romanian and Bulgarian citizens in 2010[18]. Another case would be the Italian state's attempt to introduce the mandatory fingerprinting of Romani children. Major inclusion of subnational levels could help to reduce negative framing: Involvement of supranational actors, such as EU insitutions, could include Romanis in developing a shared identity across community markers. Also, access to local and regional stakeholders such as subnational and local authorities or NGOs could potentially prevent framing of Romani communities as cultural deviants.

On the subnational level, policy-making and its outcomes are closer to both Romani and non-Romani citizens, who can collaborate on topics affecting their daily lives. Besides the collaborative effort towards specific goals, communicating and exchanging common experiences can also help overcome prejudice. Inclusion into policy-making as well as implementation is also easier to achieve on local grounds, where less contested issue areas can be discussed, and the shared involvement can help to create identity-shaping processes for all participating actors. However, while the local level comes in as an important means of connecting and involving different stakeholders, important policy decisions are normally made elsewhere. A strong connection between supranational and subnational actors could help balance this development, and present a way to successfully implement common European goals on the ground in the member-states and local communities.

2. Multi-Level Governance: A Possible Avenue for Inclusion

European integration leads to developments in policymaking that go beyond the traditional decision-making in sovereign states. By providing an additional European level of policy-making, the Union can interact with different actors and levels, taking on new ways of political impact that would not be possible in the traditional context of international relations between nation states. Governance in the EU therefore encompasses a multi-level system of different levels of authorities or institutions (supranational, subnational, civil society, NGOs, etc.) which are involved in the policy-making process and contribute to transform the character of the political system as such. Phillip Schmitter defines Multi-Level Governance as

> an arrangement for making binding decisions that engages in a multiplicity of politically independent but otherwise interdependent actors—private and public—at different levels of territorial aggregation in more-or-less continuous negotiation/ deliberation/ implementation, and that does not assign exclusive policy competence or assert a stable hierarchy of political authority to any of these levels.[19]

For the theoretical context of this paper, the "multiplicity of interdependent actors at different levels of territorial aggregation" as well as their state of "continuous negotiation/deliberation/implementation" need to be stressed. While the actors are independent, they are interdependent in their decisions, and collaborate with each other across different levels and contexts. The EU can set common goals, but cannot make for effective implementation of these goals without a collaborative effort from national polities or local entities, and needs their judgment on the fit of a certain policy measure for the specific territory. In order to achieve such close collaboration, continuous contact and deliberation on the objectives and their implementation needs to be sustained—as outlined by the EU in its evaluation of the national integration strategies and work with the national focal points.

Multi-Level Governance (MLG) encompasses challenges to the state boundaries from above, below and within. It questions the existence of the unitary, sovereign state and takes place at the levels of political mobilization (politics), policy-making arrangements (policy) and state structures (polity)[20]. This gives room for civil society groups addressing different levels for their lobbying (e.g. NGOs turning to Brussels for support), as well as the Commission closely collaborating with local and regional entities and authorities and other organizations to monitor on-the-ground implementation of the common goals. If, as it is often the case in minority protection policies, the national level is reluctant or refuses to act on the matter, the European and regional or local levels may come together to find different strategies regarding the issue, and use their respective competences to lobby for a change in the current situation.

Different levels of government are traversed by actors moving freely across levels of government and spheres of authority; MLG can therefore be seen as an actor-centered approach. As noted by the Commission, civil society and local authority collaboration are vital for a successful implementation of Romani policies and their mainstreaming into different fields. An MLG system of policy-making allows for a much larger extent of such involvement than a traditional nation state environment would. In a multi-level system, actors such as NGOs or transnational advocacy groups can cross the boundary between international and domestic freely, as the state no longer fulfils its gatekeeper function; therefore, growing devolution movements and growing civil society movements are viewed as interrelated. A way of successfully connecting the domestic or subnational to the international levels could be via committees:

> Committee governance [...] is particularly attentive to the creation of trans-national deliberative communities of experts who, far from acting as the agents of their national principals, contribute to the creation of micro-regimes for the ideation, implementation and evaluation of policy solutions.[21]

When working together on specific issues, NGOs, civil society, Romani activists and other stakeholders may act as a community of experts; the European level provides them with a forum to meet and collect information as well as exchange best practices. When meeting under these circumstances, actors are no longer agents of their respective national principals, but create a different network of policy making and implementation, where national provenience is not the main criterion of alignment anymore. In this context, various actors from different levels are not congregating to represent national interests, but to share ideas and common notions in a supranational arena of the Union. Romani policies represent an issue with a strongly transnational dimension, which does not only encompass different levels but also different policy areas, and thus cannot be appropriately tackled on a purely national basis.

Involvement of supranational actors and the crossing of state boundaries may be desired and instigated from below, above, or both levels. In the case of Romanis, this could mean that NGOs or advocacy groups turn to the Commission or other actors on the European level for assistance in certain areas, or that the Commission may directly be involved with local entities if it desires to do so. Regarding Romani policies, an on-the-ground involvement of the Union is specifically outlined in the *Framework*, for both civil society actors and local authorities, which need to be involved in policy-making as well as implementation of measures. In the free movement across levels typical for MLG, state boundaries can be challenged by a forming transnational civil society (e.g. via lobbying for their causes at the EU-level); or on the other hand, the Commission could be seeking allies for its policies and especially their implementation at the subnational level. A multi-level collaboration could therefore be attained in an either "bottom-up" or "top-down" way. "Bottom-up" can be defined as subnational actors reaching out to the supranational level: "they request the freedom to interact across borders and converge in Brussels to receive funds, share experiences, devise cooperative agreements."[22] "Top-down" consists in supranational actors seeking cooperation with the subnational level, because they are aware that "[...] subnational actors can act as direct and often crucial links between themselves and the member-states."[23]

For the Romani issue, the "bottom-up" line of action could consist of local and subnational authorities as well as civil society groups asking the supranational level for assistance, or collaborating with other entities in different member states on the exchange of best practices. As outlined by the Commission in the *Framework*, the EU could take up the role of coordinator, and bring together parties interested in working together on the improvement of different issues. Regarding "top-down" procedures, the Commission may wish to seek further collaboration with local authorities and entities, especially in times of crisis where nation states can be unresponsive to demands made, and especially on sensitive subjects such as minority protection and minority policies. By directly addressing the local level, implementation procedures can be analyzed where they actually happen, and in more direct connection to the citizens and their preferences. As the nation state no longer fulfills its gatekeeper function, collaboration between local and supranational levels on certain topics has gradually become easier, especially in areas where local or regional authorities retain competences, and where the Union has taken on a clear policy and set common goals for all member states. In the identified target areas, the measures that directly impact Romani citizens can often be set by local entities (such as ensuring access to healthcare, or granting local housing projects, as well as primary school education and the fight against segregation). While larger goals and measures may be set at the national level, local and regional authorities are often the ones who most thoroughly impact people's daily lives, and can provide concrete measures that may seem of small-scale impact, but make way for larger developments, as they are most directly connected to the individual citizen and their preferences.

An MLG structure allows for both subnational authorities and civil society organizations, as well as for the Commission on the European level, to seek means of collaboration with each other. Coming together to work on a certain issue area—maybe in the structure of committees mentioned above—could make way for a better implementation of European policies, and for the provision of better fit to the needs of certain regions or policy fields. Additionally, issues could be addressed that are not in primary national interest, and would thus not usually make it on the agenda of national politics. Along the centre-periphery cleavage, minority issues are traditionally located in the periphery; protection and empowerment of minorities is therefore not a primary concern for the centre in most cases. If a state is neglectful, bringing in the supranational level could be helpful to raise awareness for minority issues, and eventually lead to pressure for compliance from outside. Even in cases where the state level cannot be involved successfully, regional development aid in the form of funding or transfer of expertise could help subnational policy makers to better respond to a situation or issue. As Imig and Tarrow (2001) argue:

> In a world without important transaction costs or variations in resources, citizens would automatically bring their claims to the agents most directly responsible for their grievances. But when these agents are distant, indirect, and often obscure, claims are more likely to be directed at where people possess dense social networks, organizational resources, and visible political opportunities.[24]

Romani activists may try to address the nation states with their claims, but they are more likely to be successful at the more directly accessible level (such as subnational and local entities), which may provide the "visible political opportunities", as well as the supranational level, where "dense social networks" and "organizational resources" are located. Dense networks and opportunities, especially for interests not shared by the whole nation-state population such as minority issues, might be easier to find on the European level. In the case of Romani representation, there is a dense and organized framework of organizations, experts, and civil society representatives involved in working and lobbying for the issue in close cooperation with Brussels.

Peter Vermeersch notes that "the EU's attempt to improve things for the Roma has received support from a wide range of internationally organized NGOs, who scrutinize state practice in individual member states and add pressure 'from below' to the pressure that is already brought on these states 'from above'"[25]. As is described in models of international norm diffusion,[26][27] transnational advocacy networks can reinforce an agenda by moral consciousness raising and by monitoring domestic change. The set common goals can therefore be scrutinized regarding their practical implementation by local entities and NGOs, who have a first-hand overview of developments and possible areas that could be further improved. Strong connections and linkages with the supranational level will provide the Union with a more complete picture of actual developments, and enable the local authorities to give a wider audience to their projects and needs. Processes that may be shifted from the focus of attention on the national level (due to the centre-periphery cleavage, or a neglectful approach on part of the nation-state) can receive more attention when analysed locally or regionally, and lessons can be drawn and/or best practices can be shared via the international forum that the EU provides.

Looking at the "top-down" perspective, European involvement might not be seen favourably by national policy makers at all times, especially when high adaption costs arise or strong veto-players are involved. While it is national-level policy makers that must transpose EU-designed legislation into national law, the subnational level should also not be neglected. As Loughlin[28] argues, regions are seen as more authentic societies than artificially created nation states. At the local and regional level, trust and reciprocity are easier to build up, providing for a sense of community. Preferences can more easily be realized without high transaction costs, and interpersonal preference maximization

is less costly at the regional than at the national level[29]. On the topic of Romanis, prejudices and stereotypes play an important role, and these can be more
easily overcome in direct interaction with the "Other" on a smaller scale than
when facing each other in larger discussions. Local level processes of preference formation have lower transaction costs, and losing "face" could constitute
less of an issue. If the framing of Romanis as "deviants"[30] can be overcome on
the local level and a sense of community can be established, this may lead the
way to an improvement of relations between Romani and non-Romani citizens,
and a shift in the debate away from mere Romani issues to a common strategy
for further development of the municipality or region.

As can be seen by looking at the EU *Framework* and implementation analyses
discussed above, the Commission extensively highlights the responsibility of
member states as well as subnational authorities in both drafting and implementing policies, and also calls for strong civil society involvement at all stages.
Again, cases in which nation states are reluctant to take action could be fertile
ground for supranational—subnational collaboration: minority protection can
be addressed in the regions where minority populations are present, and in
which they might possess leverage that they lack on the national level. Regional level support is also crucial for the measures taken not to remain paper
tigers, and to ensure on-the-ground implementation. By inviting all relevant
stakeholders to the drafting process of policies, subnational and civil society
actors can make their voices heard, and accompany the process from the first
exchange of ideas to its practical enforcement at the regional or local level.

The EU *Framework* argues for civil society to be involved in all stages of the
policy-making process; from drafting to implementation. While influence on the
norms present on paper is certainly an important characteristic, involvement in
their actual implementation will probably be of even greater importance. Actors
like the *European Roma Rights Center* have continuously warned about "the
disconnection of local authorities on the hand and the national and international
policy frameworks on the other[...]"[31]. It is therefore not enough for the EU institutions to commit the member states to the Romani issue with its demand for
action plans and implementation evaluation; the regional and local levels must
be strongly involved as well to ensure actual policy change.

A multi-level approach could therefore be of high value for guaranteeing protection, as well as empowerment; Romanis are not only recipients of protective
policies, but also actively involved in creating such measures. Direct interaction
between civil society and the international level can facilitate participation, as
well as the exchange of good practices; during the implementation phase, civil
society actors can be the "eyes" and "ears" of the Commission, who provide
information about possible difficulties that are encountered. Additionally, identity-shaping primarily takes place at the local level, and involvement in this area
could help to counter the framing of Romanis as a "part of European community", or as cultural deviants. Action on the matter can be taken by an internationally organized civil society with EU connections and access to funding, who
can then collaborate and monitor and member state or national level. Following
a different path, a national NGO or group of activists may lobby at the international level to gather support for their cause. In any case, civil society involvement is vital at all levels and during all stages of the policy process. Concrete
measures taken at the local level could lead the way for larger projects, and an
exchange of best practices facilitated by the European level may further diffuse
such successful models throughout the Union. A one-size-fits-all approach of
course cannot operate effectively, however closer cooperation on issues common to all member-states is possible.

3. Kavarna as an Example of Stakeholder Empowerment

Kavarna is a small town on the Bulgaria black sea coast, quoted by the EU[32]
and other international organizations as a prime example for Romani integration and the correct use of funding. It shows how, through strong collaboration
between local authorities and involved stakeholders, Romanis can actively par-
take in creating the policies that concern them, and therefore directly influence
their future themselves, instead of merely being recipients of measures and
funding. About one third of Kavarnas 16,000 citizens are Romanis, and they
faced severe instances of discrimination in the past, such as not being allowed
into certain restaurants or public facilities. A strong reform approach was taken
on in 2003, when Mayor Tsonko Tsonev came into office. In his first term, he

created a municipal agency for Romani integration, which also featured members of the Romani community among its staff. This means that Romanis are actively involved in the making of their own policies, and can provide input and be part of the drafting of measures on the local level, the primary entity that they are directly affected by.

The three Romani agency members are responsible for implementing the national policy regarding ethnic minority groups. About 9 million Euro were invested into infrastructure projects (renovation of schools and kindergartens, sewage systems, paving of roads etc.), half of which came from EU funding. Dropout rates among Romani children sank from 30% in 2004 to 10% in 2007. Deputy Mayor Sevinch Kasabova offers a succinct explanation for Kavarna's integration success: "City authorities are as much responsible for the positive change in the neighbourhood as the Romani community itself, which is very active and strives for a better standard of living"[33]. Collaboration between local entities and Romani activists has therefore made a difference in the situation of the local Romani community. The EU provided assistance by funding and providing a platform for exchange with other organizations and communities.

A program for best practices exchange among mayors of municipalities with significant Romani populations was started in 6 Eastern European countries, monitored by the *European Roma Grassroots Organization* (ERGO). The ERGO closely cooperated with Commission officials, and invited delegations from other member states (such as the Netherlands) to Kavarna for meetings and the exchange of best practices. Mayor Tsonko Tsonev highlights the importance of collaboration with communities in other countries and with the European level, noting that not only legal rules, but also actual implementation is supervised. In Kavarna, NGOs, Romani activists and local authorities therefore all collaborated with the supranantional level, eliminating the nation state's gatekeeper function and allowing for a free flow of ideas and exchange of experiences across different levels and actors.

Actively working together with the local level, the EU could also ensure the paths that its funding was going to, and monitor the advancement of infrastructure projects as well as other developments. In addition to its function as pro-vider of funds and monitoring entity, the Union also fulfilled its task as a forum of connection for different actors and levels, and for communities from different countries to exchange ideas and best practices in. The example of Kavarna shows that if funding is secured and if relevant actors are willing to pursue change, the local level may be very important in changing the living conditions of Romanis for the better. Activists and civil society are directly involved in the municipality and are responsible for implementing minority protection measures, which reshapes their role from recipients of aid to empowered citi-zens. Collaboration with groups in other countries and the exchange of best practices play an important part in this development, as does the involvement of the European level in the implementation of measures.

In its document *Working together for Roma Inclusion: The EU Framework explained* (2011), designed for use by "national and local decision makers"[34]—which can therefore be seen as a "manual" for local and regional enti-ties—the Commission specifically mentions Kavarna. It also once again high-lights the importance of the local level for successful policy-making: "Policies and strategies may be drawn up at national level but it is usually at local level that they are implemented as this is where public services are delivered to cit-izens"[35]. The local level is where services and policies are implemented, and where citizens feel most directly in contact with the authorities, both for positive and constructive collaboration as well as criticism if improvements are needed. The disconnection commonly experienced by citizens with the national or even supranational political class is usually not felt on the local level, which makes it easier for different opinions and actors to engage in a smaller setting, where less costly decisions are made and compromise might be easier to reach. An MLG structure allows for the European level to be in touch with the local level, and to bring common goals and aims closer to the citizens. While the EU looks for information on on-the-ground implementation and specific measures taken, the local level turns to the supranational not only for funding, but also for a transnational forum when dealing with a transnational issue, such as the topic of Romanis. In an area that is common to many member states, exchange of best practices and policies is especially important.

In the local context, Romanis may move from recipients of policies or even aid, which could often alienate them even further from the general population, to actively involved policy-makers. Through a specific department in the town council, the authorities try to more efficiently tackle Romani issues, such as high school drop-out rates. In an effort to stop negative stereotyping of Romani citizens, collaboration with local media has also been organized. The common goals are set on the European level, but strong local involvement provides for a better level of fit for policy measures, and stronger resonance of projects on the regional or local level. By involving all relevant stakeholders, measures can be taken which are directly designed for the specific local situation, while still keeping the common European background and aims in mind.

Though the tools are designed specifically for the local situation, communities with similar issues may connect through the forum provided by the EU, and, where possible, export lessons and ideas to their own local Romani situation. Through the ERGO and with help from the EU's "Thank you...." initiative, in which successful integration programs are presented, Kavarna received visits from delegations from other European cities, who are interested in sharing the best practices and maybe adopting some of them for their own policy formation. In October 2012, experiences were shared at the first *Mayors Making the Most of EU Funds for Roma Inclusion* (MERI) conference. The event, launched in partnership by the European Commission and the Open Society Foundation, aims to "provide a platform for local authorities to exchange, learn, and support each other in their efforts towards Roma inclusion" and to "bring mayors and other representatives of local authorities into the loop of the European frame-work for Roma inclusion, and highlight available European Union funds for this objective"[36].

The instalment of the MERI conference shows that the importance of local in-volvement and local authorities for the successful implementation of Romani policies has been recognized by the EU as well as other NGOs, and will prob-ably be highlighted further in its future strategies. The EU no longer only pro-vides funding, but takes an active role as a European platform for sharing ex-periences and best practices. The local level is the first level that citizens turn to with their queries and concerns, and where they are most easily involved in, as it directly concerns their daily life and the distance between elites and citizens is not felt as strongly. By interacting with the local authorities, the Union can therefore also move closer to its citizens, and prove to be a reliable partner for local communities and their issues.

In the procedure leading up to the MERI conference, 104 local practices were submitted as successful examples to the committee, of which 17 were selected and presented with awards for their work on different topics (education, housing, healthcare, Romani immigrants, and sustainable efforts towards inclusion). Kavarna was one of the award winners; the committee noted that its local integration strategy was not an own end for itself, but a vital part of the municipal local development strategy—the Roma community had become involved stakeholders at the local level, and Romani issues were being mainstreamed into different policy areas as outlined in the *Framework*. The MERI notes that

> the case is a good example of how results can be achieved in all policy fields by implementing systematic and sustainable measures. The diversification of resources, coupled with the municipality's ownership is worthy of appreciation. The Roma neighbourhood was legalized and infrastructure systems were developed, 70 Roma families were provided plots, and now only legal housing construction is allowed. Other results are increasing the number of Roma children with completed secondary school education, an awareness campaign for girls' education, and a decreased mortality rate thanks to health prevention projects, anti-discrimination measures in the local administration system, and employing five Roma in municipal offices.[37]

The successful strategy present in Kavarna is therefore in line with the EU's suggestions: A systematic mainstreaming of Romani issues into all areas of policy-making, strong involvement of civil society, local authorities and Romanis themselves as active stakeholders, present both in the community as well as in the local administration. The EU level directly interacts with local authorities, making it a prime example for the free alignment of actors possible in a MLG setting.

The nation state's role in this setting appears to be limited, and in line with the principle of subsidiarity, policies of relevance to the local level are also made and implemented locally; the state's passive role may also be due to the fact that minority issues are usually not a very highly ranked topic on the national agenda, and that getting involved in this area often involves high costs but only minimal benefits. By concretely planned use of EU funding and taking owner-ship of developments in their own community, the Kavarna municipality was able to make Romanis not only beneficiaries of benefits, but actively involved citizens on the local level, and to have them participate both as activists and representatives of the local authorities. On the subnational and especially the local level, lower transaction costs and easier patterns of compromise and pref-erence formation may facilitate such developments, especially if the EU takes its role as monitoring body and coordinator seriously and strongly collaborates with different levels and actors to ensure the implementation of common goals.

Conclusion

The last years have seen the EU getting involved in the protection of minorities, which can be explained from a security perspective, a migration policy per-spective, as well as an interest in the promotion of "European" values such as non-discrimination and minority equality. In the CEECs, the EU demanded mi-nority protection standards, which some of its members did not fulfil; the Un-ion's work on Romani protection therefore constitutes the first case in which the same measures are applied to the whole EU, and to a certain extent even to candidates, especially in the Western Balkans. Though the EU can success-fully act as an international forum for discussion and a monitoring entity, the on-the-ground implementation lies in the hands of member states, and espe-cially of local and regional authorities. Establishing collaboration between the European and local level is therefore vital for a successful implementation of the EU *Framework*.

The EU is characterized by a multi-level and multi-actor system, providing sub-national and supranational actors with a unique possibility for collaboration, knowledge exchange, ideas on best practices and involvement of civil society. From a "top-down" perspective, the European level can draw in civil society organizations and activists, as well as local or regional level authorities, and involve them in the process. If collaboration is achieved "bottom up", NGOs or activists can decide to lobby the European level for their causes, especially if the nation state is not responsive to their ideas and claims. Free association of levels and actors also means that collaboration can be achieved on a variety of issues, and that local authorities as the primary entity connected to the citizen can function as an important link between the population and the supranational level.

While national and especially EU elites are often seen as distant, local political involvement has direct impact on the citizens' daily lives, and the threshold to be involved is lower. Preference formation and identity shaping also occur first and foremost on a local or regional level, two important processes in a topic ridden by prejudices such as the Romani issue. While national discussions and developments often involve high transaction costs, discussions and compromise on the local level are less costly and more efficient. Local authorities can transpose the common European goals into measures that display the best goodness of fit to the specific community situation, and the Union can act as a monitoring body supervising developments and providing a forum for discussion and contacts with other areas working on similar policies. The collaboration between European and local or regional decision making levels may be the best way forward for the transnational uniform approach to improvement of situations in which Romani communities find themselves.

The case of Kavarna aims to show that stakeholder involvement can indeed be the road to success, and that collaborations between the local or regional and the EU level can achieve great improvements in the situation of Romanis. Only when they are involved in the policy-making process, from drafting of ideas to practical implementation, can the Romanis become active shapers of the political and social realities surrounding them, and reframe themselves as empowered citizens, instead of mere beneficiaries of EU funding who are often seen as the "Other" by the local population.

New developments like the MERI conference show that the Union has acknowledged the great potential that lies in strong collaboration between European and local levels. Romani policies can be directly mainstreamed into general development strategies at the local level, and in many member states, the four identified target areas are indeed in the competences of regional or local entities. By adopting the mainstreaming approach suggested by the Commission, Romani issues are no longer singled out, but tackled as general improvement for the local entity, which benefits not only one group, but all citizens living in the community.

References

1   I am using the term Romanis/Roma as defined by the European Commission: "The term Roma is used [...] as an umbrella which includes groups of people who have more or less similar cultural characteristics, such as Sinti, Travellers, Kalé, Gens du voyage, etc. whether sedentiary or not; around 80% of Roma are estimated to be sedentiary" (Commission 2011). Please note that where other sources (e.g. EU-documents, scientific literature) use the word Roma instead of Romanis, I follow this terminology in the paper.

2   Sasse, G., "Securitization or securing rights? Exploring the conceptual foundations of policies towards minorities and migrants in Europe", *Journal of Common Market Studies* 43:4 (2005): 673-693.

3   Guglielmo, R. & Waters, T.W. "Migrating towards minority status: shifting European policy towards Roma", in: *Journal of Common Market Studies*, 43:4 (2005): 763-785. Also, Vermeersch, P. "Ethnic Mobilization and the political conditionality of European Union accession: The case of the Roma in Slovakia", in: *Journal of Ethnic and Migration Studies*, 28:1 (2002): 83-101.

4   Vermeersch, P. (2012). "Reframing the Roma: EU Initiatives and the Politics of Reinterpretation", in: *Journal of Ethnic and Migration Studies*, 38:8 (2012): 1192-1212.

5   Sigona, N. & Trehan, N. "Introduction: Romani politics in neoliberal Europe", in: Sigona, N. & Trehan, N. (eds.) *Romani Politics in Contemporary Europe: Poverty, Ethnic Mobilization and the Neoliberal Order.* (Houndsmills: Palgrave Macmillan, 2009), 1-20.

6   *Charter of Fundamental Rights of the European Union* (2000).

7   European Commission. *Communication from the Commission to the Council, the European Parliament, the European Economic and Social Committee and the Committee of the Regions: The Social and Economic Integration of the Roma in Europe.* COM(2010)133.

8   Council of the European Union. *Draft Council Conclusions on the Inclusion of the Roma.* Brussels, 28 May 2009.

9   European Commission. *The Social and Economic Integration of the Roma in Europe.* COM(2010)133.

10   European Commission. *Communication from the Commission to the Council, the European Parliament, the European Economic and Social Committee and the Committee of the Regions: An EU Framework for National Roma Integration Strategies Up To 2020.* COM(2011)173.

11   European Commission. *An EU Framework for National Roma Integration Strategies up to 2020.* COM(2011)173.

12   Ibid., 3.

13   Ibid., 12.

14   European Commission. *Communication from the Commission to the Council, the European Parliament, the European Economic and Social Committee and the Committee of the Regions: National Roma Integration Strategies: A First Step in the Implementation of the EU framework.* COM(2012)226.

15   Ibid., 17.

16   Vermeersch, "Reframing the Roma".

17   Vermeersch, "Reframing the Roma", 1197.

18 van Baar, H. "Expulsion fever in Europe: The case of the Roma", *Nationalities Blog*, 26 September 2010.
19 Schmitter, P. "Neo-Functionalism", in: Wiener, Antje & Diez, Thomas (eds.) *European Integration Theory*. (Oxford: University Press, 2004), 49.
20 Piattoni, S. *The Theory of Multi-Level Governance: Conceptual, Empirical and Normative Challenges*. Oxford: University Press, 2010.
21 Ibid., 30.
22 Piattoni, The Theory of Multi-Level Governance, 60.
23 Ibid., 60.
24 Imig, D. & Tarrow, S. (eds.) *Contentious Europeans: Protest and Politics in an Emerging Polity*. (Lanham: Rowman & Littlefield, 2001), 17.
25 Vermeersch, "Reframing the Roma", 1197.
26 Keck, M. E. & Sikkink, K. *Activists Beyond Borders: Advocacy Networks in International Politics*. Ithaca & London: Cornell University Press, 1998.
27 Risse, T; Ropp, S. C. & Sikkink, K. *The Power of Human Rights: International Norms and Domestic Change*. Cambridge: University Press, 1999
28 Loughlin, J. "'Europe of the Regions' and the 'Federalization' of Europe", in: *Publius: The Journal of Federalism*, 26:4 (1996):141-162.
29 Scharpf, F. W. "Community and Autonomy: Multi-Level Policy-making in the European Union", in: *Journal of European Public Policy*, 1:2 (1994): 219-242.
30 Vermeersch, "Reframing the Roma".
31 Vermeersch, "Reframing the Roma", 1209.
32 European Commission—Justice. Working Together for Roma Inclusion—The EU Framework Explained. 2011.
33 Dzhambazova."In Bulgaria's Rock City, Roma also Thrive", Roma Buzz Monitor, 2011.
34 European Commission—Justice, *Working together for Roma Inclusion*, 2.
35 European Commission—Justice, *Working together for Roma Inclusion*, 14.
36 Szekeres, Silvana. Mayors Making the Most of EU Funds for Roma Inclusion. Open Society Foundations, 8 November 2012.
37 Ibid.

Roma as a Pan-European Minority?
Opportunities for Political and Legal Recognition

Sara Memo

University of Trento

The academic debate on Roma in Europe has largely considered them as a unique social group in light of a number of distinctive features. First and foremost, Roma represent the biggest minority group of Europe. According to official estimates of the Council of Europe (CoE), presently there are approximately 10–12 million individuals, about the same numerical proportion of a middle-size European country such as Belgium or Greece.[1] Moreover, Roma are regarded as a unique social group in all European countries, with three other main distinctive features:

non-territoriality i.e. the impossibility of identifying the Romani community/communities in Europe in connection with one precise territory, the Romani thereby being a diffuse minority;[2]

historical tie with the European territory as a whole. Although nomadic, Roma have been living within the European continent for more than ten centuries;[3]

overall exclusion from mainstream societies which have traditionally perceived Roma as "Others, as foreigners in their home countries."[4]

Williams has more effectively described the overall social status of Roma in Europe by emphasizing elements of "immersion" within territories inhabited by other populations, "dispersion" within different territorial areas and "illegitimacy" as the general mainstream perception of Roma by other social groups.[5]

Indeed, a strong antiziganist prejudice has historically been attached to Roma in Europe, as they have been traditionally perceived as habitual criminals, social misfits and vagabonds.[6] Such an antiziganist attitude has progressively exacerbated the overall socio-economic exclusion of Roma and contributed to recurrent waves of discriminatory attacks. In some cases, discriminatory perception has turned into assimilation policies, in other cases it has even turned into annihilation policies.

For a long time, European countries managed the "illegitimate" presence of Roma in Europe exclusively as a "domestic affair" affecting the spheres of internal security and public order.[7] Only in the last decades, thanks to the pressure of civil society, have international organizations working for the protection of human rights in Europe progressively included Romani issues into their agendas. In particular, these organizations have committed themselves to act for the improvement of the socio-economic conditions of Roma, as an fundamental benchmark of democracy.[8]

In 2005, while condemning the widespread phenomenon of antiziganism in a Resolution on the situation of Roma in the European Union, the European Parliament defined Roma as a "pan-European community".[9] This holistic definition has put pressure on member states to adopt a "comprehensive approach" to efficiently fight discrimination against this social group at the European level. In 2007, the same definition of Roma as a "pan-European minority" was also adopted by the CoE and by the Organization for Security and Cooperation in Europe (OSCE).

More specifically, in the "Statement on Roma and Sinti" presented at Working Sessions 6 and 7 of the Annual Human Dimension Implementation Meeting of the OSCE-ODIHR held in Warsaw in September 2007, the European Roma and Traveller Forum (ERTF),[10] openly referred to Roma as a "pan-European minority". In the same statement, the ERTF also highlighted that Roma are "the most disadvantaged ethnic minority group in Europe, suffering from human rights violations and being a particular target of racism throughout Europe".[11]

This paper analyses the implications that the definition of Roma as a "pan-European minority" entails at the political level and—more deeply—at the legal one. Indeed, this holistic definition of Roma as a "pan-European minority" may open new legal scenarios, allowing the transcendence of national borders and nationalistic definitions which still constrain Roma within a territorial paradigm considered to be largely inadequate to address the needs of this minority group. In particular, this paper discusses how legal status affects social recognition, non-discrimination policies and the empowerment of Roma in Europe. To this regard, the paper proposes a critical reflection on the opportunity of enhancing the socio-economic rights of Roma, thought as an essential prerequisite for the empowerment of this social group. In its final section, the paper considers the opportunity of complementing the "pan-European" recognition of Roma, currently arising at the political level, with a parallel "pan-European" recognition, developing from a legal perspective.

1. Assessing the Political Level of European Recognition

The official recognition of Roma as a "pan-European minority" has contributed to a more systemic consideration on the life conditions of Roma in Europe, at least at political level. Especially at the EU level, programmes addressing the social inclusion of Roma have started to develop in the last decade. In 2008, the European Commission (EC) established the "Roma Action Group" within the DG Employment, Social Affairs and Inclusion. The "Roma Action Group" was created with the specific mandate of bringing together EU desks responsible for coordinating and monitoring investments of the European Social Fund in relation to projects aimed at improving employment, equal opportunities and social inclusion for Roma.[12]

Moreover, in the same year, the EURoma Learning Network was founded, also within the EC's framework with the aim of exchanging good practices among the twelve participating states. In particular, the network aimed at a most efficient use of EU structural funds in relation to national policies, targeting the inclusion of Roma, especially in the areas of training and employment.[13] Furthermore, also in 2008, during the first European Roma Summit, EU member-states created the "European Roma Platform" whereby member-states, Romani civil society, EU policy-makers and independent experts exchange good practices and experiences on the subject of Romani social inclusion.[14]

In 2011, the EC promoted a Framework for National Roma Integration Strategies up to 2020 which set the basis for the adoption of a comprehensive policy commitment for the socio-economic integration of Roma in a medium term perspective. Through this framework, the EC has aimed to address the needs of Roma by means of a targeted approach with "explicit measures to prevent and compensate for disadvantages they face".[15] This approach has hinged on the idea that positive measures are urgently needed to foster economic and social rights for Roma in line with the "comprehensive approach" advocated by the European Parliament in 2005.

According to the Racial Equality Directive,[16] the principle of equal treatment embedded in national legal systems does not in fact prevent member-states from maintaining or adopting specific measures to prevent or compensate for disadvantages linked to membership in racial or ethnic community. The EC has thus required EU Member States to adopt National Roma Strategies (NRIS) in order to meet EU targeted goals in the areas of education, employment, health and housing. The EC's idea of NRIS has been "borrowed" from the Decade of Roma Inclusion (2005-2015), which involved twelve countries, all of which have a significant of Roma living in a disadvantaged economic and social position.[17] Along the lines of the Decade's goals, the NRIS as well aims at intervening in the areas of education, employment, health and housing.

2. Assessing the Legal Level of European Recognition

Notwithstanding the advancements that the recognition of Roma as a "pan-European minority" has entailed at political level, a parallel "pan" definition of Roma has not yet entered the legal sphere. The EU has in fact focused more on a political recognition of Roma rather than on the improvement of its legal framework. Nonetheless, the widespread exclusion of Roma from European mainstream societies as well as their overall position of socio-economic inferiority as a non-dominant group, not only depends on antiziganist attitudes and xenophobic policies of mis-recognition which have been taking place at the domestic level. It does also depend on the legal mis-recognition of Roma legal status and rights.

Presently the European minority rights framework is built on soft-law documents and hard-law instruments developed at the level of the OSCE, the CoE and the EU. In each of these organizations coexists a double-layered set of legal instruments that focus both on human and on minority rights.[18] The number of human and minority rights instruments has reinforced the view that Europe is the geo-political region that most intensively protects the rights of minorities in the world.[19] Notwithstanding its highly promotional attitude, the European legal framework presents a number of gaps in the protection of minority groups. These gaps mostly ensue from a territorial Westphalian concept. In fact, national systems founded on this paradigm continue to identify minority groups exclusively in connection with territorial areas.

According to legal doctrine, the existing legal frameworks protect and promote minority rights by targeting two kinds of minority groups: the so-called "old" minorities i.e. "historical, traditional, autochthonous minorities" and the so-called "new" minorities i.e. "new minority groups stemming from migration".[20] While the first category mostly refers to communities that became minorities as a consequence of the re-drawing of international borders, the second category refers to groups of individuals who left their original homeland to emigrate to another country. This second category specifically includes the mass-migration of people that has become a distinguishing feature of the globalization process.

It is interesting to highlight that both legal categories ("old" and "new" minorities) and the legal instruments ensuing from them, protect and promote minority groups which can be comprised within a territorial scheme.[21] The same legal categories are unable to comprehensively identify and to fully protect non-territorial minorities since they fall outside the Westphalian paradigm.

The recognition of the legal status of Roma is affected by the "nationalistic trap"[22] since this group's intrinsic nature as a "historical" and, at the same time, "non-territorial" minority fails to assign them to one of the available legal categories. On the one hand, since they have historically lived in Europe also with (an increasingly) sedentary lifestyle, Roma can be considered a "traditional minority". On the other hand, Roma might also be considered as "migrants" since a consistent percentage of them engage in migration and/or occasionally adopt a nomadic lifestyle.[23]

The condition of "legal limbo" in which Roma fall, directly influences the recognition of rights provided by every domestic legal system to this social group. Given the lack of an international binding definition of "minority" and of "non-territorial minority", European states do not always recognize Roma as a minority group. When a legal definition exists to identify Roma, such a definition generally reflects *ex negativo* the conception of "ethnos" and "demos" around which each European state has formed. The legal status attributed to any social group has to be considered of key importance since, aside the question of recognition, it strongly influences their coexistence with other social groups as well.[24] In other words, legal recognition is strongly influential, in the sense that it (pre-)determines political and social recognition.

Accordingly, the recognition of Roma in Europe can be summarized by reference to four general models identified in the comparative analysis of the legal recognition of diversity in Europe as pertaining to (a) repressive national systems, (b) liberal agnostic systems indifferent to differences, (c) promotional systems and (d) multinational equal systems.[25] More specifically in the case of Roma, these constitutional approaches have recently been re-modulated on the basis of the status of ratifications of the Framework Convention on National Minorities (FCNM).[26]

The FCNM is the most important legal instrument providing protection to minority rights at the CoE level. Among the 47 Member States belonging to the CoE, currently only eight countries (four of which belong to the EU) have not explicitly recognized any minority group within their legal systems, Roma included.[27] Among the remaining 39 countries which recognize minorities within their legal systems,[28] four constitutional approaches have been identified which address the domestic recognition of Romani minorities: exclusionist countries, agnostic countries, mildly promotional countries and highly promotional countries.

"Exclusionist countries" have been identified as those countries which completely exclude Roma from the legal protection of the FCNM, given that this social group has not been recognized as a "national minority". The non-recognition of Roma as a "national minority" has been justified, at the ratification stage, with different sets of reasons. Among EU member states, Denmark explained the lack of recognition in light of a (supposed) full integration of Roma within its society; the Netherlands and Portugal argued that they could not include Roma within the category of "national minority" due to the lack of clear territorial features identifying this social group; in Cyprus, instead, Roma are not recognized since they are regarded as part of the Turkish-Cypriot community which, in turn, is also not recognized.[29]

The doctrine has identified as "agnostic" those legal systems that do not formally recognize Roma as a "national minority", such as Italy and Slovenia. Other countries do not recognize Roma in terms of "national minority" but through other legal definitions (e.g. "ethnic minority"): these countries have been deemed to be potentially included within this category of "agnostic states". In some cases, such as in Poland, the variety of legal definitions is merely formal since the distinction between "national" and "ethnic" minorities does not substantially affect the enjoyment of minority rights given that both social groups are de facto entitled to the same set of rights.[30]

A third group of countries that has recognized Roma as a "national minority" has been defined as "mildly promotional" since it has limited the enjoyment of minority rights to the citizens of the State only. The vast majority of European legal systems can be included in this model when addressing the legal recognition of Roma. Germany is the most emblematic example: The category of "national minority" has not been extended to Roma who are not German citizens because of the opposition of the "autochthonous" Romani German citizens.[31] Another interesting case that is worth mentioning under the category of "mildly promotional countries" is that of Spain. This State has recognized as "national minority" under the scope of the FCNM only the Spanish Romani social group (gitanos). Indeed, Spain has not recognized any other social groups as a "national minority", although different linguistic groups have historically claimed autonomy because they allegedly belong to a different social group other than the "Castilian" majority.[32]

The fourth constitutional approach addressing the constitutional recognition of Roma has been identified in the group of "highly promotional" States. These countries have recognized as a "national minority" all Romani individuals living within their national territories regardless of the citizenship criterion. This is especially the case of United Kingdom and Ireland, both countries that do not formally distinguish between citizens and non-citizens when applying the category of "national minority" under the scope of the FCNM.

Indeed, the United Kingdom has recognized Roma as a "national minority" under the judicial interpretation of the *Race Relations Act* of 1976. Ireland has extended the recognition of the rights guaranteed to "national minorities" also to Romani individuals who are not Irish citizens.[33] Sweden is another interesting case that is worth highlighting in a discussion of the group of "highly promotional countries". At the moment of ratification, in fact, this country has omitted a detailed specification of the categories of minority groups benefiting from the protection of the FCNM. The practice has shown that Swedish authorities apply equally the set of rights enshrined in the Convention to Swedish citizens as well as to non Swedish-citizens.[34]

The picture emerging from this short analytical overview provides some general insights for the comprehension of the heterogeneity of legal definitions identifying Roma in each European domestic jurisdiction. Nonetheless, a further element should be considered when reflecting more deeply on the reasons underlying the different legal definitions of Roma. A glance to the numerical proportion of Roma *vis-à-vis* the overall majority national populations appears in fact essential to contextualize the development of each political-legal framework on a "practical" level as well.[35] However, this is not a general rule since in some cases the political-legal framework totally disregards the existence of minorities in spite of their numerical presence.[36] For this reason, it might be useful to provide a general picture of the numerical presence of Roma in Europe before engaging in a "definitional" analysis.

According to Piasere, a simplified but immediate numerical representation of Romani presence in Europe can be provided through the identification of the so-called "Gypsy-Europes".[37] The first "Gypsy-Europe" is the "core area" of the European Romani presence, and it comprises the states belonging to the Carpathian-Balkan area. The states registering the highest number of Romani population are all connected by an "imaginary line" linking almost vertically Slovakia to Macedonia.[38] In these countries, the average rate of Roma is around 9,5 percent of their total population.

The second "Gypsy-Europe" identified by Piasere comprises the Atlantic Region with Spain as the country with the highest rate of Romani population,[39] followed by Ireland, France and Portugal.[40] The peculiarity of this second "Gypsy-Europe" is that all alone it comprises almost the eleven percent of the overall Roma population in Europe. Finally, the third "Gypsy-Europe" is characterized by the remaining European countries where the average rate of the Roma population is below 1 percent of the total population.[41] The number of Roma living in the first "Gypsy-Europe", has been explained by Piasere in light of social and political frameworks characterizing Central and Eastern Europe at the time of the first Romani migrations in that area.

While Western European countries have always had a "totalitarian exclusionist attitude" towards Roma, Eastern European countries traditionally placed Roma at the lowest positions of their social stratification scales but, at the same time, provided them with a certain degree of freedom. In particular, this freedom regarded the opportunity to choose to adopt a sedentary life-style (either in cities or in the countryside) or to remain nomadic as long as they were regular tax-payers.[42]

In the second "Gypsy-Europe", Spain appears as a "numerical exception" in Western Europe in light of the historical development of its political institutions. In the post-Westphalian era, Spain adopted a very peculiar model of "inclusion" of Roma.[43] While a substantial majority of European countries promoted a "general expulsion" of Roma and, in the worst cases, committed genocide, Spain allowed the existence of this social group within its territory, at a high price, though: the "ethnocide" i.e. the complete cultural assimilation of Roma within mainstream society. Since the "classic" Western model "regulating" the presence of Roma through expulsion was not leading to the desired outcome,[44] the Spanish model was shaped around another strategy: it prohibited Roma from gathering collectively, speaking Romanes, wearing traditional Romani dresses, performing in traditional dances and following a nomadic lifestyle. Moreover, to pursue an implicit *"divide et impera"* policy, Spain also banned Roma from living together in the "Spanish districts" of the most populated cities and towns with less than 200 inhabitants.[45] Even though the "Spanish model" totally annihilated Romani collective cultural identity, it nonetheless provided a very small space for the individual existence of Roma.

The model of cultural assimilation initiated by Spain started to be rapidly exported. In particular, during the Enlightenment it was firstly adopted by Maria Theresa of Austria, mainly in the Hungarian regions of the Empire where Roma were pushed to a sturdy sedentarisation. Since the 19th century, the model was permeated by antiziganist stereotypes which increased until reaching the highest peak in the physical annihilation of Roma during the *Porajmos*, the Romani Holocaust.

The development of the three dimensions of "Gypsy Europe" sketched by Piasere can be better understood in light of the various "migration rounds" contributing to the further movements of Romani communities in Europe. After the large migration of the Modern Age through which Roma initially spread across the European continent, a second large wave of migration occurred in the mid-19th century after the abolition of slavery in Romania. At that time, in fact, a number of Roma left the Romanian regions to migrate to other European countries as well as to central Asia and to America.[46] A third migration wave occurred during the Balkan wars of the 90s. This wave has been identified as the biggest Romani migration from the Balkans in European history.[47]

A more recent migration, which was not as large as the previous ones, was caused by Italian and French antiziganist policies, which have resulted in the eviction of non-Italian and non-French Roma from their territories by forcing them to return to their home-countries.[48] These two recent migration waves emphasize a further element of complexity of the protection/promotion of Roma rights in Europe: within the same "national" minority status (be it that of national, ethnic, linguistic minority, etc.) different legal statuses may coexist. This means that in many European States, Romani individuals who are European, non-

European, refugees, asylum-seekers, stateless or even unregistered may co-exist. Hence, when reflecting on different legal definitions of Roma, it follows that a single legal category results for a higher degree of complexity of legal statuses.

Today, Roma are legally recognized in 21 of EU member-states, with different forms of legal recognition corresponding to diverse entitlements through minority rights approach. Roma are recognized as a "national minority" in Austria, Greece,[49] Finland, Germany, Latvia, Lithuania, Moldova, Romania, Slovakia and Sweden. Hungary, the Netherlands,[50] Poland and Portugal instead recognize Roma as an "ethnic minority". In Czech Republic, Roma are identified both as a "national minority" and as an "ethnic minority".[51] In Slovenia instead, Roma are neither recognized as a "national" nor as an "ethnic" minority, but rather through the definition of "Romani community" which, practically speaking, falls between the concepts of that of "national" and "ethnic" minority.[52] In Estonia, Roma are defined through the National Cultural Autonomy Model (NCA).[53]

In France, Spain and Italy, Roma are not defined through legal definitions forming part of a "minority rights scheme" but through other legal definitions which provide them with a very minimum recognition. In France, Roma are identified through the legal category "gens de voyage". This category, though not based on an ethnic criteria, implies Romani nomadism and is de facto excluding individuals who have adopted a sedentary lifestyle. In Spain, Roma are legally defined as "gitanos"; while this legal category has provided them with a minimum set of rights, their overall legal treatment is characterized by a "deficit of citizenship" in the lack of an anti-discriminatory legislation.[54] In Italy, Roma are not recognized as a "minority" at the national level, but at the regional one some mild forms of recognition have been provided mostly through the category of "gypsy" and "nomads".[55] Finally, a last interesting case to be mentioned is that of Ireland where the legal category "indigenous people" has been applied not to the whole Romani community, but only to the social group of "Travellers".[56]

From this short overview, it follows that the various "legal definitions" of Roma ensuing from the various European legal systems have to be understood as a historical, social, political and legal process of sedimentation which over the

centuries has stratified *multi-dimensionally* both the Roma and national populations.

3. Economic and Social Inclusion of Roma at Domestic Level

An array of definitions pertaining to the legal status of Roma in national legislations results in a heterogeneity of applications for Roma rights. Among the
various sets of human and minority rights, the set of economic and social rights
is particularly susceptible of a different degree of implementation on the basis
of the legal status accorded to Roma at domestic level.

According to the OSCE High Commissioner on National Minorities (HCNM),
economic and social rights constitute the prerequisite for the legal recognition
of other sets of rights, such as cultural and political rights. In the HCNM's
words, "in the lack of minimum conditions guaranteeing human dignity, the full
social integration of Roma cannot be achieved".[57] In some cases, the "fluid
nature" of economic and social rights may extend their enjoyment beyond the
citizenship requirement, in other cases their enjoyment may also be restricted
within the citizenship requirement. This is often the case for Roma.

Indeed, the overall socio-economic living conditions of Roma in Europe have
been described as a "poverty cycle" or "socio-economic trap".[58] This "trap" can
be understood as a (vicious) cycle which connects the dimensions of education, employment, housing and healthcare.[59] For many Romani individuals, the
chain of economic and social exclusion does not only undergo constant per-
petuation but incessant exacerbation as well.[60] The majority of EU legal systems in fact do not entitle Roma to a specific set of minority rights in the socio-
economic sphere, but instead generally refer to the recognition within a general
human rights clause. Only a number of states promote economic and social
rights for Roma through a promotional system. On a merely *de jure* level, it is
nonetheless interesting to note that most promotional legal systems recognizing Roma with the widest set of economic and social rights entitlements have
defined Roma through the legal category of "national minority".[61]

A number of legal systems specifically provides minority groups with *ad hoc* socio-economic rights set by including Roma in general economic and social "minority rights" provisions. This is, for instance, the case of Austria, whereby the 1976 Austrian Federal Act did not grant to the Ethnic Advisory Boards the competence to represent, *inter alia,* the economic and social interest of ethnic groups, which according to the law, shall be taken into consideration "before issuing legal norms and regarding general planning in the area of public funding affecting the interests of the ethnic groups".[62]

Among the various spheres belonging to the spectrum of economic and social rights, the educational sphere is one of the legal areas which finds a more extensive elaboration with regard to minority economic and social rights. This right can in fact be considered multi-faceted as it embodies different legal areas: linguistic rights, cultural rights and economic and social rights. Hence, even if this right is often devised with the primary aim of protection/promotion of linguistic and cultural dimensions of minority rights, the complementary economic and social dimension inevitably appears protected and promoted as well. While, in some cases, the right to education is exclusively articulated on a linguistic dimension,[63] in other cases this right is formulated as to be guaranteed at different didactic levels[64] and through public as well as through self-organized private arrangements.[65]

As for the economic and social areas of employment and housing, it is also interesting to note that both Irish legislation and Italian regional legislation specifically mention the enjoyment of these areas in relation to a specific (although at time not exclusive) minority exercise.[66] In a very limited number of cases, the set of socio-economic rights is devised to *specifically* address the needs of Roma in the areas of education, employment, healthcare and housing.

The Slovenian Roma Community Act[67] is particularly remarkable legislation which enshrines the state's positive obligation to, *inter alia,* actively engage for the integration of Roma community members into the system of education, also by means of appropriate scholarship policies (Art.4). Specific reference to the right to education of Roma is also made in a couple of Italian regional laws[68] which foresee the opportunity to include Romani adults in specific educational projects.[69] Slovenian and Italian regional legislation are again the only two sources specifically intervening in the area of employment (in particularly by mentioning educational training[70] and by promoting traditional Romani working activities).[71] In the area of healthcare, only Italian legislation specifically mentions the needs of Roma.[72]

In the realm of housing, the legal systems of Slovenia, Ireland and United Kingdom specifically recognize the needs of Roma. In each of these three cases, such recognition requires national and/or local authorities to provide the conditions of spatial planning for Roma settlements.[73] In Ireland, the Housing Travellers Accommodation Act requires local authorities to acquire appropriate accommodation by introducing a statutory framework for housing authority loans for caravans or sites for caravans.[74]

The Irish legislation further provides for the establishment of the National Traveller Accommodation Consultative Committee on a statutory basis to advise the Minister on any general aspect of Traveller accommodation.[75] In United Kingdom instead, a Gypsy or a Traveller living on a local authority caravan site does not fully enjoy an effective protection against eviction provided that he or she has been given four weeks' written notice and a court order has been obtained.[76]

Nonetheless, when moving from a *de jure* to a *de facto* perspective in the recognition of economic and social rights for Roma, i.e. from a formal to a substantial application of the equality principle within the different domestic systems, the constitutional model that generally applies throughout the EU is the "repressive" model.

4. From Policies to Laws: Enhancing the Pan-European Framework

Even in EU Member States entitling Romani communities with specific economic and social rights, recommendations of international bodies and reports of non-governmental organizations testify the very limited enjoyment of human and minority rights by Romani individuals and Romani communities. As discussed above, the sets of rights ensuing from "Westphalian" domestic legal definitions were born as "genetically" inadequate to address Romani cultural features as a non-territorial and diffuse minority Europe.

The legal practice developed by states uses the "national minority" definition as the most common legal category to define the legal status of Roma in Europe. Although the use of the legal category "national minority" does allow for a wider "promotional opening" in addressing Roma rights *vis-à-vis* other legal categories, since it *inter alia* benefits from the legal standards enshrined in the Framework Convention on National Minorities (FCNM),[77] it attempts at non-territorial definitions of the group.[78] The analysis has also shown that this legal category appears inadequate to comprehensively address Roma rights especially in the socio-economic realm.

To this regard, the promotion of the EU Framework for National Roma Integration Strategies up to 2020 may turn in an effective policy tool to address the gap between "law in the books" and "law in action" especially with to regard to economic and social rights. Indeed, given their programmatic nature, economic and social rights need an active engagement from the state in order to be fully implemented. The National Roma Integration Strategies (NRIS) thus could contribute to the "lobbying" of EU Member States to actively engage for the substantial implementation of economic and social provisions for Romani individuals as well.

Nonetheless, the "pan-European" recognition of the Romani social group is not in itself sufficient to comprehensively address Romani needs from a holistic perspective if it merely develops from a political perspective. Especially in Western Europe where the general legal recognition of Roma has traditionally been less promotional than in Central-Eastern Europe, NRIS risk to become a "nice *but* soft reformulation" of positive obligations of the state. Their programmatic nature remain in fact totally deprived of any binding force and thus of any potential mechanism of justifiability at the legal level. As the Italian NRIS, *inter alia*, demonstrates, the full social inclusion of Roma cannot be achieved as long as a legal fragmentary system is still in place. Within this precarious legal framework the adoption of the Emergency Decree No. 181/2007,[79] which breached international and European human rights law, may jeopardize the full efficacy of the Italian NRIS.

Therefore, in order to fully eradicate discriminatory attitudes towards Romani communities in Europe as well as their social exclusion, a comprehensive recognition of status of Roma should take place at the legal level, as well as at the political one. The EU has recently acknowledged this need by proposing a Council Recommendation on effective integration of Roma in the member states.[80] The aim of this legal document is to ensure that EU member states adopt an effective approach to Roma integration and endorse goals on the four pillars of education, employment, health and housing. In particular, the EC noted a scattered and divergent regulation addressing the issue of integration at domestic level. Indeed, Roma integration is often tackled in an uncoordinated manner creating growing discrepancies in approaches across different member states.

This proposed EU legislation represents a remarkable step in the process of binding member states to a stronger commitment for implementing the sets of policy measures enshrined in the NRIS. Nonetheless, this soft-law proposal lacks the ability to tackle the inner deficiencies of the Westphalian model, i.e. the comprehensive recognition of Roma legal status. Ideally, such recognition should take the form of a hard-law legal instrument that recognizes the legal status of Roma as a "Pan-European minority" by providing member states with the power to recognize Roma by reference to a legal category that accords with their constitutional traditions. In this way, the legal recognition of Roma would build on a common minimum legal framework but, at the same time, would not disregard specific national institutional features as well as domestic responsibilities in providing and implementing Roma rights.

This "Pan-European legal recognition" would allow the "by-pass" of the limits and the contradictions inherent in the domestic Westphalian paradigm. At the same time, it would address Romani cultural identity by considering the historical tie with European territory as well as the non-territorial minority feature within domestic jurisdictions. By the same token, a pan-European legal framework would entitle Romani communities across Europe to a minimum set of rights in the socio-economic, linguistic, cultural and political spheres. In line with the principles established by the EU Framework, member states entering into this legal arrangement would be free to adopt a more inclusive and promotional approach towards Roma rights also on the basis of the experience developed at the implementation stage of their NRIS.

By framing Romani minority status and rights in a Pan-European legal framework, economic and social guarantees will be fostered through binding commitments. At the same time, such a pan-European legal instrument would avoid the risk of totally demanding protection and the promotion of Romani rights to the European level which may turn into another type of "trap". The excessive "Europeanization" of both Romani "identity" and Romani "policies" may in fact further exacerbate the exclusion of Roma in Europe. By merely representing them as a separate "nation of Europe" instead that of as a real "pan-European minority", domestic and European policies might continue to address them as foreigners rather than as citizens of EU.

References

1   See the most recent data and figures provided by the Council of Europe (updated at 14th September 2010) available at http://www.coe.int/t/dg3/romatravellers /default_en.asp (last entered on 8th December 2013).

2   In 1993, the Conference on Security and Cooperation in Europe (CSCE, now Organization for Security and Cooperation in Europe OSCE) firstly described Roma in Europe "non-territorial minorities living dispersed in more than one country". Brett, R. and Eddison, E. "The CSCE Human Dimension on National Minorities. Can National Minorities Be Considered Positively? ." Helsinki Monitor. Quarterly on Security and Cooperation in Europe 4, no. 3 (1993): 39-43, 40. The concept of "non-territoriality" is understood in contrast to "old" minority groups (such as "kin-state" minorities) whose identification has traditionally been connected to a specific territorial area of reference.

3   The first historical evidence documenting Romani presence in Europe was registered in Anatolia in the early years of 1000 A.D. Fraser, A. Gypsies. Oxford: Blackwell 1992, 45. Hence, the "historical tie" with European territory is more than a thousand years old.

4   A. Robles-Gil, "Final Report on the Human Rights Situation of the Roma, Sinti and Travellers in Europe, for the Attention of the Committee of Ministers and the Parliamentary Assembly Common DH (2006)1,"Strasbourg: Office for the Commissioner of Human Rights, 15 February 2006). §5.

5   P. Williams, "L'ethnologie des Tsiganes " in Des Tsiganes en Europe, ed. M. Stewart and P. Williams (Paris : Editions de la Maison des Sciences de l'Homme, 2011), 12.

6   Hancock, I. We Are the Romani People. Ame Sam E Rromane Džene. Hertfordshire Centre de recherches tsiganes—University of Hertfordshire Press 2002.

7   The so-called "Anti-Gypsy legislation", which for centuries "regulated" Romani presence within European States, stemmed from this "national" and "nationalistic" perspective. According to Fraser, the "Anti-Gypsy" legislation started to develop in the 15th century as a response to Roma's incapacity or unwillingness to adapt their culture to post-feudal Western European mechanisms, mostly hinging on a "commercial economy" under development. As Fraser explains: "The authorities could not come to terms with rootless and masterless men, with no fixed domicile and useless as a workforce: in their eyes that status was itself and aberration, at odds with established order, and had to be put right by coercion and pressure of the [gypsies]". A. Fraser, Gypsies (Oxford: Blackwell 1992), 130.

8   Firstly, and more prominently, the CoE, then the OSCE, and finally the EU. On the first political debates and legal texts on Roma in Europe see, inter alia, M. Danbakli, Roma, Gypsies: Texts issued by International Institutions (Hatfied: University of Hertfordshire Press 2001).

9   European Parliament Resolution on the situation of Roma in the European Union, 28th April 2005, P6_TA(2005)015, point 27.

10 The ERTF was created under the framework of the CoE as "the first democratically elected pan-European body representing "the voice of Roma in 46 countries". On the ERTF's recognition of Roma as a "pan-European minority" Statement on Roma and

Sinti at the Working Sessions 6 and 7 of the Annual Human Dimension Implementation Meeting of the OSCE—ODIHR, Warsaw, 27th September 2007, HDIM.IO/205/07.

11   Ibid.

12   See Political Groups which tabled the resolution pursuant to Rule 108(5) of the European Parliament's Rules of Procedure: PPE-DE, PSE, ALDE, Verts/ALE, GUE/NGL B6-0050/2008 / P6_TA-PROV(2008)0035. See §8-10.

13   For further information on States included in the EURoma network and on the specific activities put forward see http://www.euromanet.eu/about/index.html (last accessed on 8th December 2013).

14   See http://ec.europa.eu/justice/discrimination/roma/roma-platform/index_en.htm (last accessed on 8th December 2013).

15   COM(2011) 173 final. Section 2.

16   The Racial Equality Directive 2000/43/EC.

17   In particular, the idea of the Roma Decade emerged during the Conference "Roma in an Expanding Europe: Challenges for the Future" held in Budapest in 2003. Following this Conference, in 2005 the prime Ministers of the first eight participating governments signed the "Declaration of the Decade of Roma Inclusion" in Sofia where they committed themselves to fostering the economic and social conditions of Roma in Europe in partnership with a number of international governmental and non-governmental organizations (such as the World Bank, the Open Society Foundations, the United Nations Development Program, the Council of Europe, the Council of Europe Development Bank, the Contact Point for Roma and Sinti Issues of the Office for Democratic Institutions and Human Rights of the Organisation for Security and Co-operation in Europe, the European Roma Information Office, the European Roma and Traveller Forum, the European Roma Rights Centre, UN-HABITAT, UNHCR, the United Nations Children's Fund (UNICEF) and the World Health Organization (WHO). See http://www.romadecade.org last accessed on 8th December 2013). In line with the Decade's goals, the European Roma Strategies also aim at intervening in the areas of: education, employment, health and housing.

18   At the OSCE level, the most notable institution for the protection of minority rights is the High Commissioner on National Minorities (HCNM). This office monitors the situation of minorities within OSCE States and simultaneously assists States through recommendations and guidelines. At the CoE level, some specific legal instruments for the protection of minority rights were developed, particularly as a result of the Balkan "ethnic" conflicts of the 1990s, the CoE has adopted a more effective strategy to protect the rights of minorities. The "Venice Commission" was created as a commission of legal experts with the mandate to better assist democratization processes also by promoting minority rights. The rights of minorities are protected and promoted at the CoE level also by the 1992 European Charter for Regional or Minority Languages (ECRML) and the 1995 Framework Convention on the Rights of Persons Belonging to National Minorities (FCNM). The European Commission against Racism and Intolerance (ECRI) and the European Committee on Social Rights (ECSR) also play significant roles in this realm. At the EU level, minority rights fully entered the competence of this organization only after the entry into force of the Lisbon Treaty in 2009. Also some other legal instruments of secondary legislation developing from a larger human rights spectrum may theoretically improve the conditions of minority groups as well. In the case of Roma the Employment Framework Directive (2000/78/EC), the Long-Term resident

Directive (2003/109/EC) and Racial Equality Directive (2000/43/EC) may be mentioned in this regard.

19   M. Nowak, *Introduction to the Human Rights Regime* (Leiden : Martinus Nijhoff Publishers, 2003).

20   Ibid., 40-41.

21   "Old" minorities as traditionally belonging to the EU territory v. "new" minorities as traditionally falling outside this scheme.

22   G.M. Quer and S. Memo, "Releasing Minorities from The "Nationalist Trap": From Territorial to Personal Autonomy in a "Multiple Demoi Europe" " *Cuadernos Europeos de Deusto* 47, no. 2012 (2012).

23   ENAR/ERIO, "Debunking Myths & Revealing Truths About the Roma," (Bruxelles: ENAR/ERIO, 2011).

24   P. Bonetti, "I nodi giuridici della condizione di Rom e Sinti in Italia," in *La condizione giuridica di Rom e Sinti in Italia*, ed. P. Bonetti, A. Simoni, and T. Vitale (Milano: Giuffré Editore, 2011), 20.

25   This classification was firstly proposed by R. Toniatti, "Minoranze e minoranze protette. Modelli Costituzionali Comparati," in *Cittadinanza e Diritti nelle città Multiculturali*, ed. T. and Dunne Bonazzi, M. (Bologna: Il Mulino, 1994). and J. Marko, "Equality and Difference: Political and Legal Aspects of Ethnic Group Relations," in *Vienna International Encounter of Some Current Issues Regarding the Situation of National Minorities* ed. F. Matscher (Strasbourg: Arlington, 1997). in F. Palermo and J. Woelk, *Diritto costituzionale comparato dei Gruppi e delle minoranze (2nd Edition)* (Padova: CEDAM, 2011).

26   F. Palermo, "Rom e Sinti come minoranza. Profili di diritto italiano e comparato e di diritto internazionale," in La condizione giuridica di Rom e Sinti in Italia ed. P. Bonetti, A. Simoni, and T. Vitale (Milano: Giuffré Editore 2011).

27   So far only four countries have neither signed nor ratified the FCNM: Andorra, France, Monaco and Turkey. Whereas four other countries have signed the Treaty but not yet ratified it: Belgium, Greece, Iceland and Luxembourg. See http://www.coe.int/t/dghl/m onitoring/minorities/1_AtGlance/PDF_MapMinorities_bil.pdf last update 24th October 2008 (last accessed on 8th December 2013).

28   Such a recognition can be generally inferred from the ratifications of the FCNM provided by these countries.

29   Palermo, "Rom e Sinti come minoranza. Profili di diritto italiano e comparato e di Diritto Internazionale" 80.

30   Ibid., 159.

31   See, *inter alia*, the reports that Germany presented before the Advisory Committee of the FCNM.

32   This is mostly the case with respect to Catalans and Basques linguistic groups. For a more in- depth analysis on this issue see Palermo, "Rom e Sinti come minoranza. Profili di diritto italiano e comparato e di diritto internazionale." 161.

33   Although non-Irish citizens can benefit from a wider spectrum of rights they are not entitled to political rights. In fact, according to the *Race Relations Act* non-Irish citizens can benefit from cultural and linguistic rights as well as from right to association.

34   Palermo, 162.

35   This is the case of EU "micro-States" (Luxembourg and Malta) where, facing the quasi-total homogeneity of nationals, Roma (as well as other minority groups) do not benefit from any special recognition and, consequently, from any legal definition.

36   Especially in "agnostic legal models", such as in France, "where numbers" seem not to "warrant" it, to paraphrase the general principle regulating the Anglophone "minority" schooling system in Canada.

37   L. Piasere, *I Rom d'Europa. Una storia moderna* (Roma-Bari: Laterza, 2004).

38   The data presented in Piasere's 2004 publication have been updated according to figures provided by the last CoE data. See the statistics on Romani presence in Europe prepared by the Council of Europe and Travellers Division updated at 14th September 2010 available at http://www.coe.int/t/dg3/romatravellers/default_en.asp (last accessed on 8th December 2013). In these countries, the average rate of Roma is around 9,5 percent of their total population (Romania 8,32%; Bulgaria 10,33%; Hungary 7,05%; Slovakia 9,17%; Serbia, Montenegro and Kosovo—around 12,6% all together—Macedonia 9,95%. This "core area" of States with a high presence of Roma is surrounded by a "ring" of neighbouring countries where Roma average presence is rated around the 2 percent of the total population (Czech Republic 1,96%; Greece 2,47%; Albania 3,18%; Bosnia and Herzegovina 1,09%; Turkey 3,83%; Croatia 0,78%; Moldova 2,49%; Slovenia 0,42%).

39   With 1,57 percent of the population.

40   With the average rate of 0,9 percent of the total population.

41   In the case of Russia, average estimates of Roma population are 825.000 people, even more than in Bulgaria (750.000 people). While in the case of Russia the number of Roma individuals corresponds to 0,59% of the total population, given the extension of the country, in Bulgaria a lower number of people corresponds to 10,33% of the population.

42   Piasere, *I Rom d'Europa. Una storia moderna*, 35.

43   Ibid.54

44   The living strategy adopted by Roma during the Modern Age (and even lately) was based on the creation of settlements in the border regions where the power of nascent States was more fragile. See Ibid., 63.

45   Ibid., 54.

46   Ibid., 64.

47   Ibid., 66.

48   H. O'Nions, "Roma Expulsion and Discrimination: the Elephant in Brussels," *European Journal of Migration and Law* 13, no. 4 (2011).

49   In Greece, Roma are only partially recognized as a "national minority". Greece is, in fact, adopting an agnostic approach that formally does not recognize any minority group within its domestic jurisdiction. However, Muslim Roma of Western Thrace are the only social group recognized as a "national minority". Such legal recognition derives from the legacy of the Treaty of Lausanne and it does not formally or practically mitigate the extreme marginalization that Romani communities generally experience within Greek society.

50   Such recognition has been provided only at the "political" level since no legal recognition of Roma has yet appeared in any official document. Roma started being defined as an "ethnic minority" in 1983 in the policy formulated by the Dutch Parliament. V.

Guiraudon, Phalet, K., Ter Wal, J., "Monitoring Ethnic Minorities in the Netherlands," *International Social Science Journal* 183(2005): 76.

51   When referring to "new" groups immigrated, especially during the Balkan wars, Roma are identified as an "ethnic minority". Consequently, the Act on the Rights of Members of Ethnic Minorities distinguishes between Roma with Czech citizenship and immigrated Roma with residence permits.

52   The Roma Community Act of April 13th 2007, no. 33/07.

53   National Cultural Autonomy (NCA) is a model that was proposed in 1899 by Renner and Bauer to find a pacific solution to deal with nationalist claims which were causing the Austrian-Hungarian Empire to collapse. The NCA shifted the design and management of minority rights from a "territorial" to a "personal" conception. This model can be easily explained through the "religious simile" used by Renner: "Much in the same way Catholics, Protestants and Jews could coexist in the same city .. so members of different national communities could coexist with their own distinctive institutions and national organizations, provided they did not claim territorial exclusivity." E. Nimni, *National Cultural Autonomy and Its Contemporary Critics* (New York: Routledge, 2005), 10.

54   F. Rey, "Propuestas para avanzar en el caso Español," *El Globo Internacional, política y integración*, no. 37-38 (2007).

55   Legge regionale N. 9/88 Regione Sardegna "Tutela dell'etnia e della Cultura dei nomadi"; legge regionale N. 47/88 Regione Emilia Romagna "Norme per le minoranze nomadi in Emilia-Romagna"; legge regionale N. 77/89 Regione Lombardia "Azione Regionale per la Tutela delle Popolazioni appartenenti alle etnie tradizionalmente nomadi o semi-nomadi"; legge regionale N. 32/90 Regione Umbria "Misure per favorire l'inserimento dei nomadi nella società e per la tutela della loro identità e del loro patrimonio culturale"; legge regionale N. 6/92 Regione Liguria (no heading); legge regionale 25/02/1993 Regione Piemonte "Interventi a favore della popolazione zingara".

56   It seems worthwhile to consider the argumentation that Ireland brought before the FCNM Advisory Committee to explain the rationale distinguishing "Travellers as indigenous people" from other Romani communities: "In a range of legislative, administrative and institutional provisions, the Government has recognized the special position of Ireland's Traveller community, in order to protect their rights and improve their situation. While Travellers are not a Gypsy or Roma people, their long shared history, cultural values, language (Cant), customs and traditions make them a self-defined group, and one which is recognizable and distinct. The Traveller community is one whose members, like the Gypsies in other countries, travelled from place to place in pursuit of various different traditional vocations. Despite their nomadic origins and tendencies, the majority of the Traveller community now live in towns and cities. Their culture and way of life, of which nomadism is an important factor, distinguishes the Travellers from the sedentary (settled) population. While Travellers do not constitute a distinct group from the population as a whole in terms of religion, language or race, they are, however, an indigenous minority who have been part of Irish society for centuries". Report submitted by Ireland pursuant to Article 25 Paragraph 1 of the Framework Convention for the Protection of National Minorities ACFC/SR(2001)006 received on 13th November 2001, 15.

57   OSCE-HCNM, "Report on the Situation of Roma and Sinti in the OSCE Area," (OSCE-HCNM 2000), 15.

58   European Parliament, "Measures to Promote the Situation of Roma Eu Citizens in the European Union. Study," ed. Citizens' Rights and Constitutional Affairs Policy Department (Bruxelles European Parliament, 2011). Instead, in the past, many European States completely disregarded the dimension of socio-cultural deprivation underlying the economic and social exclusion of Roma by focusing merely on the dimensions of poverty and unemployment. S. Baldin, "Il Consiglio d'Europa e l'inclusione Sociale dei Rom e dei Viaggianti," in *Il Mosaico Rom. Specificità culturali e Governance Multilivello* ed. S. Baldin and M. Zago (FrancoAngeli: Milano, 2011), 162.

59   According to the report of the European Parliament the cycle is rooted in a limited (or on a substantially inexistent) access to the right of education. The insufficient level of education produces lack of skills which in turn brings about a high risk of unemployment, a lack of income and a limited access to social assistance. People living in this precarious socio-economic dimension easily fall into a condition of indigence which produces their social exclusion. In order to survive, these socially excluded individuals engage in informal activities which, in turn, contribute to their increasing marginalization by local communities: these individuals start in fact to be perceived as "hostile" precisely on the basis of the informal activities that they perform. The inter-related chain of circular causation eventually ends where the "trap" begins: in the limited access to the right of education.

60   See also D. Ringold, M. O. Orenstein, and E. Wilkens, "Roma in an Expanding Europe. Breaking the Poverty Cycle," (Washington, D.C. : World Bank 2005).

61   Germany, Austria, Romania, Slovakia, Latvia, Lithuania, Finland, Sweden and partially Greece (recognizing only the Muslim community of Western Trace).

62   Section II paragraph 3.1.

63   Romania Art.32.4 of the Constitution, Slovakia Art.43.2. (a) of the Constitution.

64   Hungary Art.43, Lithuania Art.2 (Interesting enough, the Lithuanian Law on minorities at Art.3, also foresees the possibility "to train specialists to respond to the needs of particular ethnic cultures in the realm of education"). At the Italian regional level this provision is enshrined in Art.9 of the Regional Law of Umbria (32/90), Art. 8 of the Regional Law of Sardegna (9/88), Art. 10 Toscana (2/2000), Art.13 Regional Law of Friuli Venezia Giulia (11/88). Some Italian regional laws promote also the adult education namely Art.8 Regional Law of Sardegna (9/88), Art.7 of the provincial law of Trento (Law jh/09).

65   Czech Republic Act on the Rights of Members of National Minorities of 2001 No107/819 Official Gazzette 273/2001.

66   Through different legislative acts, Ireland guarantees the rights to education and employment also, but not exclusively to, Travellers, namely: in the Employment Equality Act No.21 of 1998, in the Equal Status Act No.8 of 2000 for Ireland, in the Equal Status Act No. 24 of 2004 and in the Housing (Miscellaneous Provisions) Act No. 9 of 2002. Poland's legislation refers to the protection of economic and social rights of minorities through a positive obligation at Art.6.1.2 of Act of 6th January 2005 on national and ethnic minorities and on the regional languages. (Dziennik Ustaw No. 17, item. 141, with the amendment of 2005, No. 62, item 550). Latvia's legislation refers to equal rights of minorities to access work (§3) and develop material conditions of education (§10) in Law about the Unrestricted Development and Right to Cultural Autonomy of Latvia's Nationalities and Ethnic Groups, adopted on March, 19th 1991 and amended on June, 6th 1994. The Italian regional laws of Lombardia (Art.8 Law 77/89), Veneto

(Art.5 Law 54/89), Emilia (Art.10 and 12 Law 47/88) and Liguria (Art. 5 and 6 Law 6/92) also promote to the social integration of Roma in the areas of education and employment.

67   Official Gazette of the Republic of Slovenia, No. 33/07, 13 April 2007.

68   At the Italian regional level this provision is enshrined in Art.9 of the Regional Law of Umbria, Art. 8 of the Regional Law of Sardegna, Art. 10 Toscana, Art.13 Regional Law of Friuli. Art.8 Regional Law of Sardegna, Art.7 of the provincial law of Trento.

69   Art.8 Regional Law of Sardegna, Art.7 of the Provincial Law of Trento.

70   Art.4 Roma Community Act of Slovenia, Art. 8 of the Regional Law of Toscana, Art.8 of the Regional Law of Lazio, Art.11 of the Regional Law of Friuli, Art.7 of Liguria.

71   Arts 8-9 Provincial Law of Trento, Art.12 of the Regional Law of Emilia, Art.6 of Liguria

72   Art.9 Toscana, Art.4 Lombardia, Art.14 Emilia, Art.8 Liguria.

73   See, Art.5 of the Roma Community Act of Slovenia, letter a) of the Explanatory and Financial Memorandum of Housing Travellers Accommodation Act No.33 of 1998 of Ireland and Sections 7 and 8 of the Caravan Sites Act of 1968 of United Kingdom.

74   Letter h) of the Explanatory and Financial Memorandum of the Housing Travellers Accommodation Act No.33 of 1998.

75   Letter e) of the Explanatory and Financial Memorandum of the Housing Travellers Accommodation Act No.33 of 1998.

76   M. Willers, *Ensuring Access to Rights for Roma and Travellers. The Role of the European Court of Human Rights. A Handbook for Lawyers Defending Roma and Travellers* (Strasbourg : Council of Europe 2009), 65.

77   Including the monitoring activity of the Advisory Committee on National Minorities which periodically monitors the implementation of European standards at the domestic level.

78   Such as those of "ethnic minority" and National Cultural Autonomy (NCA).

79   "*Disposizioni urgenti in materia di allontanamento dal territorio nazionale per esigenze di pubblica sicurezza.*" The Decree entered into force on 2nd November 2007 and provided local prefects with the power to expel citizens of EU Member States considered to be a threat for the public order. Although not explicitly mentioned, the main targets of the decree were Romanian Roma. See C. Tavani, "La protezione delle minoranze in Italia e il mancato riconoscimento della Minoranza Rom: ragioni e conseguenze," *EDAP* 03(2013).

80   The draft text of COM (2013) 460 was finally adopted by the Council of the European Union on 9th and 10th December 2013. See http://www.consilium.europa.eu/uedocs/cms_data/docs/pressdata/en/lsa/139979.pdf (last accessed on 10th December 2013).

The Subtlety of Racism: From Antiziganism to Romaphobia

Ioana Vrăbiescu

National School of Political Studies and Public Administration

Since the 1990s the notion of discrimination has, according to Ignăţoiu-Şora, been "the most significant element associated with the situation of Roma".[1] As a result, anti-discrimination has become a policy tool to improve the situation and protection of Romanis. In addition, van Baar considers that the European-isation of Romani activism has been enhanced through the discourses of mi-nority and human rights regimes, the social policies of the European Union (EU), and the memory politics of the *Porajmos* (the Romani Holocaust).[2] As van Baar points out, "the Roma are no passive receivers of transnational con-ditions, but have been actively involved in shaping the process of constructing identities, memories, and social relations."[3]

This paper argues that over the past two decades, the anti-discrimination dis-course targeting Romanis has developed into a European governmentality tool. The anti-discrimination discourse relies on the logic of European integration and neoliberal politics, both of which showcase a considerable blind spot for racism. In this process, Romani activists cannot be deprived of their agency, having made a great contribution to shaping the discourse and terms that de-fine racism targeted at themselves and other members of Romani communi-ties. The debate over the concepts that define a Romani-centred racism started with the political action by Romanis who wanted to be perceived as equal part-ners in expressing a political identity and an ethnic culture.[4] The scholarly work on the definition of these concepts is a recent one and still in need of in-depth analyses.[5] The racism against Romanis covers multiple analytical perspectives and political stances. It is a commonplace approach in defining this special type of racism to conceive of it as a process temporarily limited and bound to differ-ent socio-political conditions. Similarly, antiracist discourses follow this process closely, contributing to the definition and as such also perpetuating antiziganist practices. This paper problematizes racialisation, which contributes to Romaphobia and enforces new forms of racism against Romanis by pointing out antiziganist attitudes in wider society.

The structure of my argument is informed by theories of racism, particularly those that explain but do not exhort the differences between biological, cultural, symbolic and structural racism. I construct my argument in three steps that will contextualize the contemporary antiziganist discourse. First, I explain racism against Romanis as a process brought to bear by European political structures. Here, theories of racism build on concepts such as biological and cultural racism; I use these to ground my argument concerning the difference between antiziganism and Romaphobia. Second, I analyse how minority rights and human rights approaches in Central and Eastern European (CEE) countries have been used to manage ethnic diversity in the region. In doing so, I examine these policies in the context of the East-West relationship and point to the importance of norm convergence across Europe.[6] Third, I discuss the role social policies have played in facilitating Romani activists' advocacy for group rights and the impact this particular political context has had on the Romani movement. In conclusion, I identify the structural constraints in European antiracist discourse as having a compound effect on the shift from antiziganism to Romaphobia in Europe.

Racism against Romanis goes back many centuries. It existed under different regimes, exerted its influence through different cultural practices and has been aggravated since the collapse of the socialist regimes in 1989. The European Commission against Racism and Intolerance (ECRI) defines antiziganism as

> [A] specific form of racism, an ideology founded on racial superiority, a form of dehumanisation and institutional racism nurtured by historical discrimination, which is expressed, among others, by violence, hate speech, exploitation, stigmatisation and the most blatant kind of discrimination.[7]

In negatively targeting Romani people, antiziganism has been consistently defined within the paradigm of biological racism, where the Gypsy was portrayed as having subhuman characteristics. Romaphobia—unlike antiziganism—is an invisible, structural form of racism built on the denial of racism against Roma-nis. Romaphobia is the systemic discrimination that remains in the aftermath of the formal political commitment to fight antiziganism (i.e. European documents etc., and nation-states' policies).

I refer to Romaphobia as a new type of racism against Romanis that cannot be tackled under the ideologies of human rights and minority rights protection. Both paradigms address biological racism in antiziganism, and during the decades of implemented antiracism legislation they determined a special kind of structural blindness. Formally, the racial and ethnic non-identification procedures and the politics of affirmative action were meant to alleviate discrimination against Romanis. While the fight against antiziganism—as was led by European institutions, Romani activists and individual member states—should have diminished racist attitudes against Romanis within European societies, some recent data points in the contrary direction.[8] Importantly, the efforts made under human rights or minority rights protection appears to be negatively balanced when compared to the cases of discrimination suffered by Romani people.[9] Romaphobia is deeply rooted and widespread in different European institutions; it becomes even more relevant for our understanding of the way European identity is articulated in cultural rather than racial discourse—through normative and practical dimensions and by the process of integration.

Racism against the Romanis,—antiziganism—has been addressed by international organisations (IOs), nation-states, non-governmental organisations (NGOs), private actors and public individuals in an array of documents and policies since the beginning of the 1990s, when the fear of ethnic conflict in Eastern Europe was at its peak. The financial, political and moral support of civil society in Eastern European countries put the accent on individual empowerment and responsibility. Both American and European influences on post-socialist Eastern Europe were grounded in the ideal of neoliberal governance and the discourse on human rights.[10]

It is my argument here that the neoliberal context instituted after the fall of the Iron Curtain, alongside the subsequent EU strategies of enlargement and integration have produced a shift from biological racism against Romanis towards

Romaphobia, a form of structural racism. European institutions foster a specific identity that "refuses to acknowledge the existence of dividing, discriminatory lines that systematically exclude some groups."[11] This, I argue, has resulted in the shift from antiziganism to Romaphobia. In addition, the Romani movement has partially contributed to Romaphobia. Romani activists have used human rights and minority rights frameworks to combat discrimination and racism. This discourse has been highly relevant to both the internalisation and exploitation of racial identity markers by subjects and objects of antiziganist practices over the decades. My paper exposes the mechanisms that maintain Romani exclusion through Romaphobia, not despite but due to an overt focus on the human and minority rights of Romani individuals.

1. Antiziganism in Europe and Structural Racism

What explains the persistence of racism against Romanis in Europe? Why does it continue to rise despite concerted efforts to counter it on several political levels, despite the existence of protection frameworks that are based on both human and minority rights? Racism is the process of dehumanising, generalising individual features and essentialising the "other" in order to maintain a hierarchy of power and privileges. In her discussion of the meanings of race, Melissa Weiner identifies indicators for racism as tools for researchers and the development of a critical theory of racism. Her starting point is the understanding of "racialisation" as the assignment of "groups to different hierarchical categories reflecting perceptions of inferiority and superiority based on perceived biological and/or cultural differences."[12] She further sums up the forms of racism as "malignant (oppressive and violent), benign (paternal and culturally ethnocentric), and benevolent (altruistic)."[13] This "new racism" or cultural racism can be considered benign or even benevolent by reinforcing individual stereotypes. Those being racialised identify themselves with the victims of racism through the stigmas applied to them. Such racism persists and damages more because it refuses to acknowledge ongoing systemic discrimination while blaming the target group for their stigma and unwillingness to adapt. Racism at the community level works both in the minds of the agents of racism as well as in minds of those subjected to racism.

Structural racism, as Étienne Balibar concisely puts it, is the "hierarchisation of labour force, with or without compensatory migrations, and corresponding ideological representations of 'different humankinds.'"[14] The economic and political system dehumanises and oppresses people to exploit their labour force, building up an ideology of culture or ethnic differences to sustain its power. Within the human rights framework these outcomes are best achieved by tapping the antiracist discourse: The formation of discourses and ascribing meanings to "race" is the privilege of the dominant.[15] Consequently, the whole framework of human and minority rights is constructed within a global hierarchy of power. As such, political communities can engage in debates about racism but they do so from *within* the very system that builds on racist attitudes. Thus, one can only speak about racism from within the inherently racist social and, as such, also political structures. Discussions of anti-Romani discrimination, antiziganism and Romaphobia, imply that there is no fatality of racism but rather a confirmation of the necessary "evil," the unavoidable "inside other" constructed and reproduced under different ideologies and regimes.

Whether cultural or structural, racism poses several interrelated challenges to academic debates.[16] The concepts used in academic studies to define anti-Romani racism are debatable, especially when considered against the background of the theory of "indexicality of race," referencing the sign that stands in for an actually existing thing.[17] The semiotic and linguistic analyses of the word "antiziganism" unveil a certain type of racist behaviour without recognizing the Gypsy as a real thing, as the exonym Gypsy refers to a racialised category of people.[18] Furthermore, first letter capitalisation could be understood as signifying a certain idea, rather than using the term as a common noun and limiting the ideologically biased usage of the concept.

Antiziganism is a concept that stands for the racist behaviour towards a constructed "other," as there is no real Gypsy but rather a superimposed image on Romanis.[19] Some scholars and Romani activists struggle not only with the naming of antiziganism but also with the meaning of racism against Romanis, a meaning similar to "differentialist", "cultural," "symbolic" and "structural" racism.[20] Antiziganism has been defined as a distinct type of racist ideology, being at the same time "similar, different, and intertwined with many other types of racism."[21]

The pervasiveness of antiziganism in Europe relies on socially embedded experiences and practices of racism. Throughout their history in Europe, the Romanis have been consistently racialised and subjected to policies of control and practices of bureaucratic surveillance. From centuries of slavery in the Romanian territories and the Habsburg politics of assimilation, to the *Porajmos* in World War II (WWII) and the sterilization of Romani women in some countries, antiziganism can be understood within the full definition of biological racism. The bodies of people labelled through perceivable distinctions and ideological reasoning were ascribed to a social category of "Roma". Though it is appealing to consider antiziganism as a form of cultural racism, the image of a hated Rom has visible biological features outlining ethnic and "deviant" characteristics. Present narratives about the civilizing missions towards the "deviant Gypsy" are complementary to the invisibility of Romanis in mainstream European culture and politics. Antiziganism perpetuates the racist identification process, adding a distinctive characteristic by homogenizing and essentialising Romani communities and by locating them precisely in the European political space.

Besides being a form of biological racism, antiziganism is strengthened by the existence of structural racism within Europe. The documents and policies targeting Romanis either tackle biological racism or else develop policies based on a Romani ethnic identity. As Robert Koulish notes, the legitimised and institutionalised race-based policies of affirmative action determine the construction of the public imaginary about the righteousness of ethnic identification and claims for minority rights protection.[22] Structural racism opens up a space for public debate on the subject of antiziganism without providing the political means to confront discrimination against Romanis. Considering the failure of affirmative measures, the denial of racism perpetuates a Romani antiracist discourse without formulating any policies to explicitly challenge antiziganism. The ongoing policies for Romanis—the Decade for Roma Inclusion, the Organization for Security and Co-operation in Europe (OSCE) Action Plan, National Roma Integration Strategies (NRISs), etc.,—neither mainstream antiracism nor do they address specific antiracist measures.

Thus, the question that needs answering in the context of prevailing structural incentives to keep antiziganist attitudes across societies unchallenged is about the role played by the Romani movement in antiracist campaigning. The anti-racist fight stays at the core of Romani political identity. Romani political identity refers to the identity built through normative (documents, policies etc.) as well as public actions (NGOs' programs, media communication etc.), where Roma-nis are the subject of political and public debate. If we accept that structural racism is a settled part of European identity and is confounding the world sys-tem of power relations as Balibar suggests, then all attempts to question racism help not so much to eradicate racism but to strengthen the existing hierarchy of power.[23]

The European counter-racist political discourse is a part of this logic of racism; a new type of racism being built on the denial of racism. Moreover, the denial of racism might be interpreted as an important ideological outcome of neolib-eral governance, being built upon a "certain level of accomplishment in imple-menting a human rights and antiracism agenda in a society," which obscures other racist attitudes and practices.[24] As long as officially and culturally that particular form of biological racism is outlawed, other racist social practices and structural patterns can be muted. While antiracist political rhetoric targets racist groups, these groups can often easily defend themselves as not being racist on the ground that their racist discourse does not fit the post-Second World War understanding of prejudices based on biological racism, i.e. a human rights framework.

Besides the homogenising and essentialising processes that create a Romani political identity, the consequences for Romani representatives and activists are circumscribed by the markers underlying their own political identity. Defini-tions of nomadism, *Porajmos* and antiziganism partly characterise Romani po-litical identity and contribute further to the construction of antiracist discourses and policies. Romani identity is built on their "otherness," being marked by their subaltern position and "their sheer invisibility as humans within European dis-cursive and social fabrics, from history books to everyday workplaces."[25] While antiziganism permeates every society in Europe, the Romani people's experience of such racism is divergent and disparate, depending on the constructed image of the "other" in a particular location.

From human rights violations to the denial of racism, an important transformation has occurred. The racism targeting Romanis which has been constructed over the last few decades has generated a particular discourse that penetrates social practices, political and institutional attitudes, and individual reasoning. The shift produced between the identifiable antiziganism and the subtler Romaphobia relies on "Roma" as a political subject. At the EU level, the "Roma" become the main character in the policies which address antiziganism, thus equating the Gypsy with "Roma". Not only does the EU address Romanis as the actually existent people and not as a construct of political invention, but the antiracist policies that shape this identity in the new political context discard the notion of the constructed character of Romani identity.[26]

The Romani antiracist discourse has risen to the liberal moral maxims of a neoliberal ideology that champions the treatment of all individuals as equals in an ethnic- and colour-blind fashion. In demanding to abolish the racial perception of the Gypsy, this ideology has ushered in the denial of racism; the Gypsy, as it were, is not hated anymore because the Romanis are "good people". The vicious circle of racism takes advantage of the counter-racist discourse. The denial of racism has been consolidated by policies against antiziganism that, in fact, legitimised the use of an anti-Romani discourse that is supposedly grounded not in a racial perception of the Gypsy but in the cultural, economic or social attitudes towards the "Roma". Dismantling the denial of racism challenges the construction of Romaphobia within European structural racism.

Romaphobia represents the consequence of a political attitude that strengthens antiziganism within existent structural racism. It is the expression of the failure of Romani antiracist discourse. In ideological terms, Romaphobia cannot be explained through the pervasiveness of antiziganism as the racial discrimination against Romanis. Rather, it is built on the wider and structural denial of racism. Romaphobia is a process and not another name for the same racist structure that dehumanises Romanis. As a process, Romaphobia holds the weight of economic-political prejudices and actions, re-signifying racism against the Romanis and relying on the human rights paradigm.

2. The Human and Minority Rights in Europe and Antiziganism

The European experience of Nazism and Fascism ushered in a universal condemnation of racist ideologies and political programmes. Antiracist politics alert to the human rights framework and pursued after the Second World War have repeatedly condemned biological racism. Clustered in nationalist ideologies, biological racism objectifies people as inferiors, and as not being able to take part in civilisation as represented by the nation. Romanis have been the object of this biological racism, which has been the basis of much of the social and territorial exclusion of Romanis practiced in modern European states. Under the development of nationalist ideology, eugenic theories explained Romanis through their "bio-psychological and psycho-moral abnormality."[27] After 1945, Western experts on Romani communities transformed the abnormality of Romanis "into a psychosocial and 'cultural' obstacle," thus dissolving biological racism.[28] Biological racism was taken over by cultural racism, whereby the Romanis were exposed through their inadaptability or failed assimilation into mainstream society and culture.[29] Although the Gypsy is depicted as capable of slowly progressing towards the accepted societal model, and "civilising" himself, the failure of Romanis to integrate is often seen as their demonstrable inadaptability, confirming the previous image of Romanis as biologically or genetically inferior.

Bringing the argument back to the human rights paradigm, this ideology perpetuates the marginality, poverty and structural racism concerning Romanis. Moreover, the universalism of human rights, implemented into European states' legislation, determines the denial of racism in society. The denial of racism has developed on both sides of the Iron Curtain, although differences exist. The political language of the principle of human rights ranges from absolute condemnation of ethnicised racist public discourses to the blindness of certain exclusionary and racist social practices. For example, the refusing of ethnic identification in some states, or ethnic recognition in the case of Romani individuals, did not erase the social or state practice of ethnicising people, but rather rendered it invisible.[30] During the Cold War, there was an evident bias in approaches to combating racism between European states, depending on their ideological differences.

The human rights approach hailing from the Western European polities was further deployed as a political tool to constrain economically and diplomatically Eastern European states. Also, those differences within the cultural and political sense of the constructed binary image of Gypsy/Roma pointed to a gap between the European liberal-democratic and centralised-communist policies developed in each country. After the Helsinki Accords of 1975, domestic politics in Eastern European states came under international scrutiny, and various governments in the region were pressured into signing and implementing the Accords in exchange for economic aid and foreign recognition.

Although in the aftermath of the Cold War social and ethnic conflicts did not multiply throughout Eastern Europe, the ex-socialist states were perceived as a political boiling pot. These tensions endangered the rebuilding of positive new relations. However, the East-West political rivalry has turned in the same pattern of relations, under EU domination. International organisations struggled to react to this frightening horizon by injecting money into grassroots projects and putting pressure on national governments in the region to adopt anti-discrimination laws. The consensual political move was towards greater human rights protection which continued despite some ethnic conflicts and general economic instability in Eastern European countries in the 1990s. This transition framework has been maintained thanks to "human rights concerns [which] would appear to have been used instrumentally by Western powers" in a process of continued "intervention in CEE states over minority rights [by the OSCE], while ignoring concerns of recognition of minorities in Western states."[31] The politics imposed by the EU on ex-socialist countries continue to grow in the unbalanced context of power relations.[32]

Looking more closely at Eastern Europe, racism has been constantly disavowed based on at least three socio-political grounds. First, during the socialist period, CEE societies could deny racism within the Communist ideology due to the conception that "race" was solely a biological and not a social construct. The socialist regimes erased race from juridical and legislative documents. Equality among all the people required by official Communist ideology led not only to homogenisation and assimilation politics, but also to the permanent denial of the existence of racism. Second, the CEE countries have seen themselves caught within the logic of human rights negotiability, which started "the moment states and financial institutions connected human rights with military and economic aid," and thereafter has justified on moral grounds—rather than on political power—intervention in the politics of other states.[33] Third, the minority rights regime, built on EU conditionality and treaties, has been imposed on CEE countries in order to create and develop national or ethnic minority policies.[34]

EU demands for integration and social cohesion emphasise the necessity of regulating minority rights and ethnic recognition in all ex-socialist states, which needed to adopt new legislations in order to conform to the *acquis communautaires*.[35] The minority rights framework intended to counter the risk of ethnic conflict (as in the countries of former Yugoslavia), to encourage political self-determination projects (as in Hungary and Romania), or to alleviate ethnicity-based social exclusion (Bulgaria, Czech Republic and Slovakia). Further, certain politics are developed together with various affirmative actions bound to the politics of difference. The EU's imposition of minority rights on CEE countries contradicts Western states' acceptance of a sovereign approach to decide and legislate ethnic politics or identification practices. Together with multicultural politics, ethnically blind politics (in the sense of denying racial identification) have been considered to be the only discursive option after the Second World War. Although there is no consensus over the concept of ethnicity, its meaning is charged with biological designation and in conjunction with a reference to "minority" makes a notional collectivity questionable for unbiased political usage.[36] Ethnicity loses its biological essential designation and becomes a cultural and behavioural feature.

The winning neoliberal ideology in the 1990s, imposed a pattern of defining and addressing racism. The bias between Eastern and Western countries is a factor and a medium for constructing the discourse on Romani discrimination.

After the fall of the Iron Curtain we might consider two stages in the relation between EU and CEE countries concerning antiracist political attitudes: in the first decade (during the 1990s), Romani NGOs and IOs developed strategies to combat antiziganism in conflict zones where a human rights pattern imposed itself as the only viable political tool. The second stage, in the decade immediately preceding EU integration of CEE states, international organisations in particular pressed for a normative engagement and combating antiziganism. This rhetoric consolidated understandings of racism as effects of social structures, and helped antiziganism to grow in intensity and manifestation on both sides of Europe.[37]

Whether in the EU or CEE countries, the pressure to monitor anti-Romani discrimination increased political awareness about the issue and imposed changes in legislation and policies, but it did not alleviate racist practices and attitudes against Romani peoples.[38] As the EU has moved forward with enlargement and societal integration processes, Romani NGOs' agendas have increasingly been thought to have failed in key political areas as regards European governance for Romani inclusion.[39]

The latest expression of political action in EU governance for Romanis is the EU Framework for National Roma Integration Strategies (the Framework). The anti-discrimination definition as found in the Framework requires member states to adopt the same language, but the prominence of an anti-discrimination discourse is not sufficient to augment antiracist political interventions.[40] The first sentence in the text portrays Romanis as being "very often the victims of racism, discrimination and social exclusion," then the document continues without identifying the racial dimension of discrimination, omitting terms such as antiziganism or Romaphobia. The documents are attesting that there is racial discrimination against Romanis, but as there no longer is the recognition that such a thing as "race" exists, it is impossible to address it politically.

The construction of the Framework is based on human rights discourse and social policy development, preserving in this respect the parameters of previous European politics towards the Romanis. Consequently, the member states in their National Roma Integration Strategies (NRISs) follow the line of the narrative posited in the Framework, adding their specific political attitudes towards antiziganist discrimination. The NRISs respond in the same pattern of rendering racism invisible. Although these antiracist policies should be addressed transversally, an analysis of NRISs documents issued by member states reveals, with few exceptions, the ways in which states avoid addressing racism against Romanis. The terms used in documents are comfortable with a wide, shallow meaning such as "discrimination". This notion is being used by almost all NRISs as the preferred expression concerning Romani exclusion. The "discrimination" mentioned in the political discourse cannot have consequences at the policy level, at least not as the terms "race" or "racism" would have. Racism is sometimes associated with the *Porajmos*, still being understood by policymakers in the sense of a form of biological racism.

The current ethnicisation in state policy towards the Romanis is a by-product of a human and minority rights approach.[41] The differences in attitudes and practices towards ethnic data collection (state identification or self-identification) or policy implementation in EU member states have not been alleviated, even after the Racial Equality Directive in 2000. Additionally, particular aspects of social exclusion and marginalisation are making the OSCE and the Council of Europe confirm Romani individuals as being in danger of conflict and having their human rights violated. In that respect, a question concerning the human rights framework remains: What are the chances that the human rights principle will support cohesion and solidarity in society, when Romani citizens of EU member states have not been protected against racial attacks, nor have been integrated or empowered within the same regime?

After the fall of the Iron Curtain, there was a clear unequal power relationship between Eastern and Western European countries. The EU imposed on CEE countries a minority rights framework in order to combat racism, especially against Romani individuals. This context led again to a denial of racism in two ways: EU countries could maintain their ethnically blind politics, even towards Romanis, and CEE candidate states should adopt the necessary legislation concerning biological racism. As with the human rights paradigm, the minority rights paradigm is a tool for economic and political action, not an instrument to eradicate racism. But it confirms once again the denial of racism in EU institutions and member states. Thus, the antiziganism becomes a favourite political subject for EU institutions and member states, precisely because it is nestled within a wider and unfettered structural racism that is defined by Romaphobia.

3. The European Antiracist Discourse and Romani Political Identity

While non-homogenous Romani identity is pushed through organisational and representational institutions to shape the political interests of different Romani communities, an ethnocentric construction of political identity is used to empower social movements and to address racism. The antiracist discourse of Romani ethnopolitical entrepreneurs built within the framework of minority rights, human rights and the European nation-states' construct raises some questions. Could the Romani movement itself have contributed to the shift towards Romaphobia? How can this contribution be defined, and what are the consequences of this shift for Romani political identity? How do the critiques challenge mainstream Romani antiracist politics?

The EU enlargement process exports a distinctive multiculturalist ideology that is presented as a minority rights framework. The EU minority rights framework imposes a political and legislative corpus on CEE states. Romani activists employ a similar language, conceiving racial issues in ready-made definitions. The vicious circle of racialised policies in Europe is revealed by some scholars who denounce Romani integration policy within the EU as being an ethnicised social issue.[42] Romani NGOs have been ideologically and financially pushed to address minority rights' issues by pressuring states to change their discriminatory attitudes towards Romanis. Negotiations between Romani activists and states in the CEE region are arbitrated by international organisations, of which the EU is the dominant party.[43] In this section I argue that the international framework within which Romani NGOs and political leaders operate imposes certain constraints on the claims these NGOs and other Romani leaders are able to make, constraints that ultimately increase Romaphobia.

Scholars disagree about the consequences of human and minority rights politics for Romanis. For the Romani movement there are at least five negative effects. First, on the basis of human rights protection, IOs (the EU, the Council of Europe, the OSCE), NGOs and human rights activists, being those "moral entrepreneurs," supported and encouraged international intervention in the domestic politics of states in order to defend Romanis against widespread abuses.[44] The political attitude addressing antiziganism was left to Romani civil society and to IOs with a human rights agenda. The collaboration between international institutions—such as Council of Europe or ECRI—and Romani NGOs (including the European Roma International Organisation, European Roma Rights Centre, etc.), became the paradigm for tackling antiziganism. They had exclusive legitimacy for seizing the issue and pressuring states to develop antiracist policies.

Second, working through Romani networks, the transnational Romani elite has used the international legal system to report human rights abuses against Romanis. Romani activists hope international organisations are able to address politically and take action against the discrimination which Romanis face. This general context made activists confident in using the human rights paradigm and embracing the antiracist discourse, both of which seemed politically correct and ideologically appealing. For example, Nicolae and Slavik explain that

> Discrimination, hate speech in the mass media, and acceptance of violent attacks against the Roma have become the lifestyle of the majority in Romania. The response and attitudes of the government and mass media reinforce and perpetuate a strong and harmful social stigma, giving an already racist and xenophobic society the clear message that segregation and continued discrimination is in the interest of the Romanian state. [...] The solution to the problem of social stigma in Romania is the growth of a culture of human rights in Romania. Some assistance can be expected from the European Union when Romania eventually joins, but that is at least five years into the future. In the meantime, it is the responsibility of Romanian civil society to fight racism against Roma.[45]

Third, as a consequence of power relations, IOs on one hand were demanding the participation of civil society and Romani people themselves to find ways to combat racism; and on the other hand, human rights organisations were making clear that the racism issue should be nation-states' concern and responsibility.[46] IOs place the responsibility on member states, which "should strive to encourage Roma social inclusion and foster peaceful co-habitation within the wider community," regardless of the lack of any coercion towards the adoption of specific legislation or budgeting policies.[47] Although the attention received from the part of international organisations lacked consistency and political practicality, a considerable number of publications have been produced to support a genuine interest in and to disseminate well-written guidelines on antiziganism.[48]

Fourth, the minority rights framework determined an ethnicised pattern of political identity. This ethnicisation of Romanis in Europe, being driven by the minority rights paradigm, leads to more segregation instead of alleviating differences. The European framework of political identity has already identified Romanis in two mutually exclusive ways: the "Gypsies and Travellers" as a group living in the West, culturally distinguished, nomadic, and marginalised; versus the "Roma", who usually live in the East, or have migrated from there, and can be identified by reference to a solid ethnic identity, are socially excluded and poorly educated. These two models of identity are constructed out of the biased treatment of two parts of Europe: the West versus the East. The ethnic identification of the Romanis is seen as a colonial tool of Western countries and the basis for an ethnically-constructed, self-determination movement. Indeed, within the European FCNM, Romani activists found the necessary endorsement for developing their political identity. They shaped a political identity by assuming and emphasizing their difference from majority populations in ethnic terms by combating antiziganism. The turning point in the politics of difference becomes a danger for the target group, because by affirming difference, "the implementation of group-conscious policies will reinstate the stigma and exclusion" of that group.[49]

Fifth, minority rights conditionality becomes the backbone for the Romani movement concentrating its efforts and actions on the possibility for increased socio-political development. At the same time, the minority rights regime becomes a tool for the non-Romani majority to identify and gauge democratic development, stigmatizing again, in different ways, Romani and pro-Romani leaders, politicians and activists for their inefficiency and inability to manage responsible and visible projects, blaming them for the failure of affirmative-action politics and accusing them of fraud. In this way, Romani people are again converted into victims and blamed for "their" failure.[50]

Moreover, the Romani movement emerged and developed under a neoliberal ideology that consolidates individual responsibility. Romani political entrepreneurs have accommodated neoliberal principles and acted accordingly through NGOs' managerial mobilisation of communities and resources. The Romani NGOs' dependence on external donors has been hotly debated,[51] especially as to whether or not these NGOs are left with too little space for action and motivation. In the hierarchy of power, Romani NGOs are indeed restrained by limited resources and a very small audience in an already crowded political space. However, the actions of Romani activists are not completely lacking agency as they have demonstrable political consequences.

The neoliberal policies enforced by development programs oblige CEE states to renounce social solidarity politics following a different redistribution principle. Moreover, the importance of competition and the promotion of individual responsibility encouraged "social inclusion" as the only solution for the politics of redistribution. Thus, Romaphobia has become a term expressing disdain for those who keep on failing when "everything" is done for them. Although Romani activists are unfairly blamed for structural gaps, still there are entire categories of people that Romani representatives and NGOs are failing to activate politically or address effectively, including Romani women, the undocumented, Romani migrants, those who hide their Romani identity and those who deny such a constructed identity. Outside the Romani movement, critics of antiracist policies have opposed multicultural policies for Romanis, arguing the depreciation of states' welfare systems. These critics point out the existence of multicultural policies allows for formal equality, but neglect the fact that multiculturalism is built on the denial of racist prejudice.

The absence of women in the debate about antiziganism reveals the deficiency of gender equality in Romani representation and could be used here as a useful illustration. Three notable concerns can be raised as regards the absence of

Romani women from the construction of Romani political identity.[52] Romani women's invisibility results from the lack of a negotiated political position, favouring instead the allocation of traditional roles; of specific gender policies within mainstream Romani issues; and of understanding discrimination within the Romani antiracist discourse as a result of structural constraints. Overall, anti-discrimination policies target an abstract "Roma," completely ignoring, among other things, intersections of class, gender, citizenship, and religious dimensions of social identities.[53] Moreover, the invisibility of Romani women points to the need for an intersectional analysis to address the multiple forms of discrimination to which women are subjected.[54] The mainstream fight against antiziganism exacerbates the discrimination faced by those who, for different reasons, are excluded from the political description of "Roma." The entire antiracist discourse in the Romani movement is apparently condemned not only to reproduce itself but also to marginalize and oppress internal minorities and individuals of "uncomfortable" categories.

The founding principle of the European system for social solidarity in welfare states is that of human rights.[55] Governance through principles of social justice based on equality reflects upon, but is not built on the value of human rights alone. It includes an implicitly normative reference to social solidarity which, as Eduardo Galeano argues, requires equality between interacting partners.[56] Charity and commitment to respect are, however, top-down processes that humiliate those on the receiving end of it, and ultimately prevents challenges to implicit power relations. Within the larger context of EU declarations for development, Romani communities are made targets of EU structural funds and the Romani minority becomes a priority of top-down policies, i.e. "the chief principle to be taken into account in the planning of policy implementation."[57]

The European Governance for Romani Inclusion finances many projects as part of its "integration" policies and calls on the involvement of local, national and international Romani NGOs. As a result, in both Western and Eastern Europe these projects are mostly perceived as a waste of money and as counterproductive campaigns with no one responsible. Without being welfare states, the redistribution of resources within Eastern European states cannot lead to integration and cohesion. Nevertheless, the allocation and distribution of financial resources has to occur within the human rights framework. The consequence of this duality of EU policy towards Eastern states is that resources have been used for interventions that have led to segregation and exclusion. Thus, Romani communities and individuals have become the real victims of the integration process coordinated by the EU in two different ways: first, by being targeted as the main recipient of EU funds and policies for social inclusion (e.g. different EU programs such as the Decade initiative); second, by being constituted as a socio-economically segregated minority group due to ethnic minority protection policies.

The top-down political pattern of minority rights conditionality and the human rights regime fails the most vulnerable within Romani communities. Taken together, the social solidarity policies and charity applied formally to Romani communities are self-contradictory, only deepening the exclusion of Romani people within societies that either do not recognize them as equals, or else keep them in a dependent situation in order to consolidate and legitimate the status quo. Despite the discourse about integration revealing the degree of exclusion of the Romani minority, Romani activists assume the politics of difference on the basis of the perceived essentialised ethnicity of the community. And as a result, Romani people themselves are made responsible for poverty and failed integration and blamed for not improving their situation. This twist in the discursive representation of structural background for the integration of Romani communities gives space for multiculturalist policies and social-inclusion funding to reason about the best courses of action to remedy the "plight of Roma" as well as to combat racism. Thus, this framework presents itself as a paradox. On one hand the framework encourages the politics of difference and multicultural ideology as charity-funding models that aim to help Romanis escape the poverty circle in which they are trapped. On the other hand, it calls upon the marginal communities themselves to do something about their exclusion without addressing the wider structural reasons for exclusion.

Conclusion

The focus on human rights established as a shared norm across post-war Europe has long played an important role in building a legislative and political bulwark to fight intolerance and racism. Once international treaties have been acceded to, it is up to states and domestic political elites to implement these regulations and ensure continued commitment to positive action in support of minority individuals' rights and prosecution of those engaging in discriminatory practices. As my paper shows, the multiculturalist approach to the management of ethnic diversity has insisted on erasing salient racial categories from public awareness, yet has upheld practices of racism, which are ubiquitously found in political institutions throughout Europe. Though different political regimes in Europe have appealed to antiracism and sought to enshrine the discourse in public sphere, the erasure of race in politics leads to the denial of racism and perpetuates structural racism.

Even Romani activists are constrained to operate within a framework of ethnicised identity. At the same time, policy-makers and scholars are essentialising Romani identity. The result is the build-up of a minority rights framework and the ethnicised issue of Romani social exclusion. For the Romani movement the consequence is the impossibility to abandon the political ethnic paradigm and the antiracism framework. The racialised subject is trapped within a racist vicious circle, and the fight against racism becomes a political tool. Thus, Romani representatives contributed essentially to the portrait of the "Roma" precisely as it has been constructed through the discourse of race and racism within the human rights and minority rights frameworks.

Romani and pro-Romani activists are caught between IOs' interests, nation-states' actions and their own struggle to have a political voice to politicize the hatred faced by Romani people in daily life. My paper maintains that local, national and transnational Romani NGOs are compelled to use the minority and human rights paradigms along with anti-discrimination policies to protect Romani citizens of nation-states. By doing this, they are circumscribing their actions and initiatives within state-driven politics and reinforce the ethnicisation and promotion of ethnic differences. Since the 1990s the pattern of dependence of

CEE states on Western Europe has been further entrenched. The evolving principles of the human rights regime observed throughout Europe were based on compliance to top-down policies targeting CEE states and societies. The result is a gradual shift, first towards minority rights, and then towards an individually-based, multicultural non-discrimination approach.

Those states falling "behind" the West, usually associated with defunct socialist regimes, had to conform to and adopt a neoliberal political agenda. Furthermore, by conforming to the shared human right norms of the EU, CEE countries aligned their internal legislations on minorities' protection to standards defined by institutions of which they were not yet a part, and thus had no input on the decision-making process. Precisely because the political and normative structures in place required only the new member states to acquiesce to these "common" standards on minority protection and human rights, Romani activists could tap into the discourse of discrimination and appeal to minority rights provisions. In light of the ongoing EU integration process, Romani representatives saw the EU integration process as their best chance to engage representatives of the majority in dialogue about the remit and application of human rights norms. However, as my discussion above shows, the overreliance on "inclusion" and the lack of commitment to specific human rights concepts reduced such dialogue to an exercise in ineffectiveness, resulting in Romani activists' withdrawal from participation in political arenas.

The construction of Romani political identity has long been shaped by opposition to antiziganism and anti-Romani discrimination. And as a political identity with relevance to political processes and institutions, Romani political identity cannot be separated from the racist pigeonholing of the majority on the basis of racial markers, reference to Nomadism, and the experience of *Porajmos*. It is therefore legitimate to see the core of Romani political action for recognition in Europe as a part of bottom-up practices against antiziganism.

Romaphobia, the structural racism of European institutions, tags Romani people and communities, while at the same time antiracist initiatives support Romani NGOs and human rights activists. It seems, therefore, that decreased state involvement in policies ensuring the allocation of group rights and the non-discrimination of individuals leaves it to Romani people themselves to facilitate integration. By the same logic, Romani people are also constrained to stop victimizing themselves. Yet, as there is no common policy for combating antiziganism in the EU Framework and EU recommendations on Romani integration, Romani activists are left only to react to attempts at defining antiziganism within EU documents.

Racism against Romanis has transcended several political regimes regardless of governmental commitments to combat discrimination. These political regimes have nevertheless been committed to human rights principles. In my paper I have addressed the paradoxical construction in which an anti-discrimination discourse, which conforms to the human rights principle, allows racism to be maintained and even be reinforced. The consequences at the political level are counterintuitive. Given that this form of racism is structural and systematic, addressing and combating Romaphobia within the traditional framework of human rights has been, and is likely to remain, ineffective.

Acknowledgements

An earlier version of this article was presented at the Conference "Antiziganism: What's in a word" in Uppsala University, October 23-25, 2013. The author acknowledges the helpful feedback received from the participants of this session. Special thanks for their careful comments and reviewing go to Chris Davis, Diana Popescu and Timofey Agarin.

References

1   Emanuela Ignățoiu-Șora, "The discrimination discourse in relation to the Roma: its limits and benefits," *Ethnic and Racial Studies* 34:10 (2011): 1697-1714, p. 1697.
2   Huub van Baar, "Cultural policy and the governmentalization of Holocaust remembrance in Europe: Romani memory between denial and recognition." *International Journal of Cultural Policy* 17:1 (2011): 1-17.
3   van Baar, "Cultural policy and the governmentalization of Holocaust," 3.
4   Nicolae Gheorghe and Jennifer Tanaka, *Public policies concerning Roma and Sinti in the OSCE region* (OSCE/ODIHR, 1998). See also, Andrzej Mirga and Nicolae Gheorghe, *The Roma in the twenty-first century: A policy paper* (Project on Ethnic Relations, 1997). Nicolae Gheorghe, "Choices to be made and prices to be paid: Potential roles and consequences in Roma activism and policy-making," in Will Guy, ed., *From Victimhood to Citizenship: The Path of Roma Integration* (Pakiv European Roma Fund: 2011). György Csepeli and Dávid Simon, "Construction of Roma identity in Eastern and Central Europe: perception and self-identification," *Journal of Ethnic and Migration Studies* 30:1 (2004): 129-150. Isabella Clough Marinaro and Nando Sigona, "Introduction Anti-Gypsyism and the politics of exclusion: Roma and Sinti in contemporary Italy," *Journal of Modern Italian Studies* 16:5 (2011): 583-589.
5   Sabrina Tosi Cambini, "Antiziganismo: strumenti interpretativi e fenomenologia contemporanea," *ANUAC* 1:1 (June 2012): 17-23.
6   The paradigm of East-West, together with my analysis of human rights during the Cold War or the minority rights paradigm after the fall of the Iron Curtain, refers on one hand to a settled perception about a multiple divided Europe, and on the another hand to a distinctive type of neo-colonialism towards Eastern European ex-socialist countries.
7   European Commission against Racism and Intolerance, ECRI (2011)37, ECRI General Policy Recommendation No.13, On Combating Anti-Gypsyism and Discrimination against Roma, (Strasbourg: Council of Europe, 2011). Hristo Kyuchukov, ed., *New Faces of Antigypsysim in Modern Europe* (Praha, 2012).
8   Barometrul incluziunii Romilor, (București: Fundația pentru o Societate Deschisă, 2007) shows that the responses regarding the ethnic identity of Romanis rather conforms to the normative than perceptive, people using racial identification conformingly to what they think is happening and not to what actually happens (p.10). See also Pro Democrația Association, *Stereotypes against the Roma*, 2010.
9   Sorin Cace, Roxana Toader and Ana Vizireanu, *The Roma in Romania. From Scapegoat to Development engine,* (Agenția Împreună, July 2013).
10   I use the term "neoliberal governance" or "neoliberalism" in the sense of market policies for regulation and the state reforms that consider public policies in terms of individual and community responsibility. Neoliberalism reduces redistribution to "social inclusion." The way the neoliberal market has influenced the mechanism of Romanis marginalisation is best tackled in Huub van Baar, "Toward a politics of representation beyond hegemonic neoliberalism: the European Romani movement revisited" *Citizenship Studies*, 16:2 (2011), 287-296. For the American influence see David Chandler, *Constructing Global Civil Society: Morality and Power in International Relations* (London: Palgrave MacMillan, 2004). Denise Horn, "Democracy, American Style: US Foreign Policy, Democratization, and Women's Political Integration in Transitional States,"

Center for Global Security and Democracy Department of Political Science (Paper presented for the panel *Gender, US Hegemony, and Interstate Conflict* at the International Studies Association Annual Convention, Rutgers University, Montreal, 17-21 March 2004).

11   Susana Martínez Guillem, "European Identity: Across Which Lines? Defining Europe Through Public Discourses on the Roma," *Journal of International and Intercultural Communication* 4:1 (2011), 23-41, 25.

12   Melissa F. Weiner, "Towards a critical global race theory," *Sociology Compass* 6:4 (2012): 332-350, 333.

13   Weiner, "Towards a critical global race theory," 334.

14   Étienne Balibar, "Europe as borderland," *Environment and planning D: Society and space* 27 (2009): 190-215, 198.

15   Ramón Grosfoguel, "Introduction: 'cultural racism' and colonial Caribbean migrants in core zones of the capitalist world-economy." *Review (Fernand Braudel Center)* (1999): 409-434.

16   Ralf Melzer and Sebastian Serafin, eds., *Right-wing Extremism in Europe* (Berlin: Friedrich-Ebert-Stiftung, 2013)

17   Kate T. Anderson, "Justifying race talk: Indexicality and the social construction of race and linguistic value," *Journal of linguistic Anthropology* 18:1 (2008): 108-129. Jane H. Hill, "Language, race, and white public space," *American anthropologist*, 100:3 (1998): 680-689. For discussion of semantics in the indexicality approach and the reference to philosophic pragmatism see Charles Sanders Pierce. For more general discussion, see Markus End, "History of Antigypsyism in Europe: The Social Causes," in Hristo Kyuchukov, ed., *New Faces of Antigypsysim in Modern Europe* (Praha, 2012), 7-15.

18   End argues that when written with a hyphen, anti-Gypsyism, the word 'Gypsy' becomes accepted and recognized, it indicates a meaning and a real referent. The same word written without a hyphen—Antigypsyism—has almost exactly the same meaning as Antisemitism. See End, "History of Antigypsyism in Europe".

19   Although I consider that the term to be used is Antiziganism with capitalizing first letter, for the reason of the edited volume I keep the editor's choice of antiziganism.

20   Valeriu Nicolae, *On Diplomacy, Roma and Anti-Gypsyism.* (New York, Amsterdam and Brussels: Idebate Press, 2007), 31-48. Jan Selling, "'A Gypsy is a gypsy': a literary construction in a long-term perspective," *Scandia* 79:1 (2013): 11-37. David T. Goldberg, *The threat of race: Reflections on racial neoliberalism.* (Wiley. com. 2009). Barnor Hesse, "Im/plausible deniability: racism's conceptual double bind," *Social identities* 10:1 (2004): 9-29. David O. Sears and Patrick J. Henry, "The origins of symbolic racism," *Journal of personality and social psychology* 85:2 (2003): 259.

21   Nicolae, *On Diplomacy,* 21.

22   Robert Koulish, "Hungarian Roma attitudes on minority rights: the symbolic violence of ethnic identification," *Europe-Asia Studies* 57:2 (2005): 311-326.

23   Balibar, "Europe as borderland."

24   Dimitrina Petrova, "The denial of racism," in *Roma Rights: Race, Justice, and Strategies for Equality* (Amsterdam: IDEA, 2002), 4.

25   Nidhi Trehan and Angéla Kóczé, "Racism, (neo-)colonialism and social justice: the struggle for the soul of the Romani movement in post-socialist Europe," *Racism Postcolonialism Europe* 6 (2009): 50-77, 51.

26   Shannon Woodcock, "Romania and EUrope: Roma, Rroma and Ţigani as sites for the

contestation of ethno-national identities," *Patterns of Prejudice* 41:5 (2007): 493-515.

27 Giovanni Picker and Gabriele Roccheggiani, "Abnormalizing minorities. The State and Expert knowledge addressing the Roma in Italy," *Identities: Global Studies in Culture and Power* (2013), 9.

28 Picker and Roccheggiani, "Abnormalizing minorities," 9.

29 Verena Stolcke, "Talking culture: new boundaries, new rhetorics of exclusion in Europe," *Current anthropology* 36:1 (1995): 1-24.

30 The examples of Western European countries should be taken into account: Spain and Portugal—do not recognize Romani as an 'ethnic minority'; the Netherlands—does not recognize Romani as a 'national minority' although other national minorities are recognized (the difference of allochthonous and autochthonous shadow ethnic discrimination, although anti-Romani discrimination is all pervasive); Italy—there is no recognition as 'national minority' for Romanis; Switzerland and UK—in 2001 the UK issued a special border policy against Romanis, yet there is no such ethnic identification of Romani in passports; France and Germany do not recognize any 'ethnic minority'; Malta, Denmark, Luxembourg—there are anti-Romani attitudes despite the fact that there are formally no Romani people registered in these countries (as examples of racism in the absence of the racialised subject), etc.

31 Chandler, *Constructing Global Civil Society*, 39.

32 Melanie H. Ram, "Interests, Norms and Advocacy: Explaining the Emergence of the Roma onto the EU's Agenda." *Ethnopolitics* 9.2 (2010): 197-217.

33 Margaret E. Keck and Kathryn Sikkink, *Activists beyond borders: Advocacy networks in international politics*, (Ithaca, NY: Cornell University Press, 1998).

34 David J. Galbreath and Joanne McEvoy. *The European Minority Rights Regime: Towards a Theory of Regime Effectiveness*, (Palgrave Macmillan, 2012). See also, Aimee Kanner Arias and Mehmet Gurses, "The complexities of minority rights in the European Union," *The International Journal of Human Rights*, 16:2 (2012): 321-336.

35 The minority rights framework is constituted of legal and political conditionality within the EU enlargement process, including the anti-discrimination and minority rights' articles in the Maastricht Treaty, Amsterdam Treaty, Framework Convention for the Protection of National Minorities (FCNM), Racial Equality Directive (Council Directive 2000/43/EC), the Anti-Racist Directive 2004 (Directive 2004/38/EC) and the ECRI Reports. Galina Kostadinova, "Minority rights as a normative framework for addressing the situation of Roma in Europe," *Oxford Development Studies*, 39:02 (2011): 163-183.

36 Gerd Baumann, *Contesting culture: Discourses of identity in multi-ethnic London* (Cambridge University Press, 1996).

37 Étienne Balibar and Immanuel Maurice Wallerstein, eds., *Race, nation, class: ambiguous identities*, (Verso, 1991). Jan Nederveen Pieterse, "Europe and its Others," *A Companion to Racial and Ethnic studies*, 1 (2002): 17-24.

38 OSCE Conference on Anti-Semitism and on Other Forms of Intolerance, Córdoba, 8 and 9 June 2005, PC.NGO/25/05, Report on Anti-Gypsyism in European Media.

39 Márton Rövid, "Roma Rights 2012: Challenges of Representation: Voice on Roma Politics, Power and Participation," http://www.errc.org/en-research-and-advocacy-roma-details.php?article_id=4174&page=1, accessed on 29th of August 2013.

40 National Roma Integration Strategies: a first step in the implementation of the EU Framework COM (2012) 226, 21 May 2012.

41 Patricia Ahmed, Cynthia Feliciano and Rebecca Jean Emigh, "Internal and external

ethnic assessments in Eastern Europe," *Social forces* 86:1 (2007): 231-255. Eva Sobotka, "Human Rights and Roma Policy: Formation in the Czech Republic, Slovakia and Poland," in Roni Stauber and Raphael Vago, eds., *The Roma: A Minority in Europe*, (Hungary: Akaprint, 2007).

42   Jennifer Illuzzi, "Negotiating the 'state of exception': Gypsies' encounter with the judiciary in Germany and Italy, 1860–1914," *Social history* 35:4 (2010): 418-438. Katherine Hepworth, "Romani Politics in Contemporary Europe: Poverty, Ethnic Mobilization and the Neoliberal Order," *Journal of Ethnic and Migration Studies* 38:1 (2012): 189-190. Aidan McGarry, "The dilemma of the European Union's Roma policy," *Critical social policy* 32:1 (2012): 126-136.

43   Others involved are the United Nations Development Programme (UNDP), the Organisation for Security and Cooperation in Europe (OSCE), the World Bank and the Soros Foundation.

44   The term "moral entrepreneurs" belong to Susan D. Burgerman, "Mobilizing principles: The role of transnational activists in promoting human rights principles." *Human Rights Quarterly* 20:4 (1998): 905-923. One of the examples is given by Bhopal analysing the Gypsy and Travellers from Ireland where the decision for relocation of a certain number of families was reflected by the UN response that insisted towards "an acceptable agreement for relocation should be reached in line with international human rights obligations" in Kalwant Bhopal, "'What about us?' Gypsies, Travellers and 'White racism' in secondary schools in England", *International Studies in Sociology of Education* 21:4 (2011): 315-329, 317.

45   Valeriu Nicolae and Hannah Slavik, "Being a 'Gypsy': The Worst Social Stigma in Romania," (2003), http://www.errc.org/cikk.php?cikk=1385, accessed on 1 May 2013.

46   Thomas Acton and Andrew Ryder, "Roma Civil Society: Deliberative Democracy for Change in Europe," (Discussion Paper for Third Sector Research Centre, February 2013).

47   Simonetta Basso and Stefania Bragato, *Combating Anti-Roma Discrimination. Knowledge and Policies* (Venezia: COSES—Consorzio per la Ricerca e la Formazione, 2010).

48   ECRI Reports.

49   Iris Marion Young, "Justice and the Politics of Difference", in Susan S. Fainstein, Lisa J. Servon, eds., *Gender and planning: A reader* (Rutgers University Press, 2005), 86.

50   Cristian Tileagă, "Representing the 'Other': A Discursive Analysis of Prejudice and Moral Exclusion in Talk about Romani," *J. Community Appl. Soc. Psychol.* 16 (2006): 19–41.

51   Martin Kovats, "The politics of Roma identity: between nationalism and destitution," *Open democracy* 29 (2003): 1-8. Nidhi Trehan, "In the name of the Roma? The role of private foundations and NGOs," in Will Guy, ed., *Between Past and Future: The Roma of Central and Eastern Europe* (Hatfield, University of Hertfordshire Press, 2001): 134-149.

52   Nicoleta Bițu, "The Challenges of and for Romani Women." *European Roma Rights Centre* (2003). Alexandra Oprea, "Romani feminism in reactionary times," *Signs* 38:1 (2012): 11-21.

53   Swati Mukund Kamble, *Towards Gender Inclusive Policy Interventions for Roma Women The 'Decade of Roma Inclusion 2005-2015' in Hungary*, Diss., (Budapest: Central European University, 2011).

54   Angéla Kóczé and Raluca Maria Popa, *Missing Intersectionality: Race/Ethnicity, Gender and Class in Current Research and Policies on Romani Women in Europe*, (Budapest: CEU Press, 2009). George Bădescu et al., *Barometrul incluziunii romilor*, (Bucureşti: Fundaţia pentru o Societate Deschisă, 2007).
55   Richard Filcák and Daniel Škobla, "Social solidarity, human rights and Roma: unequal access to basic resources in Central and Eastern Europe," in Marion Ellison, ed., *Reinventing social solidarity across Europe* (The Policy Press, University of Bristol, 2012).
56   Eduardo Galeano, *Upside down: A primer for the looking-glass world*, (Picador, USA, 2001).
57   Filcák and Škobla, "Social solidarity, human rights and Roma," 227.

Moral Exclusion and Blaming the Victim: The Delegitimising Role of Antiziganism

Diana E. Popescu
London School of Economics and Political Science

Ever since the début of the Decade of Roma inclusion (hereafter the Decade) in 2005, the problems faced by Romanis have largely been regarded as issues of social exclusion, more specifically as exclusion from four main socio-economic dimensions: education, employment, healthcare and housing[1]. This paper starts from the uncontroversial observation that, in addition to the socio-economic outcomes that social exclusion focuses on, Romanis also suffer from various forms of mis-recognition linked to discrimination, marginalisation, negative stereotypes, racism, etc. While these phenomena are often recognised as important constituents of what is known as the 'Roma problem', integration programmes have been overwhelmingly centred on minimising the gap in socio-economic outcomes between Romanis and the majority population of the countries they live in. Hence, demands for fair treatment and the accompanying efforts towards social inclusion have been mainly formulated in terms of inclusion in education, employment, healthcare and housing, losing sight of the attitudinal processes which negatively affect Romanis.

The Decade points out that bridging the socio-economic gap between Romanis and the majority population is not the only aim policy makers should have, and flags combating discrimination among the first aims in its introductory presentation.[2] This can be seen as a clear commitment to change attitudes as well as socio-economic inequalities. However, in the *practice* of the National Roma Integration Strategies (hereafter NRIS) the focus has been overwhelmingly on the disadvantages Romanis face in the four dimensions of social exclusion, and most efforts have been directed at improving the situation of Romanis with respect to them, to the detriment of concerns for improving the attitudinal dimension. The latter are only taken into account to the extent that they impact the socio-economic inequalities. Drawing attention to the attitudinal dimension of the disadvantages Romanis face would accomplish the goal of returning to the dual motivation behind the Decade and this paper will argue that this is essential for effectively addressing the social exclusion of Romanis.

In this paper I focus on antiziganism as one attitudinal component of the 'Roma problem', showing how its accompanying stereotypes and clichés effectively legitimize the forms of social injustice captured by the notion of social exclusion. The focus is not only on the notion of antiziganism, but on the interplay between the attitudinal aspects of the 'Roma problem' related to antiziganism on the one hand, and the disadvantages Romanis face with respect to social exclusion on the other. The main finding of my analysis is that the attitudinal and outcome-oriented components of the 'Roma problem' are mutually reinforcing and that the way we construe the much-studied 'vicious circle of social exclusion'[3] should be expanded to include the attitudinal dimension of moral exclusion which I analyse in this paper.

I begin by looking at a set of stereotypes and prejudices associated with antiziganism and argue that antiziganist stereotypes are not only negative, but meant to present Romanis as morally undeserving, blameworthy 'others' and are often employed to justify unequal treatment. In the second section, I look at antiziganism as a social practice using Iris M. Young's definition of the term, showing how such spurious arguments as the ones encapsulated by antiziganist stereotypes are nonetheless widely believed. Section three argues that antiziganist stereotypes are the consequences of a more fundamental phenomenon of moral exclusion which I present and discuss in relation to the situation of Romanis in Europe. Sections four and five look at the connections between moral exclusion and social exclusion, showing that the causal links run both from moral to social exclusion and, also the other way around. I explain this latter, apparently paradoxical phenomenon by using Judith Butler's notions of precarity and grievability. In the final section I argue that the dynamics between social exclusion and moral exclusion has to be included in the current understanding of the 'vicious circle of exclusion' which has been hitherto limited to the process of social exclusion alone.

1. Antiziganist Stereotypes: an Investigation

While this paper does not aim to offer a comprehensive list of antiziganist stereotypes, clichés, and prejudices, in this section I analyse a set of antiziganist
attitudes and show that, put side by side, they form a particular pattern of delegitimising Romanis through presenting them as inferior, and undeserving.
Chief among these stereotypes is the claim that Romanis themselves are responsible for the disadvantages they suffer from, a phenomenon which is
known as 'blaming the victim'[4].

Blaming the victims of an aggression, injustice, etc. for their situation is not
associated with antiziganism alone, but with a series of social problems, from
blaming the victims of sexual assault[5] to blaming (some segments of) the population living in poverty for their situation[6]. The notion that the poor are under-
serving of assistance to escape their circumstances has been forcefully formulated by Charles Murray and later advocated by Christopher Jencks, as being
that

> [i]f you set out to help people who are in trouble, you almost always find
> that most of them are to some extent responsible for their present trou-
> bles. Few victims are completely innocent. Helping those who are not
> doing their best to help themselves poses extraordinarily difficult moral
> and political problems.[7]

This accusation is often levelled against Romanis. There is a widespread belief
that Romanis not only choose—and are, hence, responsible for—their circumstances, but also that they are resistant to efforts to change those circumstances. Consequently, attempts to improve the situation of Romanis are not
only undeserved and unwarranted—they are also useless, as they would meet
resistance from them.

Examples of this way of thinking abound. In a series of articles, Christian
Tileagă analyses the attitudes middle class Romanians entertain with respect
to discrimination against Romanis[8]. A recurring theme in Tileagă's interviews is
the (partial or total) assignment of responsibility for discrimination to Romanis
themselves. When asked whether she thinks Romanis are discriminated

against, an interviewee replies that there is discrimination by the majority population, but 'only' because Romanis don't 'really' want to integrate[9]. Tileagă offers an enlightening interpretation of this statement as an instance of 'blaming the victim': "With the use of 'o(h)nly', it could be said that[...]blame is placed entirely on the Romanis. The use of 'o(h)nly' rules out any alternative explanation for the existence of discrimination and works so as to question the idea that discrimination exists"[10]. Hence, the interviewee's strategy is to place the blame for discrimination on Romanis themselves by employing the stereotype that Romanis refuse to integrate. The upshot is challenging that what is going on is 'really' a form of discrimination; discrimination is, by definition, an unjust treatment. Yet, through presenting discrimination as a legitimate response to the Romanis' alleged refusal to integrate, the applicability of the word becomes contested.

The stereotype that Romanis refuse to integrate is also employed by an interviewee who, when asked what she thinks the causes of discrimination are, answers: "I think that everything happens because of them (.) because even they don't want (.) they don't have the desire" [to integrate][11]. The use of 'everything' once again places the blame entirely on the Romanis, denying not only the responsibility of the majority, but also the existence of "any possible influences of social interactions or external circumstances"[12]. Putting the former two answers together, Romanis are the 'only' ones to blame for 'everything'. Tileagă refers to this phenomenon as "a 'redistribution of responsibility', a denial of blame on the part of the majority population and assigning of total blame on the side of Romanies"[13].

Another instance of the stereotype that Romanis do not want to integrate is analysed by Tileagă in "Representing". Here, Tileagă presents the views of an interviewee who accuses Romanis of failing to adopt 'our' 'civilised' way of life and places the blame for disadvantage on Romanis on this count: "I don't see the gypsies [sic—n.a.] as integrating themselves among us, they don't like the civilised style (.) they don't want to go to school, they don't want at all to progress".[14] Here, reluctance to integrate is connected to the stereotype that Romanis are uncivilised and backward, as well as to the stereotype that Romanis are uneducable.

This latter stereotype is re-stated by the interviewee when asked who carries the blame for the situation of Romanis: "Theirs, first of all, because [...] effectively they were dragged to school (.) they've been asked to integrate and they cannot." [They were offered a block of flats and] "they have eaten it from the ground like rats"[15]. In "Ideologies", Tileagă records a similar formulation: "To make them a communal bath, they destroy it (.) it builds them a block (.) it is destroyed (.)"[16]. Hence, the majority has attempted to integrate Romanis, and it is the latter's fault for failing to take advantage of the opportunities offered. Here, the undeservingness of the Romanis (uncivilised, uneducable, animal-like) is contrasted with the good intentions of the majority population (who have offered opportunities for education and housing which have not been taken advantage of). The exclusion of Romanis from the dimensions of education and housing is explained entirely by reference to the stereotypes that Romanis are uncivilised, unwilling to integrate, that they shun educational opportunities and are unfit for 'civilised' housing.

The above-mentioned stereotypes are directly used by members of the majority to "rationalize and delegitimize discrimination against Romanis"[17]. Stereotypes such as that Romanis are unwilling to integrate, that they are uncivilised, backward up to the point of being animal-like, uneducable and irrational are used as specious arguments for delegitimising Romanis as having a claim to equal treatment. Through this mechanism, otherwise unacceptable forms of treatment (i.e. discrimination) as well as gross socio-economic inequalities (lack of education and housing) are rendered justified.

Yet, it is not only stereotypes used in direct connection with blaming the victim that have this effect; many other antiziganist stereotypes effectively have the same delegitimising force. The commonplace ideas that Romanis are criminals, that they are dishonest, lazy, aggressive etc. depict the sort of characteristics that we typically use when blaming someone with a view to penalise their behaviour. By contrast with, for example, the stereotype that Jewish people have an ill health or that Scots are stingy, stereotypes against Romanis are not morally neutral, but carry an assumption that Romanis are deviants and blameworthy.

As anecdotal evidence of the existence of such stereotypes and of the way they are used to justify discriminatory treatment stands the following fragment from one of the most emblematic books in Romanian literature, *The Diary of Happiness*[18]. The fragment is written by a Jew persecuted under communism who subsequently became a well-known Christian intellectual, and it is note-worthy because it is used by multiple antiziganist blogs, websites and by Romania's extremist right-wing movement *Noua dreaptă* as an argument in favour of antiziganism:[19]

> Racism is folly, but—how shall I say this? Non-racism, rejecting the idea that races are different, each with its own characteristics, is preposterous. They [n.a. Romanis] are … liars, we all lie, but by idealising what is real, for them it is different, like anti-matter. And they find it proper to vouch for their lies with heavy swearing: 'Let my eyes pop out', 'let my mother die', 'I will be mad if I lie'. And you cannot please them. However nicely you talk to them, however, humbly or politely—equally useless. Lazy, they hate whoever requires an effort of them, an obstinate, violent laziness, like the preservation instinct. [...] A love of slums, an exhibitionism, a nostalgia for carnivals; and a longing for fighting, screaming and washing dirty clothes in public. Foulness. The sordid devil, the honour-less devil, the hopping devil.[20]

Many of the stereotypes Steinhardt employs in this quote are morally loaded, implying that Romanis deviate from the majority's moral order. Romanis are presented as pathologic liars ('we all lie[...]but for them it is different, like anti-matter'), as deviants from the Christian norm of not-swearing ('they find it proper to vouch their lies with heavy swearing'), as being 'violently lazy', a laziness that is, once again, presented as radically deviant ('an obstinate, violent laziness, like the preservation instinct'), and as being violent (Romanis 'long for fighting and screaming'). The passage also uses two of the stereotypes reported in Tileagă's interviews; first, the futility of attempting to provide help ('you cannot please them. However nicely you talk to them, however humbly or politely—equally useless'). Second, the idea that Romanis are uncivilised (they 'long for carnivals') and prefer their current conditions (preposterously attributed to the Romani's alleged 'love of slums'). Last but not least, the quote shows how an otherwise tolerant, moral, and enlightened person, an intellectual who had suffered various forms of persecution himself and who starts out claiming not to be a racist, ends up outright proclaiming that Romanis are the devil.

To sum up, what the various antiziganist stereotypes I have looked at have in common is that they present Romanis as undeserving and deviant. This is different from other negative stereotypes in that negative stereotypes regarding Romanis have a strong delegitimising component. In this, antiziganism matches Bernard Williams's description of racism and the justification for discrimination in the case of African Americans:

> Few can be found who explain their practice [of discrimination] merely by saying 'But they're black; and it is my principle to treat black men differently than others.' If any reasons are given at all, they will be *reasons that seek to conflate the fact of blackness with certain other characteristics which are at least candidates for relevance to the question of how a man should be treated:* such as insensitivity, brute stupidity, uneducable irresponsibility, etc.[21]

The various antiziganist stereotypes I have looked at (that Romanis are uncivilised, unwilling to integrate, uneducable, unfit for modern housing, pathologic liars and drunks, 'violently lazy', etc.) thus form a specific pattern of attributing negative characteristics that are also relevant for the question of how a person should be treated. Antiziganist stereotypes delegitimise Romanis as our moral equals while preserving the idea that the majority population is acting fairly.

2. Antiziganism as Uncritically Accepted

Another aspect regarding the way antiziganist stereotypes are employed to blame Romanis for the disadvantages they suffer from is how widespread and uncritically accepted this practice is, and how implausible the stereotypes employed (e.g. that Romanis are "like rats", that they have a "nostalgia for carnivals", etc) are. If the moral reasons offered for legitimising harm-doing are so spurious, how do they even achieve their justificatory purpose? If they are so implausible, how come people do not see through them? The answer I defend in this section is that antiziganist stereotypes are not subjected to the kind of critical reflection that would make their implausibility apparent by those who entertain them because antiziganism is a social practice. More than a set of beliefs encapsulated by its stereotypes, it is something the majority *does*.

In "Five Faces of Oppression"[22] I. Young explores the notion of a social practice for one form of oppression she focuses on, namely violence. While Young defines oppression as a "mundane and systematic"[23] phenomenon, whereas violence is exceptional and singular, violence is considered a form of oppression in the sense that it is a social practice.

Young defines oppression as a structural phenomenon, in the sense that it is "embedded in unquestioned norms, habits, and symbols, in the assumptions underlying institutional rules and the collective consequences of following those rules"[24]. Hence, a defining aspect of oppression is its reliance on 'unquestioned norms and habits', a feature Young further supports by saying that structural oppression is often the product of "ordinary interactions, media and cultural stereotypes …—in short, the normal processes of everyday life". Oppression is therefore characterised by its invisibility or appearance of being normal, and its uncritical acceptance.

Young considers violence a *social practice* because its existence is regarded as normal and as expected behaviour by everyone in society, not only by the perpetrators of violence. As Young puts it, "everyone knows [it] happens and will happen again. It is always at the horizon of social imagination, even for those who do not perpetrate it".[25] It is a social practice because it is an unquestioned part of everyday social life, whose justifiability relies on unquestioned norms about acceptable behaviour which should, upon closer inspection, turn out to be unacceptable. It is this normalisation of violence as a phenomenon encountered in society that makes it a social practice[26].

Antiziganism fits Young's description of oppression as a social practice[27], as it is a systemic social phenomenon which is widely regarded as acceptable in the societies among which Romanis live. Antiziganism is regarded as normal and expected behaviour by everyone in society, not only by those who entertain antiziganist beliefs. It is a common practice in the sense that "everyone knows [it] happens and will happen again.", and those who are caught entertaining antiziganist beliefs receive little or no punishment[28] Antiziganism is part of the daily life of societies the Roma live in, and it is never placed under close scrutiny or critical reflection because it is an inherent part of 'business as usual'.

This phenomenon can be contrasted to the way antisemitic stereotypes are regarded. Since antisemitism is commonly regarded as a form of racism, those who entertain it are regarded as racist and/or extremists. On the other hand, it is not only radical nationalists, xenophobes, or racists who entertain antiziganism attitudes. It is often the case that young, well-educated and otherwise charitable and progressive people are antiziganists themselves, or regard antiziganists as entertaining permissible or acceptable attitudes.

This point is well illustrated by the contrasts between antisemitism and antiziganism highlighted by the recent 'Jewify' initiative. This initiative was a reaction to the evictions of Romanis from Dale Farm in the UK in 2011[29]. It aims to uncover the degree of prejudice the majority entertains towards Romanis by transforming antiziganist statements into antisemitic ones through using a simple software. The software takes as input any URL of a news report and produces the article with all instances of the word Gypsy or Romani replaced by "Jew". Some of the relevant outputs were: "Italy starts controversial plan to fingerprint Jews"; "Sarkozy orders all Jews expelled from France"; "Essex Jews facing eviction threaten Big Fat Jew War on the authorities"; "Anger at Jewish invasion", etc.

What the Jewify experiment brilliantly highlights is the contrast between how unacceptable hostility and stereotypes against Jewish people are, as opposed to how commonplace and expected these attitudes are if manifested against Romanis. By transforming instances of antiziganism into instances of antisemitism, the experiment draws attention to just how embedded in everyday life antiziganism is compared to other forms of racism. As the creator of the initiative puts it,

> racism of many kinds, including anti-Semitism, is alive and well. However, in the UK, you generally won't find *official* institutions, *mainstream* politicians, or newspapers openly espousing blatantly racist sentiments—unless it's racism against Gypsies, Travellers and Roma people. This is still

a socially acceptable form of racism. This site allows you to look at articles and websites about Gypsies, Travellers and Roma people through the lens of anti-Semitism.[30]

This experiment draws to our attention the fact that "if someone had said [something like] this about a Jewish person how would you have reacted? And how come you do not have the same reaction when the same is said about a Romani?" To the reader's embarrassment, the explanation could only refer to the 'institutionalised', 'mainstream' and 'social acceptability' that accompany antiziganism.

3. Moral Exclusion and Justifying Force of Antiziganism

What my previous discussion suggests is that antiziganist stereotypes are a way of rationalizing or rendering legitimate otherwise unjustified forms of treatment. As I have pointed out, antiziganist stereotypes are not only negative, but morally loaded. Moreover, despite their implausibility, antiziganist stereotypes are widely entertained because antiziganism is a social practice. In this section I advance the claim that the idea that Romanis are not entitled to receive the same consideration as the majority population pre-exists antiziganist stereotypes. The prior phenomenon is that of moral exclusion, and antiziganist stereotypes are means through which this exclusion is rendered legitimate.

The theory of moral exclusion stems from the observation that people very often regard other human beings as falling outside the normal scope of justice concerns. It challenges the assumption shared by the overwhelming majority of theories of justice that the scope in which concerns about justice and fairness apply is universal—that the principles of justice they advocate apply to all members of society.[31] But while the assumption that fair and equal treatment is due to all persons is intuitively plausible[32], in practice some members of society do not regard principles of justice as universally applicable. Thus, some (usually privileged) members of society exclude certain groups of people from the protection of such principles. This excluded class of persons is regarded as less entitled to be covered by principles of justice and is relegated to an inferior status. As a result of suspending principles of justice for this group, unjust or unfair treatment becomes tolerable. This process is known as moral exclusion, occurring under the conditions which Susan Opotow defines as follows:

> [m]oral exclusion occurs when individuals or groups are perceived as outside the boundary in which moral values, rules, and considerations of fairness apply. Those who are morally excluded are perceived as nonentities, expandable, or undeserving. Consequently, harming or exploiting them appears to be appropriate, acceptable or just.[33]

In other words, what is defining for moral exclusion is the relegation of an individual or group to a status of an inferior, unimportant, or undeserving entity in order to justify unfair treatment towards them. Being outside the scope of justice, the morally excluded are vulnerable to a host of harms (including deprivation, exploitation, and discrimination) that come to be regarded as acceptable—either because they are "ignored" (i.e. not even perceived as such) or "condoned as normal, inevitable, and deserved" (i.e. perceived as harms, but as tolerable, even justified harms)[34].

An essential feature of moral exclusion is its appearance of being morally justified. It is not only that some people are excluded from justice considerations but, moreover, the process of exclusion itself is regarded as justified. This is done, paradoxically, through the use of moral reasons. Yet, the moral reasons provided for excluding individuals from the protection of principles of justice are specious and serve the interest of the excluding group. As Opotow puts it "[m]oral reasoning in the service of moral exclusion is typically self-serving, utilizes trivial criteria to justify harm, and implicitly asserts that particular moral boundaries are correct"[35]. In other words, *after* the morally excluded individual or group has been relegated to the inferior status, specious arguments are used to rationalise this inferior status as being justified, to legitimise the separation between a morally-included 'us' and a morally excluded 'them'.

This latter process is reminiscent of E.H. Carr's description of 'the subjection of thought to practice", the claim that the moral opinions of a group are (unintentionally) developed so a response to the interests and circumstances of that group. Carr exemplifies this phenomenon in relation to the way stereotypes regarding foreign nations tend to present those nations depending on war alliances, recalling an observation made by Bertrand Russell:

'When I was young', writes Mr. Bertrand Russell, 'the French ate frogs and were called "froggies", but they apparently abandoned this practice when we concluded our *entente* with them in 1904.'[...] In the 19th century, it was a common place of British opinion that Germans were efficient and enlightened and Russians backward and barbarous. About 1910, it was ascertained that Germans (who turned out to be mostly Prussians) were coarse, brutal and narrow-minded, and that Russians had a Slav soul. The vogue of Russian literature in Great Britain which set in about the same time, was a direct outcome of the political *rapprochement* with Russia[36]

Recalling the way antiziganist stereotypes were employed by Tileagă's interviewees to rationalise discrimination as being justified, we can see similarities with the processes described by Opotow and Carr above. Antiziganist stereotypes seem to fit this pattern of justifying depict Romanis as 'nonentities, expandable, or undeserving' with the aim of legitimising harm-doing. Stereotypes depicting Romanis as animal-like, inferior, irrational and blameworthy in a number of ways serve to justify the moral boundary between the morally excluded Romanis and the morally included majority population, rendering the harms Romanis suffer as acceptable and justified. Antiziganist stereotypes provide "trivial criteria to justify harm,"[37] using specious justification for the harms Romanis suffer. As I have shown in Section I, the discrimination and lack of education and housing affecting Romanis are justified by the Romani's alleged unwillingness or failure to integrate, lack of civilisation, irrationality, animal-like behaviour etc. The stereotype of 'blaming the victim' is by definition a way of justifying and rendering acceptable harms against Romanis.

Antiziganist stereotypes use 'trivial criteria' in two ways. First, because the stereotypes function as ready-made justifications the majority uses when confronted with the harms it perpetrates. They form a pool of specious arguments the majority taps into when rendering tolerable the injustices Romanis suffer. Second, the stereotypes are a trivial form of justification in the sense that they are meant to replace all other possible explanations for the resulting injustice—even, as Tileagă observed, those which could be explained by reference to

external factors. Hence, antiziganist stereotypes are a 'trivial' form of explanation not just because they are specious in themselves, but because the way
they are employed to justify harm-doing is specious too.

As I have shown, the stereotypes employed by antiziganism are morally
loaded, providing moral reasons for excluding Romanis from the applicability
of justice concerns. What is more, these moral reasons are "self-serving" (or
better said, they serve the interests of the majority population) in the sense that
they re-affirm the moral superiority of the majority population over Romanis.
This phenomenon could be clearly observed in Tileagă's interviews in which
the inferior, undeserving, and animal-like status of Romanis was contrasted
with the benevolence of the majority population: the majority offered Romanis
a block of flats, but the Romanis tore it down "like rats"[38]. In this, the moral
reasoning used by the majority satisfies the final defining criterion of moral exclusion: it "implicitly asserts that particular moral boundaries are correct" by
using the rationalisations it produced to justify the initial exclusion.

As further evidence of the connections between moral exclusion and antiziganism, the characteristic manifestations of moral exclusion as defined by researchers working on this topic closely resemble phenomena often associated
with the 'Roma problem'.[39] I will not dwell on describing the full list of these
manifestations here, but merely underline the processes that make it particularly relevant for the case of the Romani minority.[40]

One aspect of moral exclusion regards the way in which the majority group
places itself with respect to the excluded group. This aspect manifests itself
through a biased evaluation of groups ("Making unflattering comparisons between one's own group and another group; believing in the superiority of one's
own group"), entertaining double standards ("Having different sets of moral
rules and obligations for different categories of people"), making unflattering
and/or self-righteous comparisons which bolster the (moral or otherwise) superiority of one's own group as opposed to the excluded group, and fear of
contamination ("perceiving contact with others as posing a threat to one's own
well-being")[41]. These aspects are instantiated by the manifestations of an-

tiziganism I have looked at. Antiziganist stereotypes depict the majority as benevolent, superior and deserving, while Romanis are presented as ill-intentioned, inferior and undeserving. Moreover, the moral obligations of the majority towards Romanis are systematically downplayed, and the moral superiority of the majority group over Romanis is frequently asserted. Finally, the stereotype that Romanis are 'dirty' and 'like rats' indicate that Romanis are perceived as contaminating.

Another aspect of moral exclusion regards a cluster of related problems: derogation ("Disparaging and denigrating others by regarding them as lower life forms or inferior beings—e.g. barbarian, vermin"[42]; dehumanization ("Repudiating others' humanity, dignity, ability to feel, and entitlement to compensation" or "Denying others' rights, entitlements, humanity and dignity"; and condescension ("Regarding others as inferior, patronizing others, and perceiving them with disdain—e.g. they are childlike, irrational, simple". The 'dehumanising' nature of stereotypes about Romanis and their relation to forms of violence against ethnic groups has been studied both in direct relation to antiziganism[43] as well as in relation to expulsion and extermination of Romanis in the early modern period[44]. Valeriu Nicolae explicitly links de-humanisation to the representation of Romanis as childlike and irrational, while Miriam Eliav-Feldon focuses on the contamination associated with de-humanisation (through the use of terms such as "swarming", "infesting", "plaguing" or "flooding").[45] The stereotype about Romanis being uncivilised, irrational and animal-like also emerged in C. Tileagă's interviews I have analysed in the section one.

A third aspect of moral exclusion regards the way responsibility for harm to the excluded group is placed. The phenomena refer to the process of blaming the victim which is, by now, familiar. The specific manifestations identified by Opotow are "displacing the blame for reprehensible actions on those who are harmed", "denying one's own contribution to perpetuating the social problems faced by the excluded party", "concealing the effects of harmful behaviour", "disregarding, ignoring, disbelieving, distorting, or minimizing injurious outcomes to others"[46].

Interestingly, Opotow links the phenomenon of blaming the victim we looked at to the fact that the majority population is blind to the mere possibility of bearing such a responsibility, automatically and uncritically assigning blame to the victims themselves. This is consistent with the way in which William Ryan describes the phenomenon of blaming the victim[47], as something that happens unconsciously and is more akin to entertaining a certain ideology which carries this interpretation than intentional harm-doing. For Ryan, as for Opotow, the problem is the way the majority population becomes blind to alternative explanations for the harm suffered by a victim other than the ones that involve assigning the blame to the victim itself. Specifically, the majority population becomes blind to the possibility of explanations for harm to a victim that involve placing the responsibility on the majority itself.

The phenomena of "concealing the effects of harmful behaviour", "disregarding, ignoring, disbelieving, distorting, or minimizing injurious outcomes to others" Opotow links to blaming the victim are done through the use of 'euphemisms'. Euphemisms such as "masking, sanitizing, and conferring respectability on reprehensible behaviour by using palliative terms that misrepresent cruelty and harm"[48]) are used in the case of Romanis to justify certain forms of geographical exclusion by claiming it is done for the Romanis' own good.[49] For instance a Romani community in northern Romania was encircled by concrete fences over two meters high on the justification that it will stop children from running into the street and getting hit by cars. Also, another community was relocated by force to a decommissioned factory on the justification that their previous abode was not suitable. By pushing Romanis away from the city and/or secluding them in a ghetto they are impeded from accessing many social sectors by simply making it too difficult to reach them (due to poverty many Romanis do not own a car).

The case of the Romani minority matches these manifestations of moral exclusion quite closely and, as mentioned previously, the motivations members of the mainstream society usually provide (when challenged—or when trying to challenge sympathizers of the Romani cause) feed on antiziganist beliefs and stereotypes. Yet, the discussion of moral exclusion shows that it is not the case that Romanis are initially regarded as being covered by the same principles of justice and fairness that apply to the majority, but lose this standing as a result of the alleged faults that antiziganist stereotypes depict. Rather, through moral exclusion Romanis are perceived as not being covered by principles of justice in the first place; the accompanying stereotypes of antiziganism are conjured up mainly to provide *post factum* justification for this situation, but the perception of undeservingness precedes these explanations. Hence, more than a set of accompanying stereotypes, antiziganism comprises a fundamental perception that Romanis are not entitled to the same considerations of justice as the majority population.

4. From Moral to Social Exclusion

So far, my analysis has focused on the attitudinal dimensions of antiziganism: the nature of antiziganist stereotypes, the way antiziganism is entertained in society, the justifications for harm-doing that antiziganism provides, and the upshot of morally excluding Romanis from the domain where considerations of justice apply. Yet, these attitudinal components also have important practical consequences with respect to the exclusion of Romanis from the domains of education, employment, healthcare and housing. Simply put, the moral exclusion antiziganism entails leads to the social exclusion of Romanis.

Firstly, the fact that antiziganism renders discrimination, marginalisation, non-intervention, etc. as justifiable is a direct enabler of social exclusion. Romanis will be discriminated against in employment by those who entertain the stereotypes that Romanis are 'lazy', 'liars', 'thieves', etc. Romani entrepreneurs will have trouble finding customers if the notion that Romanis are 'dirty', 'violent', 'cheating' etc. is widely entertained. If Romanis are regarded as 'uneducable', 'animal-like' and 'irrational', Romani children will be regarded as far less capable students than majority children, which, in practice, leads to the problem of segregating Romani children in classes for children with special needs[50]. Moreover, since the high drop-out rate of Romanis is explained in terms of 'unwillingness to integrate', the exclusion of Romanis from education will be regarded as the natural consequence of Romanis' own choices. Providing adequate housing will not be a priority for those entertaining the stereotype that Romanis are 'uncivilised' and that they tear down their houses 'like rats'; such efforts would be futile and housing resources would be better spent on members of the majority population.

The consequence of this discussion for fighting the social exclusion of Romanis is that such attempts, in focusing on integration in socio-economic outcomes alone, overlook one important cause leading to those outcomes, namely antiziganism. Hence, equalisation of conditions between Romanis and non-Romanis will be short-lived: since the mechanisms producing these inequalities in the first place remain, they will act so as to reproduce social exclusion. Including Romanis in the labour market at a certain moment in time, for instance, will be short-lived if Romanis remain the first employees to be fired in the event of a downsizing. Creating opportunities for Romani entrepreneurs will be short-lived if majority individuals refuse to buy their products or services as a result of their antiziganist attitudes. Similarly, including Romani children in regular (as opposed to special needs) classrooms will be short-lived if teachers continue to see the poor educational outcomes of Romani children[51] as an indication of lack of intelligence or learning capacity instead of the result of, among other things, poor learning conditions, reduced motivation for learning, distrust in mainstream education, etc. Hence, teachers are likely to treat Romani children as having a learning disability instead of suffering from socio-economic disadvantages that affect every aspect of their lives, education included. Romani children will be treated as having special needs whether they are officially segregated in special needs classes or not.

One could object that these examples are unconvincing as they are not cases of true integration. Since the inclusion was only transient, we cannot rightly claim that real social inclusion had been achieved in the first place; it only appeared to have been achieved. Yet, the only way to defend such a position would be by claiming that job insecurity (the fact that the worker will be the first one to be fired), for instance, is a sufficient criterion to count as socially excluded. Nothing in the definition of social exclusion warrants regarding that individual as being excluded for the period in which he is in actual employment: he is participating in mainstream employment, receives healthcare benefits available through being employed, can support himself, etc. Hence, the only reason why his situation is still sub-par with respect to mainstream society is the insecurity of his job. However, claiming that job insecurity is sufficient for counting as being socially excluded over-generates socially excluded individuals: all members of mainstream society for whom losing one's job is a possibility would count as socially excluded. The same over-generalisation of socially excluded individuals can be observed by applying the proposed criterion to educational outcomes: all children at risk of having their performance considered subpar and risking special treatment on this count would be regarded as socially excluded. Hence, the criticism misses the real difference between socially excluded Romanis and non-Romanis, which is that the motivation for exclusion was based on antiziganist attitudes.

Secondly, in addition to the fact that moral exclusion causes and perpetuates unfair treatment in the first place, moral exclusion also acts as a barrier to alleviating social exclusion when sustained efforts towards inclusion are made. As I have shown in previous sections, the defining feature of moral exclusion (realised through producing demeaning stereotypes) is that of rendering harmful and otherwise unjust behaviour as legitimate, even deserved. In this, the false rationalisations provided by antiziganism act as a justification for maintaining existing inequalities, enacting unseen barriers to regarding the social exclusion Romanis suffer from as the unjust process it really is.

As I have shown in previous sections, antiziganism not only leads to unequal socio-economic outcomes, but it also creates the false perception that these outcomes are justified and that Romanis are to blame for them. An outcome of this is that efforts to minimise the social exclusion of Romanis are regarded as undeserved, even unjust. As the statements made by Tileagă's interviewees show, the fact that Romanis are excluded from education or housing was regarded as being the Romani's own fault, and the blameworthy Romanis were contrasted with the benevolent Romanians (who gave Romanis opportunities for education and housing that the latter failed to take advantage of). Moreover, the pre-eminence of moral exclusion means that social inclusion's appeal to principles of fairness in order to justify the minimisation of exclusion will not be accepted by the majority population. The attitude encapsulated by moral exclusion simply is that it is legitimate not to apply principles of justice to Romanis in the first place.

The effect of antiziganist stereotypes on social exclusion of Romanis will be that such attempts will be considered undeserved at best and unfair towards the majority at worst. Due to the stereotype that attempting to help Romanis is futile (which we have encountered both in Tileagă's interviews and in Steinhardt's fragment) and the accompanying stereotype that Romanis do not want to integrate, attempts to include Romanis in mainstream education, employment, healthcare and housing will be perceived as a waste of resources and, moreover, as something Romanis do not deserve. Why should the majority pay for the inclusion of people who do not want to be included, if the Romanis' animal-like behaviour and essential irrationality will render such attempts futile anyway? As such, attempts to socially integrate Romanis will be perceived as naïve at best and unjust towards the majority at worst. While social inclusion may continue to be realised through formal mechanisms such as the NRIS, the majority population Romanis live among will not join in the effort. This greatly limits the potential success of attempts to reduce the social exclusion of Romanis as they are currently conducted.

Moreover, as long as no attempt is made to combat moral exclusion, the majority will remain blind with regards to the responsibility it bears for the social exclusion of Romanis. Due to moral exclusion's potential of re-interpreting an atrocious reality as acceptable through engaging 'euphemisms' (I return to this point when discussing Butler's views on precarity below), simply emphasising the severity of the outcomes of social exclusion is not enough to move public opinion in the direction of empathising with Romanis. As long as antiziganism persists and its accompanying stereotypes are used to fuel moral exclusion, these outcomes—however harmful, atrocious, and unacceptable they may seem—will continue to be perceived as normal and justified. The extent of social exclusion will always be minimised, euphemised, and obstinately disconnected from the responsibilities for the exclusion that the majority has. Raising awareness of the way in which Romanis have been systematically seen as not entitled to be considered the moral equals of the majority, the way this has been rationalised through creating false stereotypes and the large-scale phenomena it has prompted will draw attention to the responsibility the majority has had on creating and perpetuating the Romanis' exclusion.

5. From Social to Moral Exclusion

The fact that morally excluding someone from normal considerations of justice leads to that person suffering multiple socio-economic disadvantages (i.e. that moral exclusion produces social exclusion) may seem unsurprising upon closer inspection; failures of regard are often translated into sub-par socio-economic outcomes. What is more surprising, however, is the fact that the reverse process—of morally excluding a person as a result of that person being socially excluded—can also be encountered in the case of Romanis.

This process seems paradoxical because witnessing the severe disadvantages a person suffers from is usually thought to prompt sympathy for that person's situation. For instance, images of mal-nourished children from poor African countries are supposed to make us empathetic and charitable. Thus, quite the contrary from enacting moral barriers between us and the vulnerable person whose unfortunate situation we are witnessing, the expected reaction would be to break down such barriers and empathize with the severely disadvantaged or deprived individual. So, why would witnessing the Romanis' severe deprivation and social exclusion actually lead to morally excluding them from the majority's moral universe?

Judith Butler's study of frames of war[52] (and the subsidiary question: when is life grievable?) could be used to explain this phenomenon. Butler introduces the notions of precarity and grievability to describe the way enemy deaths, which represent a violation of one of the most fundamental human rights—namely the right to life—are rendered justifiable in times of war. Butler defines a precarious life as a life that is perceived as always in danger of suffering harms of various sorts—including 'failing social and economic networks' and differential exposure to poverty, disease, starvation, and violence without protection"[53]. In the same place, Butler mentions as additional characteristics of precarity "starvation, under-employment, legal disenfranchisement, violence and death."

While many of these material disadvantages are familiar to those aware of the Romani struggle, there are some that resemble the problem of social exclusion quite specifically. The failings of social networks resembles exclusion from society itself, while the more specific characteristics such as failing economic networks, poverty and starvation, on the one hand, and heightened risk of disease on the other resemble exclusion from employment (with its detrimental economic effects) and differential results in the domain of healthcare.[54] Hence, Romanis would count as being 'precarious' under Butler's definition of the term.

While the precarity of a subject's life is a "material reality", grievability is a "failure of regard"[55]. Butler claims that lack of grievability or failure of regard for a fellow human's life depends on our perceived precarity. Precisely *because* precarious lives occupy a "lost and destroyed zone" (Butler, *Frames*, xix), they are perceived as "already lost and destroyed"[56]. When these lives actually become destroyed in war, nothing is lost and, hence, there is nothing to be grieved. The idea that a life is precarious makes harmful behaviour acceptable, because it is an expected reality. In this way, even the loss of one's life becomes acceptable and normalised.

For Butler, the fact that there is a "differential distribution of precarity" between the lives of our co-nationals and the lives of people in distant countries leads to the emergence of a difference in grievability. That is to say, because the lives of enemy populations are presented as more precarious than the lives of those back home, the lives of those in distant countries will also be considered less grievable, whereas the lives of those back home are "eminently grievable". The crucial idea, then, for Butler (which is first mentioned in Butler, *Precarious life*, but later developed in Butler, *Frames*) is that precarity forms the basis on which differential grievability is framed, resulting in differences among groups between "populations who are eminently grievable, and others whose loss is no loss"[57].

This interplay between precarity and grievability is also studied by Butler in *Precarious life*[58]. The connection is that the material deprivation intrinsic to precarity creates the perception of a delicate existential condition which has the potential of both humanising and de-humanising a subject at the same time. This ambivalence can then be manipulated by normative schemes which "establish what will and what will not be human, what will be a liveable life, what will be a grievable death" [59]. That is to say, the condition of precarity can be manipulated to present a subject as less than human, although it also has the potential of making one sympathetic to the condition of the deprived individual.

This interplay can be distinguished in the case of social and moral exclusion. Just as precarious individuals are considered less worthy of being grievable because of the manipulations their precarious status allows with respect to their humanity and their claims to equal regard, the deprivation socially excluded individuals suffer from can be manipulated to frame these individuals as inferior and as not warranting equal regard. Just as precarity has the potential of both drawing attention to our common humanity and singling out the other as vulnerable and inferior, acknowledging that one is socially excluded has the same dual potential. On the one hand, there is the reaction (which many would consider natural) of regarding the victim of exclusion as someone deserving our empathy and support. On the other hand, there is the potential of treating the socially excluded as inferior through a certain 'normative frame' which obfuscates the first possibility.

Antiziganism accomplishes this latter goal through the negative stereotypes meant to discredit the claims to equal regard for Romanis and to thereby justify unfair treatment. By blaming the deprivation Romanis suffer from on Romanis themselves, the material reality of social exclusion fuels moral exclusion. To account for the fact that Romanis lack proper housing, they become perceived as unsuitable for such housing; to account for the fact that Romanis lack proper education, they are seen as uneducable; to account for the inferior economic conditions and social standing, they are regarded as intrinsically inferior and less entitled to equal standing. In this regard, the stereotype of blaming the victim can be connected to the literature on "belief in a just world", which studies the way in which the general perception that the world functions justly leads to assigning blame for disadvantage on the disadvantaged party.[60]

In conclusion, attempting to raise sympathy for the Romani cause by drawing attention to the severe deprivation which characterises the lives of many Romanis is bound to fail in the absence of parallel efforts of disproving the stereotype of blaming the victim. As long as the responsibility the majority has in pro-ducing and reproducing these outcomes is systematically unacknowledged, the response in the fact of witnessing even the most atrocious conditions will be to take those conditions of further evidence for how blameworthy and infe-rior Romanis are. Thus, insisting on the degree of deprivation of Romanis risks being not only an inefficient, but potentially a harmful strategy for socially in-cluding Romanis.

6. The Circle of Social and Moral Exclusion

In addition to the existence of causal connections from moral to social exclu-sion on the one hand, and from social to moral exclusion on the other, Butler's analysis draws attention to an interesting consequence of this phenomenon, namely that it makes it impossible to establish which phenomenon came first in practice. In Butler's words: "it would be difficult, if not impossible, to decide whether the 'regard'—or the failure of 'regard'—leads to the "material reality" or whether the material reality leads to the failure of regard since it would seem that both happened at once"[61]. With applicability to the case of the Romani minority, it would be difficult to say whether the fact that Romanis were contin-uously among the precarious members of society led to the formation of nega-tive stereotypes about them which prompted failures of moral regard for disad-vantages that Romanis face or whether, to the contrary, the fact that the major-ity population morally excluded Romanis from the application of norms of jus-tice led to Romanis ending up in the circumstances described by social exclu-sion.

Therefore, social and moral exclusion form a vicious circle: moral exclusion leads to individuals becoming socially excluded, and the mere fact that these individuals are excluded then fuels negative stereotypes about their alleged inferiority all the more, making the degree of their exclusion from the majority's moral universal ever greater. The much discussed 'vicious circle of social ex-clusion', where faring badly on one count automatically leads faring badly on other dimensions as well, could easily be extended so as to include moral ex-clusion in its bounds, as moral exclusion behaves in the same cyclical and progressively aggravating manner. This circle would explain the apparently paradoxical situation we can see in the case of the Romani minority: the most disadvantaged minority in Europe, for whom the inequalities in terms of education, employment, healthcare and housing when compared to other members of society are undeniable, is also the minority that attracts least sympathy, charity, or even protection from violence.

In this paper I have shown that antiziganism, through its accompanying stereotypes denigrating Romanis, plays the role of a false justification which is used to legitimise gross inequalities and harmful treatment against the Romani minority. Antiziganism contributes to making majorities blind to, tolerant towards or, in some cases, self-righteous about, the inequalities that adversely affect Romanis in their communities, having a delegitimising role. An important conclusion this analysis points to is that antiziganism is deeply connected to the widely researched topic of social exclusion. Hence, the 'vicious circle of exclusion' that is postulated in relation to social exclusion should be enlarged to also include some of the attitudinal dimensions of 'the Roma problem' that antiziganism encapsulates. As I have argued in sections III and IV, social and moral exclusion are mutually reinforcing and a proper treatment of each requires a detailed analysis of the causal mechanisms behind the other.

A related implication, with potentially wide consequences for how support for the Romani cause should be raised, is that the current strategy of restating how disadvantaged Romanis are with the aim of raising awareness about the minority's difficulties might not be productive when moral exclusion is widespread. Such a strategy could either have no or little effect or, what is worse, it could even lead to an even further deterioration of the problem. Firstly, simply mentioning the disadvantages Romanis face could fail to work in gathering support because, in Butler's words, in the presence of unfavourable attitudinal dimensions "counting simply does not count". This resistance in the face of fact suggests that the frames in place remain unmoved even in the face of statistics which we objectively consider outrageous. This provides one possible explanation for why progress on integrating the Romani minority has been slow, even despite the awareness it raises with respect to the grave inequalities and injustices Romanis face.

A worse outcome would be the actual deepening of disregard. As I have shown in Section IV, when moral exclusion is present, a correlation with the outcomes of social exclusion can reinforce stereotypes about the targeted group as being inferior, dependable, etc. thus leading to an even greater disregard.

Hence, this paper challenges the widespread belief that perceiving another person as suffering from multiple social and economic disadvantages will have the effect of drawing sympathy, compassion, and charity for that person, by showing that this perception could fuel moral exclusion even further by re-enforcing stereotypes. What is needed, more than narratives about the poor educational, employment, healthcare and housing outcomes the Romani minority faces, are narratives about the role played by the majority population in creating and perpetuating this situation. Otherwise, the material reality of gross inequalities will be 'framed away' as something the victims themselves are to be blamed for.

In addition, a more worrisome phenomenon can be noticed. In this paper I have shown how antiziganism is related to moral exclusion, a phenomenon initially introduced to explain extreme violence and genocide during WWII, and that social exclusion is similar in effect to the precarity of the victims of war. This pattern of violence, expulsions, genocide, and war, shows that Romanis are perceived by majority population as a threat, an enemy, and as dependable victims. This draws attention to the fact that, more than inclusion in the domains of education, healthcare, housing and greater employment rate, in dealing with 'the Roma problem' it is also necessary to manage a potentially dangerous form of ethnic conflict.

One suggestion as to how this can be done emerges from Butler's analysis of the situation of migrants, whose relation with the majority population tends to be seen by the latter as a "war at home". Butler notes that the route for minorities to take would be to form alliances between minority and majority populations on common issues, such as "an alliance focused on opposition to state violence and its capacity to produce, exploit, and distribute precarity"[62]. This suggestion of forming alliances that cut across ethnic lines is coherent with the view that the efforts for Romani inclusion should put more emphasis on common citizenship and on opportunities for promoting cooperation among Romanis and non-Romanis on common interests[63].

Acknowledgements

I would like to thank the participants of the "Stereotype, cliché and prejudice" panel of the "Antiziganism: What's in a word" conference, which took place in Uppsala 23-October 2013, for their very helpful questions and comments on a preliminary version of the paper. I particularly want to thank Anne Minken, my perceptive discussant, Julja Sardelić, who sympathetically presented my paper, as well as Timofey Agarin and Matthew Kott for their helpful feedback and for the engaging format.

References

1   See, e.g. the description of the Decade at http://www.romadecade.org/about-the-decade-decade-in-brief accessed on 16/12/2013, the European Parliament's Policy Department C : Citizens' rights and constitutional affairs, *Measures to promote the situation of Roma EU citizens in the European Union Country Reports* PE 432751 (Brussels January 2011) and the European Commission, *Communication from the Commission to the European Parliament, the Council, the European Economic and Social Committee and the Committee of the Regions: An EU Framework for National Roma Integration Strategies up to 2020,* COM (2011) 173 (Brussels 5.04.2011)

2   "The Decade of Roma Inclusion 2005–2015 is an unprecedented political commitment by European governments to eliminate *discrimination* against Roma and close the unacceptable gaps between Roma and the rest of society. The Decade focuses on the priority areas of education, employment, health, and housing, and commits governments to take into account the other core issues of poverty, *discrimination,* and gender mainstreaming." http://www.romadecade.org/about-the-decade-decade-in-brief accessed 16/12/2013, my emphasis.

3   For a theoretical treatment, see Duncan Gallie, Serge Paugam and Sheila Jakobs "Unemployment, poverty and social isolation: is there a vicious circle of social exclusion?" *European Societies* 5:1 (2003): 1-32.

4   See William Ryan, *Blaming the Victim* (Pantheon Books: London, 1971).

5   See, e.g., Mark A. Whatley, "Victim characteristics influencing attributions of responsibility to rape victims: A meta-analysis", *Aggression and Violent Behaviour* 1:2 (1996): 81-95, and P. Heaven, J. Connors, and A. Pretorius, "Victim characteristics and attribution of rape blame in Australia and South Africa", Journal of Social Psychology 138:1 (1998):131-33.

6   See Michael Katz, *The undeserving poor: From the war on poverty to the war on welfare* (New York: Pantheon Books, 1990).

7   Christopher Jencks, *Rethinking Social Policy: Race, Poverty, and the Underclass* (Cambridge, Mass.: Harvard University Press, 1992), 88 and Charles Murray, Losing Ground: *American Social Policy 1950-1980* (New York: Basic Books, 1984).

8   Christian Tileagă, "Accounting for extreme prejudice and legitimating blame in talk about the Romanies", *Discourse & Society* 16 (2005): 603-624; Ch. Tileagă, "Representing the 'Other': A Discursive Analysis of Prejudice and Moral Exclusion in Talk about Romanies" *Journal of Community & Applied Social Psychology* 16 (2006): 19—41; Ch. Tileagă, "Ideologies of moral exclusion: A critical discursive reframing of depersonalization, delegitimation and dehumanization", *British Journal of Social Psychology* 46 (2007): 717–737.

9   Tileagă, "Accounting", 611

10   Tileagă, "Accounting", 612

11   Tileagă, "Accounting", 615

12   Tileagă "Accounting", 616

13 Tileagă adopts this term from Teun A. Van Dijk's *Communicating Racism: Ethnic Prejudice in Thought and Talk.* (London: Sage, 1987).

14 Tileagă "Representing", 34

15 Tileagă "Reresenting" 34.

16 Tileagă "Ideologies of moral exclusion", 704.

17 Tileagă "Accounting", 613

18 N. Steinhardt *Jurnalul Fericirii* (Bucharest: Dacia, 1972/1992) my translation.

19 See, e.g. http://roncea.ro/2010/09/20/nicolae-steinhardt-despre-tigani-in-jurnalul-fericirii-via-catalin-mihuleac-rasismul-este-o-dementa-nerasismul-este-o-nerozie/ and http://blog.nouadreapta.org/2010/09/nicolae-steinhardt-despre-tigani/#respond acessed 18/12/2013.

20 Steinhardt, *Jurnalul*, 205.

21 Bernard Williams, *Problems of the Self* (Cambridge: Cambridge University Press, 1973), 233, my emphasis.

22 Iris M. Young "Five faces" in Iris M. Young, *Justice and the Politics of Difference* (New Jersey: Princeton University Press, 1990).

23 Young, *Justice*, 196

24 Young "Five faces", 41.

25 Young "Five faces", 57.

26 "The oppression of violence consists not only in direct victimization, but in the daily knowledge shared by all members of oppressed groups that they are liable to violation." (Young "Five faces", 57).

27 While the form of oppression I have looked at is 'violence', in the rest of my analysis of antiziganism as a social practice, I do not claim antiziganism itself is a form of violence—while, of course, group-directed violence can be observed against Romanis. While the study of this latter phenomenon in Young's framework would surely be enlightening, in this section I focus on the way Young characterises a 'social phenomenon', leaving its relations with group-directed violence aside.

28 Young "Five faces", 57.

29 See http://dalefarm.wordpress.com/ accessed 18/12/2013.

30 http://www.theguardian.com/media/greenslade/2011/apr/27/roma-gypsies-and-travellers-dailymail, accessed 5.12.2013, my emphasis.

31 However, Susan Opotow claims that some theorists of distributive justice are aware of the existence of certain limitations to this universal principle, yet downplay their real importance for the way theories of justice are applied. She mentions Michael Walzer's work on the role played by the community in the willingness to distribute advantages (Michael Walzer, *Spheres of justice: A defence of pluralism and equality* (New York, NY: Basic Books, 1983), but we can also add to this list David Miller's argument about the solidarity felt by the members of the nation state towards each other and its importance for redistribution (David Miller, *On Nationality* (Oxford: Oxford University Press, 1995). See Susan Opotow, "Moral exclusion and injustice: An introduction", *Journal of social issues* 46:1 (1990): 1-20

32 What is more, theorists of justice and/or equality attempt to capture our everyday intuitions about equality rather than come up with their own views as to who should be considered as out equals (e.g. Jan Carter, "Respect and the Basis of Equality", *Ethics*

131:3 (2011): 558-571).

33   Opotow, "Moral exclusion", 1.

34   Susan Opotow et al., "From moral exclusion to moral inclusion: Theory for teaching peace", *Theory into Practice* 44:4 (2005): 303-318.

35   Opotow, "Moral exclusion", 8.

36   Edward H. Carr, *The Twenty Years' Crisis* (New York: Palgrave Macmillan, 2001), 67.

37   Opotow, "Moral exclusion", 8.

38   Tileagă "Representing" 34

39   As Opotow puts it, the aim is to "create a codebook of symptoms that would define moral exclusion operationally for empirical research." (Opotow, "Moral exclusion", 9).

40   A full list can be found in Opotow, "Moral exclusion", 10-11, and Opotow et al., "From moral exclusion to moral inclusion", 307, where the category names in between quotation marks offered below are taken from.

41   Opotow "Moral exclusion", 10-11, and Opotow et al., "From moral exclusion to moral inclusion", 307.

42   This is assumed implicitly in the category 'fear of contamination' as well.

43   See in Valeriu Nicolae, "Words that Kill", *Index on Censorship* 35 (2006): 137-141. And http://www.ergonetwork.org/media/userfiles/media/egro/Towards%20a%20Definition %20of%20Anti-Gypsyism.pdf , accessed 28.02.2014.

44   See in Miriam Eliav-Feldon et al., (eds) *Origins of Racism in the West* (New York: Cambridge University Press, 2009).

45   I would like to thank Anne Minken for this very useful historical reference.

46   Opotow "Moral exclusion", 10-11, and Opotow et al., "From moral exclusion to moral inclusion", 307.

47   Ryan, *Blaming the victim.*

48   Opotow "Moral exclusion", 11, Opotow et al. "From moral exclusion to moral inclusion", 307.

49   This could be interpreted as evidence that perceptions of Romanis as being child-like may be used to justify *prima facie* paternalistic interventions which actually serve the interests of the majority group.

50   "When 'special' means 'excluded': Roma segregation in special schools on the CEE/CIS region", UNICEF—Regional Office for Central and Eastern Europe and the Commonwealth of Independent States (UNICEF 2009) http://www.romachil-dren.com/wp-content/uploads/2011/11/When-Special-Means-Excuded.pdf (accessed 30/1/2014).

51   I leave aside the fact that even high achieving students might be discriminated against based on Romani ethnicity.

52   Butler, *Frames.*

53   In Butler's words, "Precarity designates those politically induced conditions in which certain populations suffer from failing social and economic networks of support and become differentially exposed to injury, violence, and death. Such populations are at heightened risk of disease, poverty, starvation, displacement, and exposure to violence without protection." (Butler, *Frames,* 25-26).

54   An important difference between precariousness and social exclusion is that precari-ousness refers not to *actual* failings from the above-mentioned outcomes, but to being

"in (*potential*—n.a.) danger of suffering harm" (Butler *Frames,* 25). Hence, while a socially excluded person actually lacks employment, for instance, a person whose status is precarious could be employed, but the prospects of remaining employed would be very insecure (e.g. because that person would be a day labourer). I do not focus on this difference in my analysis of an analogy between social and moral exclusion on the one hand and precariousness and grievability on the other because these discussions on actuality and potentiality or certainty and uncertainty do not play a role in Butler's explanation of the dynamics between precariousness and grievability.

55 Butler, *Frames,* 25
56 Butler, *Frames,* xix
57 Butler, *Frames,* 24
58 Butler. *Precarious Life: The Powers of Mourning and Violence* (London: Verso, 2004).
59 Butler, *Precarious life,* 134
60 See Melvin J. Lerner, *The Belief in a Just World: A Fundamental Delusion,* (New York: Plenum Press, 1980., Melvin J. Lerner and Sally C. Lerner (eds.) *The Justice Motive in Social Behavior: Adapting to Times of Scarcity and Change,* (New York: Plenum Press, 1981), and, more recently, Aaron C. Kay, John T. Jost and Sean Young (2005) "Victim Derogation and Victim Enhancement as Alternate Routes to System Justification" *Psychological Science* 16 (3), 240-246.
61 Butler, *Frames,* 26
62 Butler *Frames,* 32
63 For views of this sort see Will Guy's recently edited volume, *From Victimhood to Citizenship: the path of Roma integration* (Budapest: CEU Press, 2013), and especially Martin Kovats's paper "Integration and the politicisation of Roma identity" (pp.101-128) in that volume.

Antiziganism as Cultural Racism:
Before and After the Disintegration of Yugoslavia

Julija Sardelić

University of Edinburgh

This paper traces the discursive practices[1] of antiziganism in different historical and regional contexts of the former Yugoslav space. Although antiziganism was one of the prominent topics discussed in relations to Romani minorities[2] in Central and Eastern Europe[3] as well as in the context of the European Union (EU)[4], both comparative and contrastive analyses on the occurrence of antiziganism across the states that have emerged after the disintegration(s) of the socialist Yugoslavia (SFRY) have not yet been conducted. All the Post-Yugoslav states can namely be considered as very different localities at present since some have already joined the EU, while others are either with or without the EU candidate country status, or even considered "contested states", as is Kosovo[5].

Furthermore, unlike in other former socialist states, the transition in the former Yugoslav space coincided with violent state disintegration and reconceptualization of citizenry[6]. This also had an impact on the repositioning of Romani minorities[7]. However, as I will discuss below, antiziganism is not a product that emerged at the point of SFRY disintegration, but could claim origins in earlier historical constellations. I will point to some of such discursive practices before the emergence of the Socialist Yugoslavia and show in what ways was antiziganism also present in SFRY[8]. Moreover, this paper overviews some of the manifest discursive practices of antiziganism in the Post-Yugoslav space. I understand these manifest discursive practices as the escalation of different forms of discernable violence directed against Romani minorities. On the other hand, I will also highlight some of the less obvious, i.e. latent discursive practices of antiziganism. These are systemically incorporated into different societies and states in question and indirectly contribute to the marginalization of Romani minorities. The paper argues that antiziganism in different post-Yugoslav spaces is a conglomerate produced by the intertwining of local positioning of Romani minorities with more global trends (as described in the next section of this paper) shaping attitudes about these minorities. In order to provide theoretical understanding and methodological tools for my analysis, I conceptualise antiziganism as one of the forms of the so-called *cultural* or *differentialist racism*. But before, and in order to provide a starting point for comparisons, let me overview approaches to antiziganism and how it is usually examined in the context of Central and Eastern European states and the EU as the whole.

1. Embedding Discursive Practices of Antiziganism into Broader Societal Dynamics

Throughout the European continent (both within and outside the EU), individuals and groups identified as belonging to different Romani minorities have been targets of different extremist hostile practices: from hate speech[9] to violent attacks motivated by anti-Romani sentiments[10]. As some have argued, extremist practices directed against Romani minorities have been on the rise especially in times of macro-societal changes, which also profoundly affected the position of the Roma. This argument was used widely to explain events during the post-socialist transition after which, according to the World Bank report by Dena Ringold, Roma found themselves in a predicament as one of the most vulnerable groups across post-socialist area[11]. Similarly, as Will Guy points out, after the turn of the millennium Roma were identified "as 'the biggest losers' of the transition from communism to neoliberal capitalism"[12] in the predominant public discussion. As many socio-economic analyses have shown, including the one conducted by Gábor Kertesi in Hungary, most of the individuals identified as belonging to Romani minorities became unemployed after the collapse of state socialism [13]. Furthermore, as indicated above, there is also a prevailing argument that post-socialist transition has also been accompanied by an increase in racist violence directed against Romani minorities[14].

It has also been often argued that after the global economic crisis started in 2008[15], antiziganism has been on the rise[16] and increasingly coupled with the emergence of right-wing extremist political groups with explicit racist rhetoric[17]. However, although antiziganism can be perceived as being on the rise in the case of macro-economic changes, some scholars questioned the assumption that it merely correlates to the abrupt downfalls of the economy[18]. They namely argued that also wider societal dynamics needs to be considered. Here, for example, the EU enlargement processes coupled with the EU conditionality also have to be taken into account.

In this context, the Copenhagen Criteria also emphasised the respect of minorities and protection from discrimination of the most vulnerable such as Roma, as one of the conditions for candidate countries to join the EU[19]. Melanie Ram argued that although the EC set itself the goal to improve the position of Romani minorities in Central and Eastern Europe, it contributed to the visibility of these populations, but not necessarily to the improvement of their position[20]. Furthermore, according to Peter Vermeersch, a side effect of EU initiatives is that they have a different echo in local contexts, thereby creating additional boundaries between Romani minorities and majority populations, which often perceived Roma as outsiders privileged by the EU and not as co-citizens[21].

Moreover, there was a critique that anti-Romani racism is not merely a domain of right-wing extremist groups and movements on the margins[22], but has deeper roots in different societies. It is also questionable whether all specific features of different localities can be simply reduced to a European-wide common denominator in order to explain this phenomenon and hence the marginalized position of Romani minorities in different contexts, as is argued by Vermeersch[23]. Following these two assumptions, the question this paper addresses is whether any of these factors are present as practices of antiziganism in the Post-Yugoslav space and whether the occurrence of these practices should be understood as an expression of cultural racism.

2. Conceptualizing Antiziganism as a Form of Cultural Racism

Before proceeding to a discussion on antiziganism in Post-Yugoslav space, in order to clarify terminology and avoid conceptual confusion, I explain my theoretical approach to of antiziganism as cultural racism that I use throughout this paper. There are of course different understandings of antiziganism as well as racism itself, which to explicate would go beyond the scope of this paper. However, I will offer a short overview of how antiziganism and cultural racism are linked to one another to offer the theoretical conceptual apparatus for further analysis of selected case studies.

According to the understanding of different international organizations[24] as well as international NGOs pursuing Romani rights advocacy[25], antiziganism[26] is usually associated with direct extremist hostilities lead against the Roma. Similarly, Pierre Tanguieff was one of the first to use the term cultural racism in the analysis of right-wing extremist movements in France[27], which targeted alleged cultural differences instead of biological race that was mostly discredited in the public debate at the time. Using Tanguieff's concept of cultural racism, Romani activist Valeriu Nicolae[28] argues that manifestations of antiziganism are closely related to this new form of racism, which encompasses hostile majority attitudes towards the stigmatised minority, as characterized by Judith Okely[29].

Another understanding of antiziganism as cultural racism can be traced back to Paul Gilroy's concept and is also present in wider British Cultural Studies[30]. According to Gilroy, "[r]acism does not, of course, move tidily and unchanged through time and history. It assumes new forms and articulates new antagonisms through time and history"[31]. Therefore, Gilroy claims that it would be more suitable to talk about racisms in plural[32]. To talk about racisms in plural means that the addressees of racism are not simply 'blacks', but also other populations[33], which were constructed as culturally distinct. The constructed cultural difference was in turn, used to legitimize their hierarchical positioning within their own society. Therefore following Gilroy's argument, if we understand antiziganism as cultural racism, we also have to take into account that it is not simply on the surface of society. It also needs to be observed how it is more latently[34] embedded within the tissue of society itself, which I will also do in the following sections of this paper.

Antiziganism can also be seen as one of the forms of what Antonio Negri and Michael Hardt described as postmodern form of racism[35]. While modern racism was based on biological determinism, postmodern racism (similarly to modern anti-racism) neglects the existence of biological race, and instead operationalizes cultures as "historically determined". Hence, the postmodern racism embraces cultural differences as essentialist absolutes or is, as Gilroy would argue, based on ethnic absolutism[36]. Negri and Hardt based their understanding of postmodern, i.e. differentialist racism, on Deleuze's and Guattari's theory according to which

> [differentialist racism] functions rather through first engaging alterity and then subordinating differences according to degrees of deviance from whiteness. This has nothing to do with the hatred and fear of the strange, unknown Other. It is hatred born in proximity and elaborated through decrees of differences of the neighbour. [...] This is not to say that our societies are devoid of racial exclusions; certainly they are criss-crossed with numerous lines of racial barriers, across each urban landscape and across the globe. The point, rather, is that racial exclusion arises generally as a result of differentialist inclusion.[37]

A similar definition of *racism without races* was also given by Étienne Balibar[38]. However, Balibar argued that although such phenomenon is considered to be new, it is deeply rooted in the history of Europe and can be observed in different historical periods[39]. Balibar later on acknowledges that the Roma are also one of the main addressees of cultural racism[40]. All in all, antiziganism can therefore be understood as one of the particularistic forms of cultural racism[41], that is what some have named as anti-Romani racism[42]. In the next two sections, I will discuss some of the occurrences of antiziganism in its manifest and latent forms before and after the disintegration of SFRY.

3. Romani Minorities before the Disintegration of Yugoslavia

The position of Roma and their political representation was not at the forefront of Yugoslav public debates until the formation of the Romani movement in the late 1960s[43]. However, representations of Romani minorities in cultural imagery revealed that they were not usually considered a foreign population. One of the most famous depictions of Romanis in the region of the former Yugoslavia comes from a Nobel laureate Ivo Andrić. In his novel *The Bridge on the Drina*[44], Andrić describes how a group of Gypsies[45] led by a Gypsy blacksmith Merdžan were paid by Turkish overlords for the execution by impalement of Radisav, who was portrayed as an Orthodox peasant[46]. This impalement was one of the most brutal descriptions in the novel. According to some interpretations, it represents cultural divisions between the two groups[47]. While there were many different theories on how Radisav's impalement was according to popular belief interpreted as collective victimization of the Serbs[48], the role of the Gypsies in such imagery of the Ottoman Empire is rarely thoroughly discussed. However, we can observe that the Gypsies in this scene are hierarchically positioned between these groups and by both of these groups. They are portrayed as living among Orthodox peasants, but also as doing the 'dirty work' for the 'Turks'.

Although the literary portrayal included in Andrić' novel does not depict actual historical events, it offers a reflection that different acts of antiziganism also draw their legitimization from such widely spread representations of the Romani position in semi-mythological past. Nevertheless, investigations by historical scholars shown that some antiziganist discursive practices existed in both the Ottoman as well as in the Austro-Hungarian Empire, where the Kingdom of Serbs, Croats and Slovenians (later known as the First Yugoslavia) was subsequently established. For example, a historian David Crowe investigated that although many Roma in the Ottoman Empire converted to Islam, a Sultan sent out a decree in 1605 requiring them to pay a non-Muslim tax[49]. Despite the fact that there is no historical record of why Muslim Roma were required to pay the non-Muslim tax Crowe remarks: "[w]hile it is difficult to determine, why Muslim Roma were now required to pay a non-Muslim tax, at least one of the scholar has speculated that it was because Turks viewed them as schismatics"[50]. Differentialist racism therefore can also be attested to an earlier historical period when Roma were not perceived as foreign, but as culturally distinct and hence deviant[51] by state representatives and also by other, more dominant members of the society.

Discursive practices of latent antiziganism were not unique to the Ottoman Empire. Romani minorities were also perceived as deviant in the Austro-Hungarian Empire. Their deviancy however, was targeted by discursive practice of assimilation[52] as an act that would eradicate types of behaviours considered to be linked to the 'Gypsy identity', such as nomadism[53]. In consequence the aim was to erase the 'Gypsy identity' itself. According to some historical records of the Austro-Hungarian Empire, assimilationist policies included taking Romani children from their homes and also forbidding Romanis to marry among themselves[54].

There are very few schematic accounts on how Romani minorities were positioned after World War I (WWI) and during the interwar period in the First Yugoslavia. However, it is clear that one of the most evident and systemic manifestations of antiziganism occurred during World War II (WWII), especially in the area occupied by the Nazi-puppet state of the Ustaša regime. This regime first introduced legislation that included antiziganist laws[55]. After 1941 "Rom property was seized by the Croatian government, while most of the republic's Gypsies were arrested and sent to Ustaša concentration camps. Over the next two years, some Croatian Roma were sent to the death camps in Germany and Serbia, while others were executed 'in reprisal for Partisan and Četnik activities in the NDH'"[56].

After WWII, many socialist states developed a set of policies that also represented an assimilationist approach whereby Romani minorities were recognized as a social, and not as an ethnic group. As a social group they were to be equally included in the citizenry by way of their integration into the working class[57]. Stewart observed the following about such assimilationist policies: "Indeed, repression and discrimination could not have been further from the thoughts of the early Communist reformers. But the desired end was surprisingly close to the fascist dream: The Gypsies were to disappear"[58].

On the other hand, as argued by most of the scholars, the policies of the second Yugoslavia were diametrically opposed to those of other socialist countries. Romani contribution to the partisan movement was acknowledged[59] and they were afterwards regarded as part of the Yugoslav ethnic mosaic[60], hence they were either formally or informally recognized as an ethnic group in most of the Yugoslav republics[61]. Furthermore, the League of Communists of Yugoslavia (LCY) actively supported the inclusion of Romani minorities in their membership[62] as well as of the Romani elite, who from the beginning of the 1970is were the most prominent leaders of the Romani movement[63]. After the first Roma World Congress near London, the official Yugoslav politics as well as many Yugoslav media outlets respected the decision of their Romani delegates and replaced the usage of the term Gypsy with Roma[64]. Furthermore, while many Romani individuals were included in working processes and in the labour force, their alternative niches were also tolerated as their cultural specificity[65]. Moreover, Romani cultural organizations and the media flourished especially in the parts of SFRY where Romani minorities were most numerous[66].

Nevertheless, as argued by Judith Latham, it would be misleading to portray SFRY as a paradise for Romani minorities[67] since some latent discursive practices of antiziganism were systemically incorporated into an array of state policies. Firstly, the positioning of Romani minorities differed from one Yugoslav republic to another. What is more, it was also often influenced by how the territories of these republics were positioned in the empires before WWI and how Romani minorities were treated in that context. Romani culture and the media flourished especially in the Socialist Republics of Macedonia and Serbia, which were part of the Ottoman Empire. Nonetheless this was also possible due to legislative support[68] and not simply due to large Romani populations.

On the other hand, the Socialist Republics of Slovenia and Croatia were still more inclined to assimilationist Romani policies[69]. Though these policies had assimilationist intent, they worked off the assumption that Romani minorities were culturally and socially different. Therefore, they were marked by hierarchical inclusion. Many Romani individuals were placed in schools for children with special needs. According to the interviews I conducted with such individuals in Slovenia, they were usually placed in this parallel school system with the argumentation that they were not socialised enough and that they did not have sufficient knowledge of the majority language[70]. Similar argumentation about language knowledge was given for the introduction of segregated Romani-only classes in Croatia[71].

Other Socialist Republics and Provinces, such as Serbia along with Kosovo and Macedonia were considered to have more tolerant policies towards Romani minorities. However, here Romani individuals were often victims of latent discursive practices that can be labelled as antiziganist. For example, after the devastating earthquake in Skopje in 1963, large part of the old Romani quarter of Topaana was heavily affected. However, most of the Romani minorities, who used to live in this central neighbourhood, were then moved to the outskirts of Skopje, where the famous Romani municipality of Shuto Orizari was created as a result. Even in the area in which Romani culture flourished and was supported by state policies, Romani minorities usually lived in substandard conditions when compared to other non-Romani Yugoslavs[72].

The majority of individuals identified as belonging to Romani minorities were never included in the working class[73]. Part of the reason lies in the fact that their alternative unofficial economic niches were at least tolerated to a certain extent. However, such toleration did not simply arise due to the integration of Romanis into the Yugoslav society, but also due to a lack of a uniform plan on how they should be included. While Yugoslav authorities supported the development of Romani elites in the 1970s, a discussion on how to improve the position of the most disadvantaged Romani minorities began only in the late 1970s and still continued in the 1980s before the SFRY disintegration[74]. This resulted in many successful local initiatives for the improvement of the position of disadvantaged Romani minorities, though, of course, many remained on the edge of poverty[75].

Furthermore, Romani minorities were never officially recognised as a nationality (*narodnost*)[76] nor were they recognized as a constitutive Yugoslav nation although they were acknowledged as part of the Partisan movement. Even though their culture was officially nurtured, Romani individuals still felt the pressure to rather identify themselves as belonging to the majority or a more dominant minority in their locality. Such practices had already been identified in the Ottoman Empire, when many Roma converted to Islam. This was also described by a Romani journalist Orhan Galjus, born in Prizren, Kosovo, who often declared himself either as Turk or Albanian:

> When I applied to secondary school in Kosovo, it was a part of the old Yugoslavia, and everywhere there were ethnic quotas. The first time I applied, I wrote I was Romani. I was not accepted. Then I applied again as Turkish, because my name is Turkish, but they again rejected me. So I applied a third time as an Albanian and I was accepted. [...] When it was a part of the former Yugoslavia, many official documents were bi-

or even trilingual: Turkish, Albanian and Serbian, but never Romani. We were not considered as important—as a Rom you had no real status. To be recognized by the authorities, we had to declare ourselves as Albanian or Turkish, to record ourselves as such on official documents such as birth certificates. My family still has documents from the old times that say we are Albanian and some that we are Turks.[77]

In the socialist Yugoslavia, there was some awareness of Romani minorities as part of its societies for centuries so Roma were usually not considered to be a foreign population. While many efforts were made to ensure the inclusion of Romani minorities, these efforts were marked by differentiation and hierarchies that I attribute to latent antiziganist attitudes that were inherited form the past, but were reshaped with the arrival of new ideologies. Many Romani individuals actively responded to such reshaping. This was also described in the above quoted paragraph written by a Romani journalist Galjus. Nevertheless most of the Romani individuals could not have anticipated what awaits them after the disintegration of Yugoslavia.

4. Post-Yugoslav Antiziganism(s)

Many discursive practices that occurred during the period of the socialist Yugoslavia and characterised the position of Romani minorities included a more latent form of cultural racism, which can be understood in terms of antiziganism. Although there were fewer manifest discursive practices in a form of hate speech or violent attacks against Romani minorities reported, their hierarchical positioning was present within the system itself[78]. It was legitimized by perceived and even constructed social and cultural differences[79] of Romani minorities. These differences were usually systemized in a very subtle way, but they affected everyday lives of those individuals identified as belonging to Romani minorities. When they were included in official working processes, many of them carried out the lowest-paying jobs such as public utilities[80]. The fact that they could find a job usually only at the lowest end of the official economy wage scale was also perpetuated due to their placement into the educational system, where Romani minorities were often included, but segregated (Romani-only classes in Croatia, disproportional placement into school for children with special needs, etc.).

Although there was a genuine intention to include Romani minorities in the Yugoslav system, it is questionable whether such inclusion was done on an equal basis with those who were considered constitutive nations or even nationalities (*narodnosti*). However, it also needs to be noted that before the disintegration of Yugoslavia, especially in its last decade, there were many different discussion on measures to improve the disadvantaged position of Romani minorities. These discussions were not only conducted at the local and regional levels, but also at the highest official levels in Yugoslavia. Moreover, it was under serious consideration to officially recognize Romani minorities as one of Yugoslav nationalities, but also to acknowledge their underprivileged position. However, these plans never fully materialized and were no longer at the forefront of prominent public debates after the SFRY disintegration(s) and the establishment of the new states, which was accompanied by the armed conflict in many post-Yugoslav areas.

As Brubaker argued about the former Soviet Union[81], certain ethnic categorizations were also nurtured in the former socialist Yugoslavia through legislation and other state policies. However, the meaning of ethnic categorization was reformulated after the SFRY disintegration, not only due to the conflict, but also due to changing meaning of ethnicity in public discourse. This was for example the case in the drafting of new constitutions of the newly established states and was labelled by Robert Hayden as *constitutional nationalism*[82]. As Hayden claims, most of the newly drafted post-Yugoslav constitutions listed the core nation in its preamble. On the other hand, the working class, previously the most important collective identity category[83], was not present anymore. Hence, previous socio-economic solidarities and improvement of the position of the weakest were removed from national agendas.

Romani minorities were not at the forefront of the debate, although they were indirectly affected by these transformations. The changes were not visible at the national levels. Yet, they could be observed through the drastic change of discourse in many local contexts, which now included ethnic references to Romanis and in some cases manifest elements of cultural racism. For example, the media discourse in the Croatian region with the largest Romani population has changed drastically. While in 1971 the largest regional newspaper usually avoided references to the Roma as ethnicity or a distinct group or set out positive examples on how the Romanis were included in the Yugoslav society[84]. Ethnic labelling of Romani minorities as a deviant group became prominent since 1991 and phrases such as "ethnic conflict" between the Croatian majority and Romani minority were introduced. In this "ethnic conflict", Roma were described as an attacking collective body from the nearby settlement, while the Croats were named individually[85]. As it is evident from the vocabulary, which also included "ethnic conflict", terminology was transferred from the news reporting on the war conflict simultaneously occurring in other parts of Croatia. However, Romani minorities were in these discursive practices neither considered as foreign nor as "Other". Instead, they were perceived as certain threat to the ideal social order, marking one of the most outstanding features of differential racism[86].

The documentation on Romani minorities and their position during the war conflicts in the process of multiple disintegrations of Yugoslavia is still very partial and needs to be examined further. Romani as ethnicity were not considered in details since they were not initiators of the conflicts. Furthermore, they were never considered as a destabilizing factor in any of the post-Yugoslav states. However, they were often caught between competing narratives of nation building[87].

In some instances, Romani individuals joined the armed forces. For example, according to reported data, 2176 Romani individuals were in the Croatian army during the 1991—1995 war in Croatia. But, they were never formally recognized as the defenders of Croatia[88]. Moreover, in one of the violent attacks against Roma in the village of Škabrnja located in the Dalmatian inlands in the years after the war, the mob that wanted to evict the local Roma forcibly, chanting and calling them Serbs[89] and Četniks. The response of Roma in question was that they are Catholics and Croats, who moved here from other parts of Croatia.

This was not the only example of Romani minorities not only being considered as deviant from the in-group, but also as the ones who are siding with the enemy. According to available sources[90], some Romanis in the war in Bosnia and

Herzegovina in fact joined the Bosnian Serbs troops, while others were in the BIH armed forces. However, many Romani civilians suffered similar atrocities as Bosniak civilians: many of them were sent to concentration camps and they were also victims of the massacres in and around Srebrenica, which is rarely mentioned in the Bosnian as well as international public debate. They were equally attacked in the war, but were left unrecognized as victims in peace. This can be interpreted by the numbers game, which meant that Roma were counted as Bosniak victims. On the other hand, it can also be explained by the discursive practices of cultural racism since Roma were not recognized as a full subject to be counted as victims.

Romani minorities also found themselves caught between the Serbian and Albanian sides in the Kosovo war conflict. This paradoxically tightened the divisions between the three different Romani minority groups, i.e. Roma, Ashkali and Egyptians[91]. While it was reported that some Roma, Ashkali and Egyptians joined the Kosovo Liberation Army (KLA)[92], there was a widespread belief that the Roma usually sided with the Serbs and were doing the 'dirty work' for them against the Albanian population[93]. Ashkali and Egyptians, whose native tongue was Albanian, were considered to be closer to the Albanian community[94]. In reality, it is documented that all three groups were attacked by both sides, thereby forcing many Romani individuals to seek refuge in the neighbouring countries or in Western Europe, while many more became (initially) internally displaced in Serbia and Montenegro. Their position was complicated further when Montenegro and subsequently Kosovo declared independence[95].

Many Roma, Ashkali and Egyptians, who remained in Kosovo, were subjected to antiziganist violent attacks (forced evictions, stoning, etc.). They were living in fear for their lives even many years after the war in Kosovo concluded[96]. In addition, some Romani individuals, who were internally displaced, lived in the camps set up by the international community on contaminated soil with seriously damaging effects on their health[97]. The plan to resettle them in more appropriate housing did not start before harsh criticism from the civil society[98]. After the Kosovar declaration of independence, Roma, Ashkali and Egyptians were recognized as communities in Kosovo. However, although they gained official political representation, their plight remained under-addressed. Therefore, they were considered invisible[99] or abandoned[100] minorities, which is again a paradox derived from antiziganist elements. They were visible during antiziganist attacks from different sides, both in war and peace, but abandoned and left invisible afterwards.

Due to the discursive practices in Kosovo based on antiziganist elements, many Romani individuals were never able to return to their homes and remained displaced, either with a refugee status[101] (in Croatia, Macedonia, Bosnia and Herzegovina, EU, etc.) or with a internally displaced person status in Serbia and Montenegro. The position of displaced Romani minorities in Montenegro became even more complicated after Montenegro declared independence[102]. Although forced Romani migrants did not cross any internationally recognized borders at the time of the Kosovo conflict, they found themselves in a newly independent state with new political reality after several years. However, the regulation of their status in Montenegro[103] has proven to be far from simple, especially due to political juggling both in the state of origin (previously Serbia, now Kosovo) as well as in the destination state. While most residents in Montenegro were able to regulate their status either as citizens or residents, many Romani individuals were left with a precarious status due to inability to obtain personal identity documents. Although they were not directly targeted by citizenship status debates in Montenegro, they were one of the most affected populations. One of the largest refugee camps in Europe is still located in Konik on the outskirts of Podgorica; its residents are mostly Romani minorities[104] not being able to return home, but also not being able to fully integrate into their host society.

Besides the displaced, another challenge in regards to Romani minorities emerged: in many post-Yugoslav states, especially Serbia, Romani minorities have found themselves in a specific predicament of legally invisible persons for decades. This group mostly if not solely consisted of Romani individuals as revealed by NGOs dealing with their status[105]. This became an intergenerational problem for many Romani individuals due to a lack of birth certificates. Although one of the main arguments was that this could be attributed to the

Romani way of life, they were left without basic documents such as birth certif-icates. It is questionable why the states where they resided did not initially in-vest more efforts to register them as their own citizens. One of the interpreta-tions could be that they were citizens of unwanted ethnicity for countries in question.

This can also be corroborated by manifest antiziganist attacks and forced evic-tions of Romani minorities. One of such attacks in the post-Yugoslav Serbia happened when an angry mob was heading to attack a Romani settlement in Zemun Polje since it was reported that its inhabitants have scabies. The mob was chanting a very familiar slogan *"Ubij, zakolji, da Cigan ne postoji"* [Kill, Slaughter so that there are no longer any Gypsies!][106] . In addition, many Rom-ani individuals in Serbia, who had access to their personal documents and hence citizenship, changed their names after the war from Albanian or Bosniak to Serbian so that they could hide their identity with the following argumenta-tion: "In the last years, the Roma who fled from Kosovo have been changing their Albanian names into Serbian due to the belief held by the majority popu-lation that *'šiptar'* [derogative word for Albanian] Gypsies were killing Kosovar Serbs'"[107].

The protection of Romani minorities became more prominent topic during EU integration processes. Under the EU conditionally rules formulated in the con-text of the Copenhagen Criteria, the protection of vulnerable minorities, such as Romani, became more salient. The prominence of hierarchical inclusion has become visible in cases such as Bosnia and Herzegovina, where Roma are still second class citizens since they are unable to run for presidency or other important political posts due to clear ethnic divisions, which award such rights only to the constitutive nations of BIH[108]. Such ethnic divisions multiply in eve-ryday practices, where Romani children can choose to go either to a Bosniak or a Croat school, while in reality most of them are still excluded from the edu-cational system as many do not possess birth certificates and are hence legally invisible.

Before the start of EU integration processes, the problem of legally invisible Romani individuals and those without personal identity documents was placed on the agenda due to visa liberalization processes. According to Simonida Ka-carska, one of the benchmarks of visa liberalization for Schengen countries was also to provide access to personal documents for vulnerable minorities such as Roma and consequently protect their minority rights[109]. This started a process in which many Romani individuals, who were previously without doc-uments, were able to acquire them. However, there were not efficient control mechanisms in place to determine whether minority rights of the Romanis are sufficiently protected[110]. After the visa liberalization process was launched in Macedonia and Serbia, Western European countries reported an increase in 'bogus' asylum seekers from these two countries, many of them identified as belonging to Romani minorities. In 2013, the European Parliament therefore introduced a visa waiver suspension mechanism, which would allow the rein-troduction of the visa regime to the countries in question in case too many asy-lum seekers were coming to the Schengen area.

The assumption behind it was that if the countries in question did more to pro-tect minority rights of Romanis, the asylum seekers flow would decrease. How-ever, this in fact indirectly supported some of racist discursive practices di-rected against Romanis whose freedom of movement was not impeded since in many reported cases they are not allowed to leave the country when trying to cross borders[111]. Romani minorities were again unequally positioned as cit-izens of their own countries due to their perceived collective features as 'abus-ers' of the system harming all other citizens. The fact that Romani minorities are subjected to antiziganist discursive practices (including the impeded free-dom of movement) in their own countries was simply ignored.

Conclusion

In this article I argued that antiziganism cannot be simply explained with a sim-ple social correlation to a single factor in the society. Antiziganism is not simply a product of transition, economic instabilities nor the absence of peace. As I have pointed out to the analysed discursive practices of antiziganism before and after the collapse of the socialist Yugoslavia, I claimed that local seman-tics, historical constellations, but also wider contemporary trends of attitudes towards Romani minorities have to be taken into account.

In the post-Yugoslav space Romani minorities were not considered as strangers or the Other *per se* and that was not usually the legitimization for the occurrence of antiziganist discursive practices. However, as Romani minorities were in fact drawn away from firm ethnic and other categorizations, they were never considered to fully like 'Us' and hence were always the easiest target from all sides in conflict both in war and peace. As I have connected antiziganism to the understandings of cultural or differentialist racism, I also showed that the discursive practices of antiziganism are not only present in its manifest forms, but also latently embedded deeper into the tissue of the post-Yugoslav societies, which perpetuate such position of Romani minorities, who are included, but excluded at the same time.

Acknowledgements

This work was supported by funding from the CITSEE project (The Europeanisation of Citizenship in the Successor States of Former Yugoslavia), based at the University of Edinburgh, UK. CITSEE is funded by the European Research Council under the European Union Seventh Framework Programme, ERC Grant no. 230239, and the support of ERC is acknowledged with thanks.

References

1   In this paper, I use the concept of discursive practices as comprehended by Ernesto Laclau and Chantal Mouffe: "Our analysis rejects the distinction between discursive and non-discursive practices. It affirms a) that every object is constituted as an object of discurse, insofar as no object as no object is given outside every discursive condition of emergence" (Ernesto Laclau and Chantal Mouffe, *Hegemony and Socialist Strategy: Towards a Radical Democratic Politics* (London, Verso, 2001), 107). Discursive practices that were chosen for analysis in this paper are based on discursive conditions, which carry the elements of antiziganism.

2   I use Romani minorities in plural to emphasise the heterogeneity as well as hybridity (Annabel Tremlett and Aidan McGarry, "Challenges facing Researchers on Roma Minorities in Contemporary Europe: Notes Towards a Research Program—ECMI Working Paper #62/2013," http://www.ecmi.de/uploads/tx_lfpubdb/Working_Paper_62_Final.pdf accessed on 15th January 2014) of the populations especially in the post-Yugoslav space. Besides Roma, I also include Egyptians, Ashkali, Sinti, Bayash, Vlach Roma, etc. I use Romani minorities in those cases, where I want to stress their non-dominant position and power relations in a given context.

3   Will Guy, ed. *Between past and future: the Roma of Central and Eastern Europe* (Hertfordshire: University of Hertfordshire Press: 2001).

4   Michael Stewart, ed., *The Gypsy Menace: Populism and the New Anti-Gypsy Politics* (London: C.Hurst & Co., 2012).

5   Gëzim Krasniqi, "State Borders, Symbolic Boundaries and Contested Geographical Space: Citizenship Struggles in Kosovo," *Transitions* 522 (2013): 29–51.

6   Igor Štiks „" A Laboratory of Citizenship: Shifting Conceptions of Citizenship in Yugoslavia and its Successor States. CITSEE Working Paper 2010/02," (Edinburgh, University of Edinburgh,2010), http://www.citsee.ed.ac.uk/__data/assets/pdf_file/00 09/108828/179_alaboratoryofcitizenshipshiftingconceptionsofcitizenshipinyugoslavia anditssucces.pdf last accessed on 15 January 2014.

7   Julija Sardelić, "Romani minorities on the Margins of Post-Yugoslav Citizenship Regimes. CITSEE Working Paper 2013/31," (Edinburgh: University of Edinburgh, 2013), http://www.citsee.ed.ac.uk/working_papers/files/CITSEE_WORKING_PAPER_2013-31a.pdf last accessed on 15 January 2014.

8   This paper does not in any way imply that all discursive practices directed against Romani minorities in SFRY or any other given historical moment were necessarily fuelled by anti-Roma sentiments and can be thus labelled as antiziganist. The aim of this paper is also not to give a linear history presentation of antiziganism in the current Post-Yugoslav space, but to introduce some of the patterns that have been present, and that have a significant influence in the position of Romani minorities.

9   European Roma Rights Centre (ERRC), "ERRC Condemns Hitler Hate Speech Against Roma," http://www.errc.org/article/errc-condemns-hitler-hate-speech-against-roma/4173 last accessed on 15th January 2014.

10   ERRC, "Hungary: Police Fail to Act Against Racist Violence as Football Fans Target Romani Schoolchildren," http://www.errc.org/article/hungary-police-fail-to-act-against-

racist-violence-as-football-fans-target-romani-schoolchildren/4189 last accessed on 15 January 2014.

11   Dena Ringold, *Roma and the Transition in Central Europe: Trends and Challenges* (Washington, D.C.: The World Bank, 2000), V.

12   Will Guy, "EU Initiatives on Roma: Limitations and Ways Forward," in Nando Sigona and Nidhi Trehan, eds., *Romani Politics in Contemporary Europe: Povery, Ethnic Mobilization and the Neoliberal Order* (Houndmills, Basingstoke, Hampshire: Palgrave Macmillan), 3.

13   Gábor Kertesi, *The Employment of Roma—Evidence from Hungary. Budapest Working Paper No 1* (Budapest: Institute of Economics, HAS—Department of Human Resources, Corvinus University, 2004), 44.

14   Michael Stewart, *The Time of the Gypsies* (Boulder, Oxford: Westview Press, 1997), 232.

15   Kamelia Dimitrova, "The Econoimic Crisis Closes in on Bulgarian Roma," *Roma Rights Journal* 1 (2009): 40-43.

16   Rob Kushen, "Economics, Extremism and Roma Rights: A Dangerous Linkage," *Roma Rights Journal* 1 (2009): 1-3.

17   Andrzej Mirga, "The Extreme Right and Roma and Sinti in Europe: A New Phase in the Use of Hate Speech and Violence?," *Roma Rights Journal* 1 (2009): 5-9.

18   Michael Stewart, " Populism, Roma and the European Politics of Cultural Difference," in Michael Stewart, ed., *The Gypsy Menace: Populism and the New Anti-Gypsy Politics* (London: C.Hurst & Co., 2012): 9.

19   Maria Spirova and Darlene Budd "The EU Accession Processes and the Roma Minorities in New and Soon-to-be Member States," *Comparative European Politics* 6 (April 2008): 81-101.

20   Melanie H. Ram, " Legacies of EU Conditionality: Explaining Post-Accession Adherence to Pre-Accession Rules on Roma," *Europe Asia Studies* 64:7 (2012): 1215.

21   Peter Vermeersch, "Reframing the Roma: EU Initiatives and the Politics of Reinterpretation," *Journal for Ethnic and Migration Studies* 38:8 (2012): 1209.

22   Nando Sigona and Nidhi Trehan, "Introduction: Romani Politics in Neoliberal Europe," in Nando Sigona and Nidhi Trehan, eds., *Romani Politics in Contemporary Europe: Poverty, Ethnic Mobilization and the Neoliberal Order* (Houndmills, Basingstoke, Hampshire: Palgrave Macmillan, 2009), 9.

23   Vermeersch, " Reframing the Roma", 1209.

24   Michel Guet, "Anti-Gypsyism in Today's Europe," http://www.coe.int/t/dg3/romatravellers/archive/documentation/discrimination/antigypsism_en.asp last accessed on 15 January 2014.

25   Dimitrina   Petrova,   "The   Roma: Between   a   Myth   and   the   Future," http://www.errc.org/cikk.php?cikk=1844 last accesses on 15th January 2014.

26   Different designations for antiziganism

27   Pierre André Tanguieff, "The New Cultural Racism in France," *Telos* 20 (1990): 109-122.

28   Valeriu Nicolae, "Towards a Definition of Anti-Gypsism," http://www.ergonetwork.org/media/userfiles/media/egro/Towards%20a%20Definition%20of%20Anti-Gypsism.pdf last accessed on 15 January 2014.

29   Judith Okely, "Constructing Difference. Gypsies as 'Other'. *Anthropological Journal of European Cultures* 3:2 (1994): 55-73.

30   Paul Gilroy, ed., *The Empire Strikes Back: Race and Racism in 70s Britain* (London: Routlege, 1982).

31   Paul Gilroy, *There Ain't No Black in the Union Jack: The Cultural Politics of Race and Nation* (London: Hutchinson, 1987), 11.

32   Gilroy, *There Ain't No Black in the Union Jack*, 38.

33   Paul Gilroy, "Stepin' out of Babylon—race, class and autonomy," in Paul Gilroy, ed., *The Empire Strikes Back: Race and Racism in 70s Britain* (London: Routlegde, 1982), 288.

34   Nicolae (2006) acknowledges that there are also institutional practices of antiziganism. Here he argues that not recognizing the Roma as a national minority constitutes one of such practices.

35   Michael Hardt and Antonio Negri, *Empire* (Cambridge, MA: Harvard University Press, 2000), 190-195.

36   Gilroy, *There Ain't No Black in the Union Jack*, 13.

37   Hardt and Negri, *Empire*,194.

38   Étienne Balibar, "Is there a 'Neo-Racism'?," in Étienne Balibar and Immanuel Wallerstein, eds., *Race, Nation, Class: Ambiguous Identities* (London: Verso, 1991), 23.

39   *Ibid.*

40   Étienne Balibar, " Foreword," in Nando Sigona and Nidhi Trehan, eds., *Romani Politics in Contemporary Europe: Poverty, Ethnic Mobilization and the Neoliberal Order* (Houndmills, Basingstoke, Hamshire: Palgrave Macmillan, 2009), x.

41   *Ibid.*

42   Nando Sigona and Nidhi Trehan, "Introduction: Romani Politics in Neoliberal Europe" in Nando Sigona and Nidhi Trehan, eds., *Romani Politics in Contemporary Europe: Poverty, Ethnic Mobilization and the Neoliberal Order* (Houndmills, Basingstoke, Hamshire: Palgrave Macmillan, 2009), 7.

43   Donald Kenrick, "Former Yugoslavia: a patchwork of destinies," in Will Guy, ed. *Between past and future: the Roma of Central and Eastern Europe* (Hertfordshire: University of Hertfordshire Press, 2001), 406.

44   Ivo Andrić, *Na Drini ćuprija*, http://www.skolest.com/wp-content/uploads/2013/06/Nadrini-cuprija.pdf last accessed on 15 January 2014.

45   Here I use the term 'Gypsies' because Andrić was using it in his book. When I use the term Gypsies in this section, it is only in a reference to the literature, where other authors have used this term. Similarly I use the term Turks as it has been used in the references.

46   *Ibid.*

47   Tomislav Z. Longinović, *Vampire Nation: Violence as Cultural Imaginary* (Durham: Duke University Press, 2011), 132.

48   *Ibid.*

49   David Crowe, *A History of the Gypsies of Eastern Europe and Russia* (Houndmills, Basingstoke, Hampshire: Palgrave Macmillan, 2007), 198.

50   *Ibid.*

51   Negri and Hardt, *Empire*, 194.

52   Crowe, *A History of the Gypsies*, 201.

53   *Factsheets on Roma: Austro-Hungarian Empire*, http://romafacts.uni-graz.at/index.php/history/state-policies-integration-forced-assimilation-deportation/austro-hungarian-empire last accessed on 15 January 2014.

54 Ibid.
55 Crowe, The History of the Gypsies, 220.
56 Ibid.
57 Zoltan Barany, The East European Gypsies: Regime Change, Marginality and Ethno-politics (Cambridge: Cambridge University Press, 2002), 114.
58 Stewart, The Time of the Gypsies, 5.
59 Crowe, The History of the Gypsies, 222.
60 Barany, The East European Gypsies, 122-123.
61 Sardelić, Romani Minorities on the Margins, 6-7.
62 Barany, The East European Gypsies, 137.
63 Kenrick, "Former Yugoslavia," 406.
64 Crowe, A History of the Gypsies, 226.
65 Sardelić, Romani Minorities on the Margins, 7.
66 Barany, The East European Gypsies, 123.
67 Judith Latham, "Roma of the former Yugoslavia," Nationalities Papers: The Journal of Nationalism and Ethnicity 27:2 (1999), 207.
68 Sardelić, Romani Minorities on the Margin, 6.
69 Julija Sardelić, Kulturne reprezentacije manjšin: Slovenski Romi pred osamosvojitvijo in po njej (PhD Thesis, 2012), 340.
70 Ibid.
71 Ibid.
72 Crowe, A History of the Gypsies,
73 Sardelić, Romani Minorities on the Margins, 7.
74 Crowe, A History of the Gypsies, 227.
75 Ibid.
76 Sardelić, Romani Minorities on the Margins, 7.
77 Orhan Galjus, "The last Yugoslavs," http://www.errc.org/article/the-last-yugoslavs/804 last accessed on 15 January.
78 Gilroy, There Ain't no Black in the Union Jack, 11.
79 Balibar, "Is there a Neo-Racism", 21.
80 Sardelić, Kulturne reprezentacije, 343.
81 Rogers Brubaker, National Self-Determination and Secession (Oxford: Oxford University Press, 1998).
82 Robert Hayden, "Constitutional Nationalism in the Formerly Yugoslav Republics," Slaviw Review 51:4 (1992), 654-673.
83 Vojin Dimitrijević, "The 1974 Constitution and Constitutional Processes as a Factor of Collapse of Yugoslavia," In Payam Akhavan and Robert Howse, eds., Yugoslavia, Former and Future. Reflection from Scholars from the Region (Geneva: The United Nations Research Institute for Social Development, 1995).
84 Julija Sardelić 2011, Constructiong or Repositioning Roma in Post-Socialist Slovenia and Croatia?—MA Thesis (Budapest: Central European University, 2011), 74
85 Ibid. 79.
86 Negri and Hardt, Empire, 193.
87 Nando Sigona, "Between Competing Imaginaries of Statehood: Roma, Ashkali and Egyptian (RAE) Leadership in Newly Independent Kosovo," Journal for Ethnic and Migration Studies 38:8 (2012): 1213-1232.

222   Julija Sardelić

88 "Romi branitelji u borbi za Hrvatsku," http://vojnapovijest.vecernji.hr/broj-8-vp/romi-branitelji-u-borbi-za-hrvatsku-907782 last accessed on 15 January 2014.
89 Božana Sliviĉić, "U Škabrnji žicom ogradili doseljene Rome: Nismo ni ĉetnici, ni životinje," http://www.slobodnadalmacija.hr/Zadar/tabid/73/articleType/ArticleView/articleId/173077/Default.aspx last accessed 15 January 2014.
90 "Romi Bosne i Hercegovine, http://gfbv.ba/index.php/Romi_BiH.html last accessed 15 January 2014.
91 Sigona, "Between Competing Imaginaries", 1218.
92 ERRC, *Abandoned Minority: Roma Rights History in Kosovo* (Budapest: European Roma Rights Centre, 2011), 16.
93 *Ibid.,* 17.
94 *Ibid.,* 15.
95 Sardelić, *Romani Minorities on the Margins,* 17.
96 ERRC, *Abandoned Minority,* 24-25.
97 *Ibid.,*60
98 *Ibid.,* 61.
99 Gëzim Krasniqi, *Equal citizens, uneven 'communities': differntiated and hierarchical citizenship in Kosovo. CITSEE Working Paper 2013/27* (Edinburgh: University of Edinburgh, 2013), 20.
100 ERRC, *Abandoned Minority.*
101 Sardelić, *Romani Minorities on the Margins,* 16.
102 Jelena Džankić, "Montenegro's Minorities in the Tangles of Citizenship, Participation, and Access to Rights," *Journal on Ethnopolitics and Minority Issues in Europe* 11:3 (2012): 40-59.
103 Sardelić, *Romani Minorities on the Margins,* 17.
104 *Ibid.* 17.
105 PRAXIS, "Legally Invisible Persons in Serbia—Still without a Solution," http://www.praxis.org.rs/images/praxis_downloads/praxis-report-legally-invisible-persons-Ci-still-without-a-solution-published.pdf last accessed 15 January 2014.
106 Blic, "Rasistiĉke demontracije u Zemunu: Oko 200 graĊana šetalo uz povike 'Ubij, zakolji, da Cigan ne postoji!'", http://www.svet.rs/top-vesti/rasisticke-demonstracije-u-zemunu-oko-200-gradana-setalo-uz-povike-ubij-zakolji-da-cigan-ne-postoji last accessed on 15 January 2014.
107 Persa Vuĉić, "Sumoran život nevidljivih ljudi," http://www.republika.co.rs/428-429/13.html last accessed 15 January 2014.
108 Sardelić, *Romani Minorities on the Margin,* 20.
109 Simonida Kacarska, *Europeanization through mobility: visa liberalization and citizenship regimes in the Western Balkans. CITSEE Working Paper 2012* (Edinburgh: University of Edinburgh, 2012). 9.
110 *Ibid.* 16.
111 *Ibid.* 20.

The Root Cause of Romani Exclusion and the European National Roma Integration Strategies

Timofey Agarin

Queen's University Belfast

The European Union (EU) has a set of strategic goals, reflecting the organisation's fundamental commitment to communication with and engagement of European citizens in policy making as well as in policy implementation. Romanis across Europe—in the EU and beyond—are, however, the most likely individual members of any group to be excluded from general avenues available for participation and policy input. Whether because of their lack of employment, limited access to education and health provisions, or destitute housing conditions, Romanis do not participate in public life to the same extent as members of the majority community in their country of residence do. According to the Fundamental Rights Agency, Romani exclusion from accessing institutions of public life hampers their engagement with communications, access to information and input into policy making in regional, domestic and European arenas[1].

The lack of Romani participation further exacerbates perceptions found in most European societies that individual Romanis are dependent on welfare, locked into an intergenerational poverty cycle and are agents of both petty and organised crime. Indeed, Romani individuals often lack skills valued by the majority society, are widely marginalised, suffer endemic discrimination, and are objects of widespread hatred. In order to support Romani individuals and assist the community as a whole to participate in public life, the European Commission has recently identified Romanis as "the biggest minority group of Europe"[2]. The European Parliament, too, has repeatedly drawn attention to the stark differences between Romanis and non-Romani EU citizens, and sought to make the improvement of living conditions of Romani people a responsibility of the EU, while identifying "Roma as a truly international minority"[3].

Across European societies, Romani individuals face social, economic and political exclusion in states that de facto, if not always de jure serve cultural, linguistic and religious majorities. The fact that 'the Roma' have become the focus
of European public policy has had positive effects on public awareness about
the situation of Romani communities. The Council of Europe (COE) and the
Organisation for Security and Cooperation in Europe (OSCE) have been particularly strong advocates for the recognition of Romani communities as national minorities[4]. Since 2004, the European Parliament (EP) has explicitly focussed on Romani exclusion in the context of non-discrimination, specifically
with regards to the promotion of social inclusion and combating poverty in the
EU. My contention, however, is that the very notion of "inclusion" is elusive
because it implies that those to be "included" have no access to, and thus cannot determine the criteria of their own "inclusion". Allowing members of Romani
communities to engage to a greater extent in decision making both domesti-
cally and at the EU level—thus ultimately averting their social exclusion—was
anticipated to provide Romani communities support from states of which they
are citizens[5].

And yet, Romanis remain largely unaffected by European efforts geared toward
their inclusion. Whilst many EU member states and candidate states have put
in place policies to facilitate Roma integration and participation[6], Romani communities have seen little improvement in the general practices of their inclusion
across a range of EU states[7]. While accepting that some progress has indeed
been made, this paper contends that one is unlikely to see better progress
because of the underlying structural conditions that prevent inclusion of multiply marginalised communities, such as Romanis. Thus while I focus on Romani
exclusion specifically, the implications I draw upon are much broader and reflect the paucity of both policy and academic debate on the nature of envisaged
"inclusion".

Literature on the effectiveness of public policy has long been criticised for failing to identify the inequality of actors regarding their resourcefulness when they
engage with political opportunities so as to entrench their interests, join in the
competition for resources, and increase actor-specific returns. Much of the
work into policies which specifically target marginal communities in societies

confirms that the preferences of individual beneficiaries of policies are rarely taken into account, but rather are projected by the authors of such policies. In either case, the authors of such policies are themselves rarely aware of the inherent limitations they impose on the (projected) beneficiaries, as both sets of actors are locked into an institutional context, from within which they anticipate policy effectiveness and the scope of its application. These structural conditions determine the auxiliary interests of actors in any given situation when choices are to be made. In short, mapping policy effectiveness requires at least an appreciation of agents' intent. Furthermore, it is the limitation of an institutional framework that accounts for all nodal actors involved in policy delivery: the making, the implementing and the target audiences.

Participation in and drawing positive lessons from the opportunities offered by the National Roma Integration Strategies (NRIS), for example, requires at least the informed choice of those individuals who are to be engaged in inclusion[8]. Policies aimed at the inclusion of minority/marginal/multiply-excluded groups often fail to achieve their core objective of participation, largely because they misrepresent the type of exclusion faced by individual Romanis.

The lack of equal access to structured resources in which to participate is the core identity marker for individual Romanis, and is used to identify beneficiaries/individual members of the group who would profit from positive action. Whilst regarding groups defined by a shared identity is commonplace in EU, public policy for social inclusion and positive action towards Romani individuals on the basis of a notional overlap of identities is built on several presumptions that act against Romani inclusion. I will discuss the three core issues that inform many of the NRIS and related policies to structure the argument of this paper. The following sections of the paper will reflect on the reasons for the persistent failure of inclusion policies that primarily (a) focus individual preferences to avail of the socioeconomic and political opportunities on offer, (b) frame her or his exclusion as a result of contingent factors of social circumstances, and ultimately (c) dispense of an individual's ability to identify in an open social context. All of these reflect the core constraints of the liberal democratic approach the EU takes on social inclusion, based on offering a choice to those excluded to reverse the decline of Romani social participation, and enhance individual agentic abilities in the market-like "forum of opportunities".

1. Social Exclusion as Romanis' Individual Choice?

One of the most potent criticisms of the human rights-driven approach on Romani inclusion policies undoubtedly comes in the guise of scepticism concerning the neoliberal economy and ethnopolitical entrepreneurship which is taking hold across many postcommunist states. Indeed, several brilliant analyses of the Romani situation in Europe attempt to untangle the complex relationship between the socioeconomic changes of the past decade from the challenges of emergent multilevel governance in Europe. Most of these bemoan the diluting political responsibility at state and regional levels, the apparent empowerment of NGOs and EU actors, and the compounded impact of the above upon the economic and political status of Romanis, their political participation and mobilisation, representation and interest formation.

It takes considerable effort and dedication to identify the origins of Romani exclusion and the subtle mechanisms by which even contemporary policies for the inclusion of Romanis have, in fact, disparaged the contribution of these communities to society. The recent fuss about anti-Roma protests attests to the fact that even the societies of former communist states of Eastern Europe are reassured by comparisons between themselves and the "Gypsies". Unsurprisingly so: The genealogical links between Romani languages and Sanskrit established by enlightenment anthropologists accepted Romanis as cultural brethren of the "Indo-Germanic" ethnic and linguistic family. Europeans often saw "Gypsies" as a useful benchmark against which to judge their own ability to retain and maintain ordered economic relations, to establish and codify state orders, and to indulge in the pursuits of culture. Ascendancy to "high culture", engagement in structured economic activities and political participation in the wider European way of life still rely heavily on an implicit comparison with Romanis and distance between Romanis and the majority. Academic research has played an important part in this process.

Since the British Gypsy Lore Society was established, ethnographers have meticulously documented Romani material culture and recorded oral traditions, allowing for the study of a group of people who were (and in some places, still are) considered "pre-modern", lacking a written tradition and almost exclusively relying on oral lore. Until the end of the 1980s, the Romanis were unanimously understood as the European "Other" par excellence. Despite their conspicuous marginalisation in the public eye, a number of excellent scholarly works on the everyday lives and customs, language and occupations of Romanis were written in this tradition. Nearly all of these studies were produced by ethnographers who observed and reported their experiences of sharing in the everyday lives of Romani individuals. The closer anthropology got to the everyday activities of Romanis, however, the greater the distance of Romanis to these academics' own cultures appeared to be, and the more efficient was the construction of difference.

Since the demise of communism in Eastern Europe, interest in Romani groups has gradually shifted from description to analyses of social processes. An increasing number of anthropologists with an eye to difference, but also with the ability to see parallels between the subject under scrutiny and their own cultural background produced vivid and sometimes moving accounts of the living conditions of Roma/Gypsy/Traveller communities. This allowed for issues accompanying social change in European societies to gain prominence in the analyses of Romani communities, their religious practices, gender relations and economic activities. A new generation of social scientists came of age in the early 2000s and repeatedly pointed to the central role of the relationship between Romani and non-Romani communities, bringing the spotlight of research to wider societal processes affecting all members of society alike.

The "big bang" EU enlargement of 2004/2007 opened the floodgates of research on Romani issues with a further consolidation of diverse strands of investigation. With the accession of Romania and Bulgaria, Romanis became the "largest minority in the EU". Scholars with detailed knowledge of and experience working with Romanis from new member states have created arenas in which they can share their long-standing research with Western scholars and—much to the consternation of wider society—debate the crucial role majority communities play in perpetuating Romani exclusion. European organisations have (with the EU and the Council of Europe at the forefront) repeatedly asserted the need for states to guarantee Romani individuals' full enjoyment of their human rights and to develop inclusionary policies in the face of Romani exclusion. Many of these policies have been informed by research. Yet, as all research is partial, often the baseline of these policies regurgitates Romani "Otherness".

The majority have always found it hard to accept Romanis because their life-style, appearance and origins have not sat well with European norms. Uncertainty about the origins of Romanis, and Romani reluctance to offer a myth of origin akin to those of European majorities, are expressed clearly in the first legends about the mysterious and distant origins of Romanis, their failure to settle in one place and their unconventional ("abnormal", in the language of the day) lifestyle, all of which were habitually seen as conducive of deviance and criminality.

In this ideational context, anthropological characteristics and ethnic particularities were successively constructed and re-constructed, the perception of an in-born proclivity to one or the other way of life playing an important role in Roma images and common representations. And because the reasons for Romani nomadism in the past, or migrations today are not well-understood by the majority, Roma easily fit into existing social, economic, and political frameworks as deviants and in need of facilitating policies, such as those in the NRIS framework. Such representations place the onus of responsibility upon the state to provide its citizens with opportunities for labour market participation and stable accommodation, excusing European organisations from assuming a greater role in determining the avenues for the inclusion of Romani communities across EU member states.

The comprehensive *Romani politics in contemporary Europe*[9], for example, leaves little doubt that the uniform commitment to the neoliberal economic order and individual-focused politics have locked Roma into marginal positions, legitimised unequal relations between Roma and the majority, and entrenched the view that Romani exclusion is the result of their own disengagement and a freely chosen 'lifestyle'. Similarly, *Between Past and Future*[10] focuses squarely on the role of political processes in postcommunism, which made a clear break with the past notion of state responsibility to all citizens, without entrenching the mechanisms which ensure political entrepreneurs' accountability to citizens affected in policymaking processes. Much the same, as Rostas' *Ten years after*[11] points out, the individualistic pursuit of upward mobility among aspiring majority individuals and institutional leverage to open access routes to scarce resources by community leaders ushers the mis-representation and non-representation of Romani interests in areas such as education and access to the labour market.

This is interesting given that much of research on the effects of Romani inclusion usually accepts the rhetoric that underlines the positive role played by resourceful Romanis in articulating the needs of their communities—often at the expense of diversity in the communities they represent. This is a process that has been observed throughout postcommunist Europe and has been referred to as *ethno-business*[12]. The issue has become particularly integral to processes whereby the politicisation of an ethnic/Romani identity results in the in-group systematic practices of 'othering'. It also makes Romani integration programmes emphasise individual choice to integrate, pitting opportunities offered by the majority against the very core of Romani identity. This approach is particularly problematic as it suggests that past experiences of state support on the basis of group rights have been largely negative. Also, it implies that viable alternatives to existing inclusion policies should opt for minimal governmental intervention, in favour of policy choices implemented by community leaders who are better able to identify areas of concern and decide where action is needed.

Though I can fully appreciate that the paradigm of Romani inclusion as it developed across Europe urges one to believe that it is a normative commitment to bettering the status of widely marginalised groups, its operational reality—and the *de facto* rationality of all actors involved in grassroots activity—is deeply economic. Van Baar, for example, is particularly vocal in this regard when making sense of responsibilities governments have when they implement neoliberal policies, such as those of social integration, that underpin the creation of European Romani initiatives [13]. Although this opens the door to select expert and elite groups from the community to negotiate the impact of domestic and European policies on individual Romanis, it also forecloses the wider participation of Romani individuals who lack resources of the economic, political, social and/or esteem kind. From van Baar's point of view, all states and international forums tend to see Romanis as a burden rather than an asset for *economic* rationality: states manage *ad hoc* the emergent problems pertaining to Romani exclusion without ever addressing the root cause of the issue, avoiding responsibility vis-à-vis their citizens in offering education, healthcare, proper housing and opportunities for waged labour[14].

Adjacent to this literature, the body of work on Romani mobilisation illustrates how Romanis could tap the institutionalised structures for interest articulation, social representation and participation in politics. In so doing, major studies in the field [15] recommend that Romanis draw upon an identity/opportunity nexus in order to enter the political arena. Yet, none of these authors treat Romanis as social actors in their own right, and even less so as having agency as a group. Authors in the edited collection by Sigona and Trehan (2010), for example, expend considerable efforts in criticising remedial approaches to and action involving Romanis, consider Romanis as agents emulating the behaviour of majority actors who were successful in the past and thus having no agentic capacity of their own.

McGarry (2010), too, tracks down opportunities for Romanis to gain access to and challenge established policymaking processes that perpetuate exclusionary practices in domestic and international arenas. However, he admits that the social and political mobilisation of Romanis is a strategy of goal attainment, which has been defined by the limits of Romani integration into overall social structures. Without reference either to the context of their strategies or the pretext for their social actions, McGarry projects the outcomes of such collective action, but fails to identify whether these patterns are a *possibility* in either a theoretical or practical sense. Hence he also fails to distinguish the 'must' implications of the author from those 'ought to' of Romanis as agents in their own right. What is lacking in these and similar representations of potentialities for action available to Romanis is that their opportunities are conceptualised as contingencies, made available by the majority. Romanis thus are agents with a free choice only in so far as they choose from opportunities offered by super-ordinate agents to them in the first place, which—in my view—severely misrepresents opportunity for action by Romani civil society groups.

Undoubtedly, the situation for the vast majority of Romanis has changed somewhat over the past century: the democratisation of state-society relations across much of Europe has allowed many marginalised and minority communities to acquire increasing recognition from both domestic and European institutions. Though different in their lifestyle(s) and practices, Romanis themselves increasingly make forays into the political arena in attempts to represent the interests of their communities and advocate their (often projected) interests.

Though I generally share the excitement about the transformative role civil society *can* play, I have considerable difficulty buying into major premises in the literature on Romani political mobilisation. Vermeersch and Sigona and Trehan, as well as Klimova-Alexander[16] and McGarry argue that the civil society activities of Romanis are mere fig leaves legitimising the gradual withdrawal of the state from responsibility for its citizens, thus leaving no institutional support available for marginal groups. Thus the emphasis on the positive role of civil society underscores the preference of resourceful members of society for a minimal state which would not intervene in their lives; however, those with no resources to fall back on and left without state support are doubly exposed to paternalistic, quasi service-providers such as NGOs.

This institutional set-up, however, continues to maintain such inequalities and does so inadvertently, rather than deliberately. Much of the extant literature fails to consider Romanis as actors, tied into the structural context in which they find themselves and which also treats them as agents that have similar pool of options to choose from as any other individual. I believe Romanis should—like any other socially-embedded actor and member of society—be thought of primarily as actors operating *inside* a social system and/or adapting patterns of their actions to social and structural constraints, rather than being freely able to choose courses of action and also their own identities.

2. Availing of Opportunities as a Litmus Test of Agentic Abilities?

Recently, large numbers of social scientists have made efforts to engage with policymakers as a means to facilitate Romani inclusion and to identify avenues for the group to evade marginalisation from public politics[17]. Many of these volumes identify similar problems faced by Romani communities, and analyse the various legal[18], political[19] and social[20] challenges that Romani groups pose to institutions in contemporary societies. Regardless of the differences between Romanis, most of the studies on Romani exclusion demonstrate an acute sensitivity to and awareness of the persistent exclusion of Romanis from social processes.

Being timely and important studies, many scholarly works lay down what can only be described as partisan claims for the greater recognition of the interests, identities, cultures, and lifestyles of Romani and Traveller communities in Europe, and use academic forums to advocate Romani inclusion. Given that Romanis do not participate in the majority society's public affairs, many academics undoubtedly exercise their duty to alert majority societies to the "plight" and "misery" pertinent to Romani social exclusion. My reading of the recent scholarship on Romani exclusion as well as my analyses of the policies which (allegedly) sponsor Romani inclusion has made me highly pessimistic regarding the acknowledgement of Romani individuals as autonomous social agents with considerable potential value (in the sense of public policy) for the societies in which they live, and who can potentially contribute to policy making.

Since there is no single and unanimously agreed-upon concept of social inclusion, participation is generally used as a substitute for the diversity of strategies and perceptions of the "desired outcomes among stakeholder communities". This makes the prevailing conceptual approach to 'Romani inclusion' as having been shaped by those advocates who are themselves already a part of the political context and can designate priorities for those who yet cannot.

Indeed, the Fundamental Rights Agency (FRA) and the reports prepared by the Decade of Roma Inclusion often point out that though practically insightful, the anticipated outcomes of Romani inclusion are not the notions derived from systematic analyses of their needs on the ground. Public policies in individual states, as well as the emerging European Governance for Romani Inclusion (EGRI) neglect to consider systematically socio-cultural entities, structures and relations, having so far merely reconstructed past actions as "good practice". International commitment to supporting Romani inclusion as a valid and legitimate goal, therefore, is important only in so far as the background upon which shared identities have been built is re-aligned with the expectation of majority group institutions (political inclusion) and culture (social inclusion). The focus on Romani communities' inclusion thus supplants the attention from inequalities as they are experienced by individuals *as* group members, and instead favours dominant groups' preferences for individual inclusion. Thus the meaning of the term "social inclusion" in general, and that of "Romani inclusion" specifically, as understood in the EGRI is contingent upon a combination of elements which do not fit the myriad of exclusionary practices as experienced by the Romani community as a whole, and by individual Romanis in diverse social/economic/political contexts as single participants.

If nothing else, the public policy approach to social inclusion leaves little room to appreciate differences between majority and marginal communities, and brackets out the inconsistencies in communication between the actors involved in implementing the (ill-defined) goals of inclusion.[21] It is therefore unsurprising that European and national institutions opt for closer engagement with non-governmental organisations (NGOs) as reincarnations of civil society groups to bridge the gap between the policy-induced targets, and the needs identified at the grassroot level in the delivery of policy goals concerning Romani inclusion. Rightly, NGOs are where citizens can be directly involved in decision-making and implementation processes. But drawing upon civil society activists to oversee, implement and monitor state-driven social integration agendas provides only some individuals with access to and experience of resources.

As such, the EGRI as a whole, and NRIS specifically, juxtapose choices between those of group exclusion and individual inclusion by identifying an individual Romani on the basis of her or his membership in a community marked by systematic exclusion. Policymakers fail to account for the limitations placed on the choices made by individual members of marginalised communities and instead place their trust in the initiatives of Romanis in general, and civil society specifically to remedy the impact of social exclusion, but without challenging the underlying structural conditions which caused their exclusion in the first place. Whether or not shifting responsibility for tackling Romani exclusion from political institutions onto civic initiatives really demonstrates that the path towards inclusion comes through individual choice is left open for the discrete interpretation of those nation-states which actually implement respective NRIS. It is beyond doubt, however, that NRIS envisage that select Roma experts will assume responsibility for implementing public policies for Romani inclusion, while having limited input into deciding upon them.

With Romanis having little power to escape exclusion other than following the terms spelt out for them by members of the majority, do policymakers perceive opportunities for inclusion on Romani terms? The logic of social integration relying on civil society initiatives imbues public discourse with the focus on individual rights making it wholly impossible to determine the place for the excluded to exert independent agency. Furthermore, there have been growing complaints that the Roma Platforms are dominated by the European Commission, are hierarchical and tightly controlled, leaving little space for Romani civil society to express its aspirations, report on progress in their home countries and, where needed, articulate frustrations [22].

From the liberal perspective, individual membership in the Romani community should be intended as a qualifying criterion for accessing scarce resources. The EGRI, in this sense, operates a "double bind" that supposes the primordial bond between the individual and the community, as well as that an individual member can make a decision about her or his own release from membership as a result of a (presumably free) choice of identity. Instead of constraining the options and choices of individual Romanis, the EGRI solicits sets of meaningful options, from within which framework the individual (who is, ultimately, embedded in multiple identities and as such, is resourceful) can be expected to autonomously determine, attribute and value her or his individual priorities.[23]

On the one hand, national programmes for Romani integration rarely address the real grievances of individual members of the affected Roma community.

Among the many national programmes for Romani inclusion, Romani integration is not defined by participation on their own group terms. Instead, national policymakers operate on the basis of resource reallocation to and redistribution of funds to civil society groups aligned to top-down defined goals.[24] On the other hand, there are limited opportunities for individual Romani interests to influence social inclusion framework programmes outside the framework of civil society consultations. The dominant majority's practices and identity is the ultimate criterion of what successful inclusion means: Romani communities are believed to have to engage in and define their group identities in the same manner as majorities do and as such their ethnic/cultural/linguistic identities should provide their individual members sets of action patterns for "inclusion".

Whilst the narrative which seeks to empower Romani civil society is most often encountered in evaluations and reports of NGOs working on the ground with Romani communities, the other, which aims to co-opt individual Romanis into decision-making on terms of the majority is clearly visible in the EU nudging member states to continue the implementation of non-discrimination legislation. Undoubtedly, both go hand-in-hand with improved access for Romani individuals to employment, education, housing and health. Yet both narratives perpetuate, rather than dismantle the perception of Romanis as failing individually and collectively to lead a life of cultural, religious and community practices in any sense translatable into categories of the majority. As such, even the positive reports on the successful implementation of education and housing schemes for Romanis play into the hand of preconceived notions about Romani difference from the majority.

So far, the logic of social integration has relied on civil society initiatives to imbue abject citizens with the awareness of and ability to access their guaranteed rights. But is it really possible to conceive of Romani participation within the existing structures of opportunity without coalescing individuals into collectivities which share a group identity?

Research into possible solutions for exclusion refers to the 'collective' as the starting point to re-focus public policy on the envisaged outcomes for target groups. As O'Nions[25] suggests, although individual autonomy lies at the core of international provisions for human rights protection, it can only be sparsely used to tackle discrimination of multiply marginalised groups. Being formed in specific social contexts, reinforced by political institutions and backed up by legal norms, the collective rights agenda as extended to minorities runs the danger of overlooking the choices and identities of individual Romanis, often retrenching the inequalities that they set out to reduce. In this context, focussing primarily on the legal benchmarks that ensure practical equality between Romanis and everyone else, legal scholarship on the Romani situation[26] is often concerned first and foremost with the implications of culture-blindness, i.e. overarching group provisions for intergroup equality.[27] The preferred strategy of minority groups across Europe has been the pathway of "group rights"[28], tightly linked to a human rights discourse, which offers opportunities to minority groups either too small, too dispersed or too stigmatised to appeal to individual rights to ensure their formal equality.

Importantly, analyses of legal benchmarking as regards specific policies of Romani inclusion suggest that policies are usually developed from the spurious analyses of needs on the ground as perceived by political elites, articulated via representatives of Romani NGOs, without the involvement of those very communities affected. Many of these policies are projected, "ideal typical" images offering local solutions to the problems of Romanis, yet exculpate cash-stripped governments from the responsibility of ensuring rights provisions for all of their citizens equally. As regards the rights of Romanis as citizens of EU member states, policies of affirmative action are arguably unsuccessful in effectuating Romani inclusion[29]. This is largely because, in societies that uphold parochial social structures, with negotiated economic constraints, and which operate in the modus of 'compliance' rather than 'dialogue', group-based policies are likely to cause intergroup competition rather than cooperation. They also enhance perceptions in the majority community of being deprived access to limited resources, usually carved out for privileged use by the state, rather than minority group individuals.

The compromise, to ensure group representation whilst preventing discrimination, would require a radical departure from the rationale that both domestic and international policymakers have pursued to date. There is a need for a pluralist-integrationist framework, to be achieved through "a complementary approach to human rights which emphasises the importance of cultural identity and autonomy in addition to the prevention of discrimination and promotion of equality"[30]. Similarly, Roughneen's legal-political analyses of the situation of the Irish Traveller community suggests that much of the promise surrounding European integration processes has not departed from the narrow understanding of group identity for policy purposes[31]. In her case study, Roughneen is largely sympathetic to the broadening of the policy focus to include a critical assessment of the "taken for granted" guarantees of rights and protection from non-discrimination bestowed upon by the majority. Hence, if group rights are about equality of access, and individual rights are about freedom to avail of access opportunities, individual autonomy to realise full equality and participate in public life should be placed centre stage in inclusion policies which target multiply marginalised groups.

Importantly, however, the debate on individual autonomy cannot be appreciated formalistically by members of the majority society, but it should be alert to and even apprehensive of limitations of the human rights-based approach for minority groups. First, human rights per se are the result of political institutional support for the *de jure* (not *de facto*) equality between individuals affected by policies either because of their place of residence, their relationships with the policy implementing agencies or as a result of subjection to breaches of their rights by other individuals. This raises the point about the object-like position of minorities as well as other groups with limited/circumscribed access to the enjoyment of their full rights alongside other citizens of their states, largely those perceived to be in the majority.

Second, the focus on human rights requires significant prerequisites for humans to enjoy their agency as norm-setting actors in a social/political environment structured and enforced by nation-states' policies. Here again, the status of those expedient objects of policymaking who are not consulted but are affected, highlights the limits of participation in public life based on the terms of the dominant majority.

Third, while we should not underestimate the importance of legal provisions in regulating the relationship between majority and minority populations, we must be aware of the fact that these provisions are not universal and, though liberal, exclude some groups of residents from enjoying their full rights from the outset. As such, much ado about Romani inclusion in fact contravenes the commitment of both domestic legislations' and international organisations' commitment to make decisions with the participation of the population affected (or, at the very least, representatives of them).

If anything, legal provisions for both individual human and minority group rights highlights the paradigmatic caveat of the liberal government which offers but a tokenistic respect for individual liberties, while subjecting marginalised groups in the populace to laws that nullify the very core of their group identity. Thus, regardless of the state's provision of non-discrimination legislation to choose a lifestyle and make decisions about how to pursue it, liberal legislations exclude the option for its citizens to avail of the right to lead life which they themselves choose as legitimate—and autonomous—individuals.

My contention here is that though much debate has been taking place about rights of Romanis, these tend to opt for formal equality, while neglecting the much more potent category of substantive equality. While the debate on minority inclusion and, of late, on Romani integration points out that the rule-setting and enforcing capacities of the state exist to ensure individual citizens' unhindered enjoyment of their normative agency, all these documents project the elegant concept of a resourceful individual onto legally—not practically—defined agency. As a result, this de facto excludes minority and marginal community members from the enjoyment of these very same provisions; potentially, it indicates that some agentic abilities inherent to marginal groups lie outside the scope of the desirable in the sense of individual autonomy. Roughneen observes that "[Irish] Travellers are members of a subordinated group and restriction on the autonomy of the Traveller further subordinates the group" [32].

But how far can one criticise the abstract discourse on human and minority rights as specifically failing those individuals with limited knowledge of (and thus the limited capacity) to make informed decisions about the available path-ways out of exclusion and the possible means to countenance stereotypical representations of their marginality?

3. Dispensable Identity as a Precondition to Inclusion

European international organisations, the EU, the Council of Europe, and the OSCE promote Romani inclusion as a legitimate goal on the basis of a pre-sumed shared identity of Romani individuals, which further highlights differ-ences between majority and Romani communities as having their roots in cul-ture. Indeed, the clarity about the identity of social actors is important to avoid conceptual ambiguity about the anticipated outcomes of/from Romani mobili-sation. Predominant narratives across the EU and nation-states' programmes aimed at Romani integration circle around non-discrimination and equal rights. All these have been identified as improving Romani *individuals'* equal access to employment, education, housing and health, but this emphasis reduces Romani individuals' own attempts at agenda setting as secondary to their mem-bership in an identity group[33].

Such deficits in thinking about the drawbacks of Romani mobilisation for rep-resentation are unfortunate as there are numerous insightful ideas that could relate better to the established literature on the nexus of representation/partic-ipation/identity. Hannah Pitkin's *The Concept of Representation* [34] has been pivotal in raising concerns of the arbitrariness and inadequacy of descriptive representation. Also, Anne Phillips, in *The Politics of Presence* [35] went to great lengths to problematize the separation of and relationship between the agent and object of representation as that of epistemological subordination of ideas to interests are referenced throughout the book.

In her *Dealing with difference*, Phillips[36] raises the argument that "the liberal emphasis on individual freedoms and rights reflected a self-protective and competitive egotism that refused any wider community that which the liberal focus on 'merely' political inequalities ignored or even encouraged gross ine-qualities in social and economic life." In this text, and throughout her early work, Phillips[37] referred often to the theoretical discussion of representation brought to the fore by Hannah Pitkin, who herself drew a distinction between political actors as both represented and representative[38]. In terms of crafting a theoretical approach to understanding the representation of marginalised communities, both authors offer a lucid theoretical entry point which has of late been embraced by researchers on Romani exclusion. The attention to the works of Pitkin and Phillips marks a critical shift in the theorisation of political exclusion that marred Romani representatives and has significant potential to impact on an academic discussion of Romani inclusion. However, while a considerable scholarship grew around Pitkin's and Phillip's idea of a politics of representation and presence[39], my contention is that nearly all researchers of Romani issues taking inspiration from these two scholars take seriously the baseline both of the politics of presence and the politics of representation. "Arguably after Pitkin no one regarded descriptive representation as important, whilst after Phillips no one regarded it as unimportant"[40].

The discourse on descriptive representation is pertinent to much of the work on Romani inclusion, but as I have demonstrated it seems that it systematically trades contempt for alternative pursuits of life as synonymous with a lack of informed choice. Ultimately, it reduces Romanis as individuals and as part of a group to objects, rather than as actors in decision making. Similar to Klaus-Michael Bogdal's analyses [41] of Romanis being characterised as "socially deviant because [they are] pathologically peripatetic" under the national socialist regime, and thus justifying mass criminalisation, we find decision making on Romani expulsions from EU member states legitimised in a similar vein.

As many detailed analyses of the policymaking process indicate, "knowledge" of "Roma" and of "Travellers" is utterly skewed to subsume a particular set of stereotypes, with "knowledge" taken as a means to regulate choices of objects of policy. Thus, as we have seen, political exclusion is increasingly going hand-in-hand with a descriptive representation which neglects the relationship between ideas and the experience of individuals targeted for inclusion. With many opportunities to participate in public life being demarcated by processes, actor preference and majority-serving institutions of states, opportunities available to multiply marginalised groups to contribute to decision making about the terms of their own inclusion have shrunk to a minimum.

This begs the question about the practical applications of the substantive as well as the descriptive representation of multiply marginalised communities, as raised by Pitkin (1967). Conceptually, we might need to return to her types of representation, first as being authorised (as in a legally authorised representation of another; second, as descriptive (as in standing in for another by virtue of a shared similarity); third, as symbolic (such as by a representative with some power of decision making), and fourth, substantive, (through advocating change in favour of preferences and interests of those who are to be represented). Imbued in these four categories is the tension between the represented and the representative, which works through an ambiguous and complex relationship of the actorness and agency on both sides of this equation. However, in the context of multiply marginalised communities, both these issues point to the importance of the context within which the choice between preferences can be made.

The origins of those preferences that co-opt, rather than resolve ambiguities ensure the hegemonic pursuit of options at the expense of more palpable alternatives. In following these lines, many studies of Romani exclusion fail to offer a conceptually clear basis for policies of inclusion and as such do not provide consistent policy advice nor proposals. At the same time they often assert that identities as defined by self-interested agents could offer a working definition of the group that is in the focus of inclusion policy. This exercise has proven effective in gauging the potential for change in the relationship between socially constructed actors without superimposing one specific concept of identity and as such, also of their agency. There is considerable need for a holistic approach to inclusion via the concept of representation, and prior to that of agent-, rather than agenda-driven participation in public life.

Conclusion

European integration has led many observers to suggest that the establishment of comprehensive antidiscrimination legislation has led to the final triumph of and the widespread acknowledgement of the fundamental importance of human rights across the European continent. The package ensuring the equal treatment of individuals and benchmarking illicit practices on discrimination has been particularly important for individuals of Romani origin subject to political marginalisation across the continent. Comparative analyses of public attitudes towards Romanis by the Fundamental Rights Agency, for example, suggest that today more than ever, many members of European societies are sceptical of this group's members' ability to participate and contribute to social, economic and political processes where they live.

As has been witnessed across many Central Eastern European states where Romani mobilisation for participation and policymaking has followed a route of reactive agenda setting modelled upon majority communities' preferences, such as in Romania and Hungary, this has resulted in a sharp rise in antiziganist sentiment. To participate in social inclusion initiatives, Romani communities have thus far engaged in and defined their group identities in the same manner as majority communities. However, as this paper has suggested, with political entrepreneurs 'authenticating' the potential and actual claims of Romanis as 'claims made by independent actors', this takes place only once they fall in line with expectations of the majority.

This puts particular stress on the importance of recognising issues central to Romani interests and ideals regarding their identities, whether they are cultural, linguistic or ethnic, but all of which define their relationships with states and societies in contemporary Europe. This paper has argued that with the structural challenges experienced by members of Romani communities when seeking recognition of their claims vis-à-vis governance structures, individuals of Romani origin need to be recognised for what they individually perceive as necessary to better their status, whilst simultaneously addressing the structural grievances which disallow their equality with the rest of society as a group. These two steps have allowed me to argue that across Europe, policies of Romani inclusion entrench, rather than avert the political and social marginalisation of Romanis. While the alignment of the marginal and majority actors could create common agents where there are yet none, it would also reverse the perception of Romani lifestyle(s) causing exclusion, rather than as products thereof.

Acknowledgements

The first ideas for this paper were collected at and presented to the Uppsala Forum in September 2012 made possible thanks to generous financial support by the Uppsala Centre for Russian and Eurasian Studies (UCRS). The paper would have not come to be if it was not for a supportive and encouraging chat over chicken curry that followed, *paldies*. A significantly more dense paper was presented at the workshop "Stereotype, cliché and prejudice" hosted as a part of the conference on antiziganism in Uppsala University a year later, in October 2013. I am particularly grateful for helpful input and suggestions on improvements to Diana E. Popescu and Ioana Vrăbiescu, as well as robust critique to Julija Sardelić and Sławomir Kapralski.

References

1   FRA, 'The Situation of Roma in 11 EU Member States. European Union Agency for Fundamental Rights', May 2012, http://fra.europa.eu/en/publication/2012/situation-roma-11-eu-member-states-survey-results-glance Accessed 02/02/2014.

2   European Commission, 'An EU Framework for National Roma Integration Strategies up to 2020 (EC/COM/2011/173 Final)', 2011.

3   European Parliament, 'European Parliament Resolution on the Situation of the Roma in the European Union, P6_TA(2005)0151', 2005.

4   OSCE, 'Report on the OSCE Supplementary Human Dimension Meeting on Roma and Sinti, Vienna April 10-11 2003', 2003, www.osce.org/odihr/42550 Accessed 02/02/2014

5   Peter Vermeersch, 'Reframing the Roma: EU Initiatives and the Politics of Reinterpretation', *Journal of Ethnic and Migration Studies* 38, 8 (2012): 1195–1212.

6   Nando Sigona, 'The Governance of Romani People in Italy: Discourse, Policy and Practice', *Journal of Modern Italian Studies* 16, 5 (2011): 590–606; Annabel Tremlett, 'Comparing European Institutional and Hungarian Approaches to Roma (Gypsy) Minorities', in *Minority Integration in Central Eastern Europe. Between Ethnic Diversity and Equality*, ed. Timofey Agarin and Malte Brosig (Amsterdam: Rodopi, 2009), 129–150.

7   Angus Bancroft, *Roma and Gypsy-Travellers in Europe: Modernity, Race, Space and Exclusion* (Aldershot: Ashgate, 2005).

8   European Commission, 'National Roma Integration Strategies: A First Step in the Implementation of the EU Framework. COM/2012/133', 2012; European Commission, 'Commission Staff Working Document: Accompanying the Document: National Roma Integration Strategies: A First Step in the Implementation of the EU Framework. COM/2012/226', 2012.

9   Nidhi Trehan and Nando Sigona, eds., *Romani Politics in Contemporary Europe Poverty, Ethnic Mobilization, and the Neo-Liberal Order* (Palgrave, 2010).

10   Will Guy, ed., *Between Past and Future: The Roma of Central and Eastern Europe* (Hatfield: University of Hertfordshire Press, 2001).

11   Iulius Rostas, ed., *Ten Years After: A History of Roma School Desegregation in Central and Eastern Europe* (Budapest: Central European University Press, 2012).

12   Andreea Carstocea, '"Ethno-business": the unexpected consequence of national minority policies on the political system in Romania', in Zdenka Mansfeldova, Heiko Pleines (eds.): *Informal relations from democratic representation to corruption. Case studies from Central and Eastern Europe.* Changing Europe Series vol. 8 (Ibidem, Stuttgart, 2011).

13   Huub van Baar, 'Socio-Economic Mobility and Neo-Liberal Governmentality in Post-Socialist Europe: Activation and the Dehumanisation of the Roma', *Journal of Ethnic and Migration Studies* 38, 8 (2012): 1289–1304.

14   See esp Huub van Baar, *The European Roma: Minority Representation, Memory, and the Limits of Transnational Governmentality* (Amsterdam, 2011).

15   Aidan McGarry, *Who Speaks for Roma? Political Representation of a Transnational Minority Community* (London: Continuum International Publishing Group, 2010); Peter

Vermeersch, *The Romani Movement: Minority Politics and Ethnic Mobilization in Contemporary Central Europe* (Oxford: Berghahn Books, 2006); Trehan and Sigona, *Romani Politics in Contemporary Europe Poverty, Ethnic Mobilization, and the Neo-Liberal Order.*

16   Ilona Klímová-Alexander, 'The Development and Institutionalization of Romani Representation and Administration. Part 3c: Religious, Governmental, and Non-Governmental Institutions (1945–1970)', *Nationalities Papers* 38, 1 (2010): 105–122.

17   Rostas, *Ten Years After: A History of Roma School Desegregation in Central and Eastern Europe*; Andrew Ryder and John Richardson, eds., *Gypsies and Travellers: Empowerment and Inclusion in British Society* (Bristol: Policy Press, 2012); Will Guy, 'EU Initiatives on Roma: Limitations and Ways Forward', in *Romani Politics in Contemporary Europe Poverty, Ethnic Mobilization, and the Neo-Liberal Order*, ed. Nidhi Trehan and Nando Sigona (Palgrave, 2010); Owen Parker, 'Roma and the Politics of EU Citizenship in France: Everyday Security and Resistance*', *JCMS: Journal of Common Market Studies* 50, 3 (2012): 475–491.

18   Helen O'Nions, 'Roma Expulsions and Discrimination: The Elephant in Brussels', *European Journal of Migration and Law* 13, 4 (2011): 361–388; Mathias Möschel, 'Is the European Court of Human Rights' Case Law on Anti-Roma Violence "Beyond Reasonable Doubt"?', *Human Rights Law Review* 12, 3 (2012): 479–507; Rachel Guglielmo and Timothy William Waters, 'Migrating Towards Minority Status: Shifting European Policy Towards Roma', *JCMS: Journal of Common Market Studies* 43, 4 (2005): 763–785; Galina Kostadinova, 'Minority Rights as a Normative Framework for Addressing the Situation of Roma in Europe', *Oxford Development Studies* 39, 2 (2011): 163–183.

19   Peter Vermeersch, 'Ethnic Minority Identity and Movement Politics: The Case of the Roma in the Czech Republic and Slovakia', *Ethnic and Racial Studies* 26, 5 (2003): 879–901; A. McGarry, 'Ethnic Group Identity and the Roma Social Movement: Transnational Organizing Structures of Representation', *Nationalities Papers* 36, 3 (2008): 449–470; Nidhi Trehan, 'The Romani Subaltern within Neoliberal European Civil Society: NGOization of Human Rights and Silent Voices', in *Romani Politics in Contemporary Europe Poverty, Ethnic Mobilization, and the Neo-Liberal Order*, ed. Nidhi Trehan and Nando Sigona (Palgrave, 2010).

20   Klaus-Michael Bogdal, *Europa Erfindet Die Zigeuner. Eine Geschichte von Faszination und Verachtung* (Berlin: Suhrkamp, 2011); Martin Kovats, 'The Emergence of European Roma Policy', in *Between Past and Future: The Roma of Central and Eastern Europe*, ed. Will Guy (Hatfield: University of Hertfordshire Press, 2001); Maria Spirova and Darlene Budd, 'The EU Accession Process and the Roma Minorities in New and Soon-to-Be Member States', *Comparative European Politics* 6, 1 (2008): 81–101.

21   One of the obvious examples, highlighted by recent research on the effectiveness of Romani inclusion, points out the mismatch in actors' goals setting: The agents of policy-aligned action for inclusion operate according to the logic of maximising returns, making them unpredictable in their normative orientations (as in cases of the 'NGOization' of inclusion programmes, policy delivery and reward-by-payment for achieved results). At the same time, those actors working on projects 'on the ground' are often operating to reverse the robust set of institutional disadvantages single Romani communities and individuals face in their social environment (ensuring access to housing, education and healthcare, providing opportunities for employment, befitting the skills and abilities of Roma as well as employers).

22   Iulius Rostas and Andrew Ryder, 'EU Framework for National Roma Integration Strategies: Insights into Empowerment and Inclusive Policy Development', in *Gypsies and Travellers: Empowerment and Inclusion in British Society*, ed. Andrew Ryder and John Richardson (Bristol: Policy Press, 2012), 187.

23   To date, the state protection of minority cultures and languages has been enforced throughout the European Union member and accession states on these very grounds, enabling members of marginalised/minority groups to benefit from rich socioeconomic resources, as members of cultural and linguistic majorities already do. Much along the same lines, Kymlicka has previously claimed that cultural groups are due respect from non-members in order to guarantee 'the dignity and self-respect of its members' (Kymlicka, 1995, 89).

24   By way of example, neither the approaches to Roma across the Central Eastern Europe sought to increase the accountability of state institutions to Romani communities and encourage majority-dominated political, economic and social institutions to accommodate variant needs of Romani communities. Instead, they provided co-opted Romani groups a marginal option to cooperate within the existing (majority dominated) institutions and the obliteration of Romani interests in public domain.

25   Helen O'Nions, *Minority Rights Protection in International Law: The Roma of Europe* (Aldershot: Ashgate, 2007).

26   Ibid.; Melanie H. Ram, 'Legacies of EU Conditionality: Explaining Post-Accession Adherence to Pre-Accession Rules on Roma', *Europe-Asia Studies* 64, 7 (September 2012): 1191–1218.

27   Often, the legal assessment of opportunities for inclusion sets positive changes for Roma rights in Europe. It offers detailed overviews of two competing discourses on the opportunities minority communities can pursue under European non-discrimination legislation as individuals, and contrasting with opportunities for members of minority communities to achieve a greater say in politics on the basis of group recognition.

28   Kathrin Simhandl, '"Western Gypsies and Travellers"–"Eastern Roma": The Creation of Political Objects by the Institutions of the European Union', *Nations and Nationalism* 12, 1 (2006): 97–115; Melanie H. Ram, 'Interests, Norms and Advocacy: Explaining the Emergence of the Roma onto the EU's Agenda', *Ethnopolitics* 9, 2 (2010): 197–217.

29   Peter Vermeersch and Melanie H. Ram, 'The Roma', in *Minority Rights in Central and Eastern Europe*, ed. Bernd Rechel (London: Routledge, 2009), 61–73.

30   O'Nions, *Minority Rights Protection in International Law: The Roma of Europe*, 279.

31   Dualta Roughneen, *The Right to Roam: Travellers and Human Rights in the Modern Nation-State* (Newcastle: Cambridge Scholars Publishing, 2010).

32   Ibid., 102.

33   Cf van Baar, 'Socio-Economic Mobility and Neo-Liberal Governmentality in Post-Socialist Europe: Activation and the Dehumanisation of the Roma'; Kate Hepworth, 'Abject Citizens: Italian "Nomad Emergencies" and the Deportability of Romanian Roma', *Citizenship Studies* 16, 3–4 (2012): 431–449; Vermeersch, 'Reframing the Roma: EU Initiatives and the Politics of Reinterpretation'.

34   Pitkin, *The Concept of Representation* (Berkeley: University of California Press, 1967).

35   Phillips, *The Politics of Presence* (Oxford University Press, 1995).

36   Phillips, 'Dealing With Difference: A Politics of Ideas Or A Politics of Presence?', *Constellations* 1, 1 (1994): 74

37 Phillips, *The Politics of Presence.*

38 Pitkin, *The Concept of Representation.*

39 Eg Iris Marion Young, *Inclusion and Democracy* (Oxford: Oxford University Press, 2000); Jane Mansbridge, 'Should Blacks Represent Blacks and Women Represent Women? A Contingent "Yes"', *Journal of Politics* 61, 3 (1999): 628–657.

40 Karen Celis and Sarah Childs, 'The Substantive Representation of Women: What to Do with Conservative Claims?' *Political Studies* 60, 1 (2012): 213–225.

41 Bogdal, *Europa Erfindet Die Zigeuner. Eine Geschichte von Faszination und Verachtung.*

ibidem-Verlag / *ibidem* Press
Melchiorstr. 15
70439 Stuttgart
Germany

ibidem@ibidem.eu
www.ibidem-verlag.com
www.ibidem.eu